The University and the City

Universities are being seen as key urban institutions by researchers and policy makers around the world. They are global players with significant local direct and indirect impacts – on employment, the built environment, business innovation and the wider society. *The University and the City* explores these impacts and in the process seeks to expose the extent to which universities are just *in* the city, or part *of* the city and actively contributing to its development.

The precise expression of the emerging relationship between universities and cities is highly contingent on national and local circumstances. The book is therefore grounded in original research into the experience of the UK and selected English provincial cities, with a focus on the role of universities in addressing the challenges of environmental sustainability, health and cultural development. These case studies are set in the context of reviews of the international evidence on the links between universities and the urban economy, their role in 'place making' and in the local community.

The book reveals the need to build a stronger bridge between policy and practice in the fields of urban development and higher education underpinned by sound theory if the full potential of universities as urban institutions is to be realised. Those working in the field of development therefore need to acquire a better understanding of universities and those in higher education of urban development. The insights from both sides contained in *The University and the City* provide a platform on which to build well-founded university and city partnerships across the world.

John Goddard is Professor Emeritus of Regional Development Studies at Newcastle University, UK.

Paul Vallance is Research Associate in the Centre for Urban and Regional Development Studies at Newcastle University, UK.

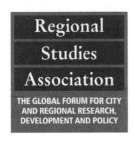

Routledge
Taylor & Francis Group

Regions and Cities

Managing Editor:
Gillian Bristow, *University of Cardiff, UK.*

Editors:
Maryann Feldman, *University of Georgia, USA,*
Gernot Grabher, *HafenCity University Hamburg, Germany,*
Ron Martin, *University of Cambridge, UK,*
Martin Perry, *Massey University, New Zealand.*

In today's globalised, knowledge-driven and networked world, regions and cities have assumed heightened significance as the interconnected nodes of economic, social and cultural production, and as sites of new modes of economic and territorial governance and policy experimentation. This book series brings together incisive and critically engaged international and interdisciplinary research on this resurgence of regions and cities, and should be of interest to geographers, economists, sociologists, political scientists and cultural scholars, as well as to policy-makers involved in regional and urban development.

For more information on the Regional Studies Association visit www.regionalstudies.org

There is a **30% discount** available to RSA members on books in the *Regions and Cities* series, and other subject related Taylor and Francis books and e-books including Routledge titles. To order just e-mail alex.robinson@tandf.co.uk, or phone on +44 (0) 20 7017 6924 and declare your RSA membership. You can also visit www.routledge.com and use the discount code: **RSA0901**

1. **Beyond Green Belts**
   Managing urban growth in the
   21st century
   Edited by John Herington

2. **Retreat from the Regions**
   Corporate change and the closure
   of factories
   Stephen Fothergill and Nigel Guy

3. **Regional Development in the 1990s**
   The British Isles in transition
   *Edited by Ron Martin and
   Peter Townroe*

4. **Spatial Policy in a Divided
   Nation**
   *Edited by Richard T. Harrison
   and Mark Hart*

The University and the City

John Goddard and Paul Vallance

Routledge
Taylor & Francis Group

LONDON AND NEW YORK

First published 2013
by Routledge
2 Park Square, Milton Park, Abingdon, Oxfordshire OX14 4RN

Simultaneously published in the USA and Canada
by Routledge
711 Third Avenue, New York, NY 10017

First issued in paperback 2014

Routledge is an imprint of the Taylor & Francis Group, an informa business

British Library Cataloguing in Publication Data
A catalogue record for this book is available from the British Library

Library of Congress Cataloging in Publication Data
Goddard, J. B.
The university and the city / by John Goddard and Paul Vallance.
p. cm.
Includes bibliographical references and index.
1. Universities and colleges—Economic aspects—Great Britain.
2. Education, Higher—Economic aspects—Great Britain 3. Urban economics. 4. Community development, Urban—Great Britain. 5. City planning—Great Britain. I. Vallance, Paul. II. Title.
LC67.68.G7G63 2013
338.4′73780941—dc23
2012030801

ISBN 978-0-415-58992-5 (hbk)
ISBN 978-1-138-79853-3 (pbk)
ISBN 978-0-203-06836-6 (ebk)

Typeset in Times New Roman
by Book Now Ltd, London

Contents

x   *Contents*

Illustrations

Figures

Maps

Tables

Acknowledgements

This book would not have been possible without the support of a Leverhulme Trust Emeritus Fellowship awarded to Professor John Goddard on his retirement. We also gratefully acknowledge the support of Newcastle University's Strategic Development Fund for our wider activities as part of the Civic University Study Programme.

Chapter 5 in this book is an updated version of Goddard, J., Vallance, P. and Puukka, J. (2011) 'Experience of engagement between universities and cities: drivers and barriers in three European Cities', *Built Environment*, 37: 299–316. We are grateful to the publisher Alexandrine Press for granting permission to reproduce this material here.

We would like to thank Chris Young for his assistance in producing the maps that appear in this book. We would also like to thank a number of colleagues in the Centre for Urban and Regional Development Studies (CURDS) for their support during the time we have been working on this book, in particular Louise Kempton, John Tomaney, Andy Pike, Susan Robson, Lottie Hann and Emma Wilson.

Finally we would like to thank everyone in Newcastle, Bristol, Manchester, and Sheffield who contributed to this book by giving up their time and thoughts for research interviews.

1   Introduction

Aims and scope

The subject of this book is relationships between universities and cities and how they shape wider processes of urban or regional development. This situates the book in a well-established field of research on the contribution that universities make to sub-national territorial development (see Lawton Smith 2007; Perry and Harloe 2007; Goddard and Vallance 2011). The focus on cities, however, suggests a departure from the previously dominant concern in this field on universities as agents of knowledge-based development in the economic and political spaces of regions. Although the boundaries demarcating cities within larger regions are almost always blurred – and indeed at points in this book we move between these and other intermediate scalar units such as city-regions – we would suggest that this shift in focus of study has a twofold significance.

On a simple empirical level, it reflects the specific location of most universities in cities of some description. The resultant spatial relationship, whether the university campus is based in the urban centre or an outlying suburb, necessarily carries social and economic impacts for the city or city-region of which it is part. For the university, this urban location – even if it is not integral to the institution's identity – forces a relationship with other institutional actors and communities that are also inhabitant in the city. It also raises challenging normative questions about the need for academic practice to be of direct relevance and value to the local contexts or, more generally, the type of social environment in which most of its practitioners live and work (see Bender 1998; Nature 2010; May and Perry 2011a).

On a conceptual level, the city as an object of study encourages exploration of a more broadly-conceived territorial development process than just that focused on economic growth and competitiveness. The relationship between the university and the city is a multi-faceted one of distinct but interrelating physical, social, economic and cultural dimensions. While interpretations of sub-national territorial planning and development more generally may accommodate multiple factors along these lines, a focus on the city – where the concentration of human life means these dimensions come into closer and more frequent contact – strengthens this plural viewpoint. This is also supported by recent theoretical imaginings of the city as a source of heterogeneous social, economic and material relations or development assets, rather than the product of a single dominant process (e.g. circulation of capital) or quality of the urban environment (e.g. agglomeration) (see Amin and Graham 1997; Storper 1997; Healey 2002). Relational views of the city as constituted through diverse (and fragmented) sets of local and non-local network linkages have also challenged understandings of its spatiality as a clearly bounded and coherent geographical or institutional entity (e.g. see Amin and Thrift 2002). A concern with the interplay of territorial and relational geographies (McCann and Ward 2010) seems germane to understanding the university as, on the one hand, a place-embedded institution with connections into the different social and institutional spheres of its locality, and on the other hand, a generative node in national and international flows of knowledge and people (especially highly-mobile students).

Elements of this relationship between universities and cities have been studied from historical, sociological and geographical perspectives in previous edited collections, journal special issues,[1] and individual papers (e.g. Bender 1988a; van der Wusten 1998; Perry and Wiewel 2005; Russo *et al.* 2007; Wiewel and Perry 2008). With this full-length monograph, our goal is to make a distinctive contribution to this literature through enabling a more comprehensive single-focused treatment of this diverse subject. In particular, across the different review and empirical parts of the book we aim to encompass and bring more fully into dialogue differing standpoints on this problem along three lines:

1   Between local economic or social impacts that follow from a university just being present within a city (e.g. related to campus developments, attraction of students to live in the city, employment of large numbers of staff and other knock-on economic effects) and those that arise from more active 'engagement' by the institution or its academic community in the development of its city.

2   Between the economic focus of most previous work on universities and regional development and a more holistic view of the varied societal interactions universities can have within their cities (relating to, for instance, community engagement, social inclusiveness or equality, urban and regional governance, environmental sustainability, health and wellbeing, cultural and civic life).

3   Between the 'external' regional and urban development role of universities and the 'internal' processes – whether in the organisational domain of institutional structures and culture or in the governance domain of state higher education policy – that enable and shape these external relationships.

These three spectrums represent the primary themes of the book that the chapters outlined below aim to address. Over the course of the book, a number of strong secondary themes emerge, several of which will be discussed together in the concluding chapter. These include:

- the differences between the university as an institution, a set of academic sub-groupings, and a population of students resident in the city;
- the role of physical sites and regeneration projects in facilitating and connecting university economic and community engagement in the city;
- the importance of inter-institutional relationships between the multiple universities (or other types of higher education institution) likely to be present in large cities;
- the interdisciplinarity of many societal 'challenges' within cities (e.g. sustainable development, public health, etc.) and the institutional tension this creates with existing disciplinary-based academic structures;
- the role of intermediary organisations or organisational units in engagement between the university and the city;
- the use of the city and its various communities as an 'urban laboratory' for academic research, engagement and knowledge transfer.

Structure of the book

The main body of this book is divided into two parts. Part I (chapters 2–5) is based on review of existing academic literature and other secondary material relating to universities and city/regional development in an international perspective. Part II (chapters 6–10) is based on original research around specific thematic areas in a selection of English cities (Bristol, Newcastle upon Tyne, Manchester and Sheffield). This sole focus on the UK in the empirical component of the book, as well as for practical research reasons, reflects our belief that university and city relations are contingent on the particular configuration of higher education and territorial governance systems, and therefore their in-depth investigation should be based in a specific detailed context (see Chapter 6). The concluding chapter summarises the unifying themes from this empirical work and discusses how they can contribute to furthering understanding of university and city development relationships more generally.

The next two chapters examine institutional-level social and economic impacts of the urban university's presence 'in the city' drawing on international examples from the academic literature. Chapter 2 focuses on how universities shape the built environment and urban social geography of cities. Chapter 3 focuses on the more 'passive' economic impacts that universities have on cities (in contrast to their 'engaged' role in innovation covered in Chapter 4). The types of social and economic impacts covered across these two chapters are institutional (e.g. through property development, employment and expenditure in the local economy) and student-based (e.g. 'studentification' of residential neighbourhoods in the city, labour market effects through migration and entry into local labour markets).

Chapter 4 turns to the more active 'engaged' role of universities in supporting innovation in urban and regional economies. The first half of the chapter reviews the economic geography literature on universities and regional or metropolitan innovation systems. This review supports a more broadly-conceived 'developmental' rather than 'generative' perspective on the role of universities (Gunasekara 2006) that emphasises their contribution to collective institutional capacity for local innovation as much as their direct commercialisation of knowledge. Related to this, in the evolutionary framework adopted for the chapter as a whole, we suggest that the diversity of knowledge, practices and organisational resources supported within universities (and not the private sector) means their place in regional innovation systems should be understood as a source of 'slack' that can add to the long-term adaptability of the economy. The second half of this chapter continues the focus on the university as a heterogeneous and decentralised set of academic sub-units by discussing the adaptation of 'loosely-coupled' internal university structures as a form of organisational innovation within the wider territorial innovation system. This involves examination of three different views of the 'entrepreneurial university' from the literature, all of which emphasise the development of specialist interdisciplinary research centres and other intermediary structures that facilitate engagement in the economy. The chapter concludes by pointing to the limits of this university adaptation approach in terms of the conceptualisation of the 'external environment' to which the university responds as an (implicitly national) higher education funding environment.

Chapter 5 begins to address this limitation by examining how the wider city and regional governance context for 'civic universities' may be elucidated. The focus shifts from the economic to the wider societal role of the university, and this is positioned in a framework of more holistic conceptual understandings of city and regional development. The main concern of the chapter is to introduce a distinction between the facilitating and constraining policy and governance conditions (here phrased in terms of drivers and barriers) that relate to university engagement in economic development and those that relate to engagement in local societal development. This argument is developed through reference to secondary material from a series of OECD reviews of higher education in city and regional development. Three European cities/city-regions are taken as our cases: Berlin, Rotterdam and Jyväskylä (in central Finland). The material reviewed points to the policy and governance drivers for extensive, sustained and strategic university involvement in local economic innovation activity being stronger than they are for engagement in activities to combat social exclusion in these cities. The chapter concludes by identifying three thematic areas that combine societal and economic development concerns and form the basis of chapters in the second half of the book: sustainable urban development, public health and medicine, and links with the cultural sector.

Chapter 6 introduces the second half of the book and outlines the UK higher education and sub-national territorial governance systems as a background to the subsequent empirical chapters. The chapter begins by outlining the original research carried out for the book and notes the importance of the rapidly-changing political and economic circumstances against which it has taken place. This also introduces material from an online survey on the research 'impacts' of individual academics that is included in this book as Appendix B and informs the thematic content of the three following chapters. The core of this chapter is three sub-sections covering: the development of the UK higher education system since the abolition of the binary university–polytechnic divide in 1992; changes in the UK (and more specifically English) territorial governance system over roughly the same twenty year period, with a particular focus on the implications for cities; and the intersections between these two distinct governance domains. This third sub-section shows that, while higher education policy in the UK is predominately spatially neutral, the incorporation of universities into regional and city-level science and innovation governance that developed under the post 1997 Labour government helped introduce some local development dimension into the mission of universities. However, the top-down and centralist form this regional architecture took meant that this dimension was limited and seemingly has not survived a recent change of government. A final section provides a brief general profile of the multi-university higher education sectors in the four cities covered in the following three chapters.

Chapters 7 to 9 explore the relationships between these universities and their cities around the three thematic areas identified above. The empirical investigation is based on a pair of cities for each chapter; matching our home city of Newcastle with Manchester for sustainable urban development (Chapter 7), with Sheffield for public health and medicine (Chapter 8), and with Bristol for links with the cultural sector (Chapter 9). The purpose is not a comparison of the two cities (although parallels and contrasts between them are employed as an analytical device), but using the empirical material from both cases to highlight key relationships and processes in relation to the particular thematic area in question. In Chapter 7, these central elements include the relationship between the institutional and academic roles of universities in sustainable urban development, and how these are mobilised by intermediary economic development or regeneration vehicles and the use of 'urban laboratory' concepts in the two cities. In Chapter 8 the main focus is how university health and medical faculty engagement with the city is shaped by their main institutional relationships (principally with the National Health Service). The two cases covered in this chapter have slightly different foci: in Sheffield our research concentrated on health research and teaching in the two universities and related engagement with the City Council as well as local NHS trusts; in Newcastle it included discussion of relationships with various regional and city agencies seeking to draw on university medical science strengths for the purposes of economic development or regeneration. In Chapter 9 the key concern is how cultural engagement by universities (whether primarily social, economic, or purely artistic in objective) takes place through specific sites or venues within the city, and how this varies between those sites that are located on or off the university campus. The first half of the chapter provides an overview of the link between key university cultural activities and spaces in the two cities. The second half of the chapter comprises more detailed examples from both cities in the area of creative media and digital technology practice;

Newcastle University's Culture Lab and the Watershed's Pervasive Media Studio in which the two universities in Bristol are now partners.

At various points throughout the book we refer to one of a number of ideal models of universities – e.g. the 'urban university', the 'entrepreneurial university', the 'civic university' – that imply varying relationships with the city. In particular, we are interested in further exploring (specifically in a city setting) the idea of the civic university, which is more centrally 'engaged' in its locality than universities that effectively just happen to be located in an urban area, and driven more by the public benefits it generates for society (see Calhoun 2006) than the business-focused entrepreneurial university. The term civic university has a specific historical meaning in relation to public universities founded in the nineteenth century (Delanty 2002), particularly in industrial cities in England (see Barnes 1996; Walsh 2009). However, more recently one of us has argued (in a UK context) in favour of the 'reinvention' of the civic university for the current day, based around principles of a constitutive relationship with the society of which it is part, the promotion of institution-wide 'holistic' engagement, and collaborative relationships with other higher education institutions (see Goddard 2009). This concern is taken up more explicitly in the concluding chapter and related to some of the connecting themes throughout the empirical chapters and book as a whole regarding the societal, economic and physical dimensions of relationships between universities and cities.

Part I

Review: international dimensions

2 The university in the city I: place and community

Introduction to the university in the city

A key subtext to this book's focus on the relationship between universities and cities is the aim of further exploring the notion of a renewed civic university, that is engaged through research, teaching and public service with the city and region of which it is part, and draws on this connection to form its identity within the global academic community (Goddard 2009). However, regardless of the degree to which an urban-located university is linked to its surroundings through these activities, it is safe to assume its presence alone within a city ensures substantial physical, social, economic and cultural impacts on the urban environment. Therefore, before proceeding to examine the more active or intentional role of institutions and academics in the economic and social development of cities or regions, the next two chapters will review existing literature on these types of institutional impacts and their relationship to urban development; focusing first on the physical and community dimensions, and second on the economic dimensions. These chapters also introduce a range of issues that are found in the empirical cases in the second part of the book.

Across these two chapters the main level of analysis is the university as an institution, instead of the smaller academic sub-units on which much of the rest of the book will concentrate. Although the impacts discussed here are seen to arise largely from the location of universities in cities, this does not necessarily denote a disengaged role on the part of the institution. In this first chapter in particular, the types of impacts covered create tensions and opportunities that the university leadership has to manage through their institutional relations with local governments, communities and businesses. Both chapters also highlight the aggregate social, economic and cultural impacts – either positive or negative – of higher education students as a group living in the city, which have become the subject of an expanding literature in human geography. As Russo *et al.* write:

> analysis of the relationship between universities and host communities should not be limited to the institutional sphere. In spite of their diverse social backgrounds, higher education students (both undergraduate and post-graduate) and, to some extent, the rest of the academic community may be

described as an urban population that establishes important economic, social, and cultural relations with other groups, modifying urban landscapes in specific ways, and ultimately determining the viability and extent of the knowledge spillover [from the university].

(Russo *et al.* 2007: 201)

The chapters are international in scope, allowing different territorial contexts for university–city relations to be reflected. Much of the research referred to is UK-based due to the geographical focus of the current literature in some of these areas, but it also draws on material related to North America, continental Europe and Australia.

Place and community

This first chapter examines perhaps the most fundamental way in which urban-located universities shape cities; as part of their built environment and urban social geography. The spatial relationship between university and city is con-stantly changing due to the active role of higher education institutions (HEIs) in shaping the urban landscape as property developers. In urban sociology, univer-sities have been defined alongside institutions such as museums and theatres as 'auxiliary players' in city growth processes; secondary to business and politi-cians in the local coalitions that form around land and property development as an economic development strategy (Logan and Molotch 1987: 75–6). In some contexts, however, where a city has a weak property market that does not attract private investment, universities may have the financial resources to themselves be major developers. The state-directed expansion of higher education systems in advanced economies during the twentieth century created an important dynamic in urban development by enabling university campuses to expand substantially through the building of new facilities for teaching, research, administration and student housing (Wiewel and Perry 2008). For older universities (particularly in Europe) with a historical location close to the centre of their city, this growth has often led to spatial fragmentation, as pressure on space forces new rounds of prop-erty expansion or redevelopment to be located in less costly suburban areas with a disconnect from the city core (van der Wusten 1998; Larkham 2000; Russo and Tatjer 2007; Wiewel and Perry 2008).

The physical arrangement of an urban university's estate can also affect the institution's relationship to the city. Different models of planning vary according to the degree to which a university's buildings are centred on one or more cam-puses, or are more dispersed and integrated into the rest of the city (Edwards 2000; Larkham 2000; van Heur 2010). The campus tradition, that originated in England but has become most prominent in the USA (Turner 1984), is associated by Bender (1988a: 3) with 'antiurbanism', although it has become a feature of some universities in larger cities as well as smaller 'college towns' (Perry and Wiewel 2005; Gumprecht 2007). A campus not only allows for functional con-centration of higher education buildings, but also creates a 'semi-cloistered'

(Bender 1988b) space in the midst of larger cities, dedicated to meeting the work and leisure requirements of student and academic communities. This space has its own distinctive character in relation to its surrounding districts and leaves a clearer imprint on the topography of cities than more integrated models of university planning. Hence, the 'campus' can be taken to signify the enduring desire for universities to form their own self-contained reflective 'place', not just for the consumption of higher education services but also for 'attendance and participation in a certain sort of cultural and social life' by its young students (Kumar 1997: 29). For universities in cities, however, the separation from society that the campus model potentially engenders can be a source of tensions with their civic mission to engage with surrounding communities that have little direct connection to higher education, but may be directly affected by their geographic expansion.

An increasing amount of attention is beginning to be paid in geography and planning to these questions about the physical development of the university, although this work has yet to form into a coherent literature (van Heur 2010). The topic has been explored most fully in two recent collections edited by David Perry and Wim Wiewel, which use property development by universities as a lens through which to view wider social and economic elements of their relations with cities. The first of these collections, *The University as an Urban Developer*, consists of case studies solely from North America, while the second, *Global Universities and Urban Development*, has an international comparative scope. In the introduction to the first of these books, Perry and Wiewel (2005) conceptually frame university real estate development practice as a matter of having to reconcile the often competing dynamics of, on the one hand, meeting the constantly-growing requirements for space and facilities of their internal constituencies (e.g. students, academics) related to the core activities of teaching and research, and on the other hand, ensuring they act in a responsible way towards their external constituencies. They outline this 'external logic' along the following lines:

> Because universities are among the largest landowners and employers in cities, as well as major consumers of private goods and public services, they have a host of external constituents. Both indirectly, in light of the institution's education mission, but quite directly and dramatically, in terms of the university's physical location, economic relations, and political demands, these constituencies often assert every bit the same level of claims on the university as they do on the firm, the church, or public agencies in the city. Therefore the role of the urban university is an important and complex one – mixing the institutional demands of both academy and city.
>
> (Perry and Wiewel 2005: 5–6)

In the rest of this chapter we will adopt this distinction between the university's internal and external 'logics' or 'constituencies' to inform our review of the emerging literature in this area. We divide this into three sections that correspond to distinct areas in this emerging literature: a mainly North American-focused literature on university and community relations around campus development; the social impacts of large numbers of students living off-campus in certain city districts; and university participation in physical economic development or regeneration projects within cities.

Community and campus development

The ethos that universities have responsibilities to their 'external' urban constituencies is particularly strong in North America, where it is reflected in characteristically American notions such as service learning (Zlotkowski 2007) or 'the scholarship of engagement' (Boyer 1996), but also in the prominence of community development concerns in the campus development practices of some HEIs. These community relation concerns are shared by urban universities located in other social and political contexts, such as the divided cities of Belfast (see Boal and Logan 1998; Gaffikin 2008) and Jerusalem (see Shachar 1998; Yacobi 2008), but relevant case studies from North America are more common in the current literature and more rooted in a rhetoric of community or civic engagement. Bromley puts this discourse in a wider context:

> The 'local stakeholder' concept is drawn from contemporary US community development parlance. It groups colleges and universities together with other local institutions and interest groups which are not footloose and must rely on the local market. This grouping links them with the municipality, the chamber of commerce, the local school district, local houses of worship and community centres, neighbourhood associations and community development corporations, and any locally-based corporations like savings banks or utilities. Recognition of stakeholder status thus serves as a rallying call, both to commit resources and to form strategic alliances with other organisations.
>
> (Bromley 2006: 11)

This concern with community relations is undoubtedly based on a degree of 'enlightened self-interest' on the part of the university, in which working to improve the local off-campus environment, particularly when the university is located amongst relatively deprived urban neighbourhoods, brings benefits in terms of the university's ability to attract students or academic staff, and increases the chances that campus expansion projects will gain consent from surrounding communities (Weber *et al.* 2005; Bromley 2006). There are, however, several additional explanations possible for the strength of the community orientation in North American HEI land and property development practice. For instance, it could represent the institutional mission of the different types of public university or college that comprise part of the mixed US higher education system (Cohen 1998). This tradition originated with the Land-Grant Institutions that were founded in each state following the *First Morrill Act of 1862*, predominately to meet the needs of agriculture and rural development, and now survive as large, socially-conscious state universities typically located outside major cities (see Kellogg Commission 1999). The US higher education system has grown to encompass many other public universities and institutions like community colleges that are located in larger cities, and whose public mission is reflected in their concern for urban development. For example, Bromley and Kent (2006) study the considerable recent involvement in neighbourhood revitalisation of four institutions in Ohio's public university system that are located in some of the state's different metropolitan areas – the University of Cincinnati (Cincinnati-Hamilton), the University of Akron (Cleveland-Akron), Youngstown State University (Youngstown-Warren), and Ohio State University, the original Land Grant Institution (which can now also be classified as an urban university due to the growth of Columbus, its host city and state capital, across the twentieth century). In contrast to the geographical neutrality of higher education policy in other countries, the metropolitan identity of some universities was formally recognised in the USA through proposals during the 1960s and 1970s to designate a system of publicly-engaged 'urban grant' universities as a counterpart to the rural-focused land grant institutions (Bromley 2006: 15). Although this plan was never realised on a national level, Bromley and Kent (2006: 50) explain how the same concern with declining industrial cities led to Ohio's state legislature creating an Urban University Programme (UUP) in 1980. They write of this programme that its:

> significance . . . is not based on the volume of the funding . . . but on the identification of eight public universities as 'urban' and having a special responsibility for urban revitalisation. Conceptually the UUP was a master-stroke in an extended period of deindustrialisation – drawing the attention of politicians, campus leaders, educational administrators and scholars.
>
> (Bromley and Kent 2006: 74)

Similarly, Bunnell and Lawson (2006: 41) describe how Portland State University has been able to redevelop its campus and an adjacent part of the city, despite not having large sources of finance at its disposal, by using its status as a locally-embedded institution to enrol other large public agencies in this project and having the 'institutional stamina' to 'sustain the planning process over a period of many years'. Barlow (1998) also describes how Concordia University in Canada adopted an explicit urban university mission to differentiate itself from other HEIs in the city of Montreal. Not all public urban universities, however, are equally committed to taking on this wider role in revitalising their city (Bromley and Kent 2006), and conversely the literature shows that some large private institutions (that may typically have more discretionary funding to spend in this area) also invest heavily in connections with local communities (Bunnell and Lawson 2006). The practical challenges of surrounding inner city decline compel a response from private universities located in cities as much as it does from public universities (Nijman 1998; Rodin 2005).

Another possible factor behind the commitment to this agenda in some US institutions is the influence of institutional leadership (Austrian and Norton

2005; Wiewel and Perry 2005). Wiewel and Perry (2008) note that one of the major differences between the case studies in their two books was the relative importance attributed to individual university leaders (normally the institution's president) in the North American cases, compared to those from the rest of the world (covering locations across Europe, Asia and South or Central America) in which 'institutional priorities and actions appear to reflect broad, ongoing planning processes more than individual agendas' (ibid.: 316). This is particularly the case in European countries where the state either owns the land on which public universities are built or regulates its use (Groenendijk 1998; Haila 2008; Peel 2008). Bromley and Kent (2006: 75) observe that the four Ohioan universities they examine in the study mentioned above are all 'associated with strong, stable institutional leadership which makes community outreach and the revitalisation of neighbourhoods around the campus major long-term institutional priorities' that do not 'get lost among the many, many different objectives and priorities of a large complex institution'. The importance of individual university leaders in North America also suggests that the strength of key inter-personal relations, for instance with local politicians or community leaders, is of greater influence in gaining support for development projects and negotiating any barriers that may arise in the planning process (see Wiewel and Perry 2005; Bromley and Kent 2006). However, the individual preferences and personal networks of university leaders will only be of consequence for as long as they are in these executive positions. As Wiewel and Perry (2005: 304) conclude 'the highest achievement... [of leadership] may be to inculcate the vision, objectives, and approach in an organization so it can be implemented consistently and steadily'. An example of this in the literature is Judith Rodin's (2005) account of the transformation of the private University of Pennsylvania under her leadership as president between 1994 and 2004. This describes a project – the West Philadelphia Initiative – to revitalise this deprived part of the city surrounding its campus, which aimed to involve the whole institution. The project included various university-supported programmes to improve local neighbourhoods, housing, retail and cultural amenities, public schools, and business and employment opportunities (by directing contracts and purchasing), but also sought to 'make the link from practice to theory' (ibid.: 247) by extending this engagement back into academic programmes, most notably by developing interdisciplinary expertise in applied urban research as part of the institution's identity.

Notwithstanding these positive stories of 'enlightened self-interest', public institutional missions and committed leadership, tensions with communities around university building projects are still commonplace. Several of the case studies featured in *The University as Urban Developer* highlight this by explaining the development of projects as the result of a longer term process that involved periods of tension and conflict with the community leading to the adoption of a more conciliatory stance on the part of the university (e.g. Deitrick and Soska 2005; Webber 2005). Marcuse and Potter's (2005) account of Columbia University's attempts during the 1980s and 1990s to convert a derelict building (the Audubon Ballroom) in the Washington Heights district of Manhattan into a biomedical science and technology facility also falls into this category (also see Zukin 1995). This project encountered opposition from African American groups because of the historical significance of this building (as the site of Malcolm X's assassination), and also required the university to ensure the development did not have negative impacts on the local Dominican population that had become the largest resident group in this area. In this case the project went ahead with the business incubator opening in 1995, thus meeting the university's requirement for more space in which scientific and commercialisation activities can be carried out in the city. Marcuse and Potter (2005) also conclude that the project has for the most part been a success from a community perspective: the new facility helped revitalise the local neighbourhood, it created retail space that served local residents, and steps to memorialise Malcolm X in the site have been taken, although they also note that some related plans (for a community centre and museum) had been delayed.

In summary, this section has examined the importance of community relations in processes of university campus development and expansion, using the case of public and private universities in North American cities. As well as discussing factors such as the strength of community stakeholdership and institutional or political leadership in this particular context, it has also highlighted the more explicit 'urban' identity of city-based universities in North America. The concern with 'external' groups that this status denotes may often be based on wanting to improve the immediate environment in which the university is located or to avoid conflict with local communities, but nevertheless indicates the potential of universities as urban development actors. The third section in this chapter returns to this theme when considering the involvement of universities in knowledge-based economic development and regeneration building projects.

Students and city communities

This second section focuses on the community impacts, not of the university per se, but its associated student population living 'off-campus' as residents in the city. This connects to the overall theme of the chapter in its concern with the way that an 'internal' expansionary logic within higher education – in this case a trend towards greater student numbers – has an 'external' effect on the use of the urban environment which is manifested in the issue of student housing.

The effects of temporary student residents on the social fabric of large cities does not generally appear to be a prominent issue in the literature on North American community and university relations discussed above. Bromley (2006: 13) suggests that many US urban universities take either the form of 'enclave' institutions 'with a high proportion of students residing on campus' and 'considerable self-sufficiency of campus services', or 'commuter' institutions with 'most students and faculty living out in the suburbs, so contact with surrounding neighbourhoods is mainly "drive-through"'. Instead, the closest equivalent to the student-dominated areas of many European cities can perhaps be found in the long-established American phenomenon of the college town; normally a smaller city with a large HEI where, in the broad definition offered by Gumprecht (2003:

51) 'a college or university and the cultures it creates exert a dominant influence over the character of the community'. Although the high proportion of students in the population can cause some tensions with permanent residents, the centrality of higher education to the economic as well as cultural life of these cities and towns – along with the widespread use of the 'campus [and its facilities] as a public space' by the whole community – indicates that town and gown are less likely to be polarised here than in other settings (Gumprecht 2003, 2007).

In other national contexts, by contrast, tensions between universities and local communities are often most heightened around the large numbers of students living in residential areas. This is particularly true of the UK where it is customary for middle-class domestic higher education students to attend university away from their hometown (Holdsworth 2009) and, following an initial year in university-provided accommodation, live in rented multi-occupancy properties that are typically concentrated in areas near to the university (Allinson 2006; Duke-Williams 2009; Munro *et al.* 2009). The government-promoted expansion of higher education student numbers over the previous twenty years (see Chapter 6), combined with a lack of any accompanying national planning policy on student housing to manage the impacts of this growth on local communities (Smith 2008), has led to certain parts of cities, including Leeds, Birmingham, Nottingham and Newcastle, and even smaller towns with a university, such as Loughborough, becoming inhabited by increasingly large numbers of temporary student residents (Hubbard 2008; Munro *et al.* 2009). The high demand for multi-occupancy rental accommodation in these areas creates the conditions for large parts of the available housing stock to be purchased by individual landlords or agencies with the purpose of letting to short-term student tenants, which can reinforce the position of the neighbourhood as a student area by pricing homeowners out of the market and reducing the attractiveness of the area to families and other groups (Allinson 2006; Hubbard 2008).

A mainly UK-centred strand of research in urban social geography has emerged (thus far largely separate from the literature on the university's campus development reviewed above) that examines these economic and social impacts by adapting concepts from the established field of gentrification studies. Hence, the neologism 'studentification' has been coined to describe the process through which urban neighbourhoods are transformed by a growing student population (Smith and Holt 2007; Hubbard 2008, 2009; Smith 2008, 2009). The distinctive consumption practices of middle and upper class students, particularly around night-time leisure activities, can form 'exclusive geographies' within their host cities based on the provision of a 'popular culture infrastructure' of bars and nightclubs specifically dedicated to this market (Chatterton 1999). It has been proposed that young students from relatively affluent backgrounds become 'apprentice gentrifiers', developing cultural capital during their first experiences of living away from home that they carry over into their future behaviour within urban housing markets (Smith and Holt 2007). Framing this discussion in the terms of gentrification has meant that much of the work on this subject has emphasised the negative social impacts associated with an influx of transient and seasonal student residents on community cohesion (i.e. inflated property prices, physical neglect of houses, anti-social behaviour, attraction of crime, withdrawal from the area during holidays, local shops and services becoming orientated towards student lifestyles, etc.) (e.g. Kenyon 1997). However, others have argued for a more nuanced position that acknowledges the opportunity for eco- nomic and cultural revitalisation of depressed neighbourhoods that student resi- dents potentially offer (Macintyre 2003; Allinson 2006; Hubbard 2008) (also Chapter 3). Other commentators have questioned whether studentification should be understood as a form of gentrification at all. For instance, Bromley (2006: 6) notes that studentification does not generally lead to a physical improvement of the neighbourhood. Hubbard (2008: 324) also argues that segments of what is a heterogeneous student population (also Christie 2007) could equally be consid- ered as relatively socially and economically marginalised in the cities where they live. A large share of higher education students have to take part-time jobs to support themselves, typically in retail or leisure sectors with relatively poor pay and working conditions (Munro *et al.* 2009).

A salient issue here is the institutional role of the university itself in the for- mation of these student geographies. For Smith (2009: 1796), a fundamental cause of studentification processes in the UK has been that 'the growth in stu- dent recruitment has not been matched by the strategic development of univer- sity halls of residence or provision of student services' leaving the surplus to be absorbed by local communities with largely unplanned social effects. The shift to most UK universities only being able to directly supply accommodation to a minority of their students can also be linked to a decline in them taking a wide- ranging pastoral responsibility for their students' wellbeing, which maybe now just associated with more traditional collegiate university models such as Oxford and Cambridge. In a paper on student communities in two continental European cities (Barcelona and Lille), Russo and Tatjer (2007) argue that there is an obser- vable trend towards the 'decoupling' of students' educational spaces (i.e. univer- sity campuses) from their main residential and leisure spaces. Depending on the institutional circumstances, this can take different forms: for instance, universi- ties located in a city centre where students can no longer afford to live, or con- versely the case of suburban-located universities whose students prefer to live closer to the city centre for lifestyle reasons. However, in contrast to this picture of a growing disconnect from involvement in student residencies, universities continue to have to meet housing requirements for a possibly growing number of both domestic and international students, and the attractiveness of this accommo- dation may be important to the competitiveness of institutions in being able to recruit prospective students. With declining state funding for higher education placing restrictions on the number of large-scale capital projects that universities can self-finance, there is a growing trend in the UK and internationally for them to partner with private investors to enable new student housing developments (Macintyre 2003; Fincher and Shaw 2009; Hubbard 2009). According to Macintyre (2003: 115–116) these arrangements can follow different models, including the university guaranteeing a supply of future student tenants (and therefore a relatively low-risk fixed return for the investor), or more speculative developments by private companies aimed at the wider student rental market in which the university may not be directly involved. It is the second of these options that Hubbard (2009) is concerned with in a paper focused on the introduction of new purpose-built housing facilities catering to well-off post first year undergraduate students in the English university town of Loughborough. This type of off-campus development has become common in recent years across cities in the UK (also Chatterton 2010), and has been welcomed by universities and local authorities as part of their strategies to address the over-concentration of students living in the existing rental sector of some neighbourhoods (Hubbard 2009: 1909). It may also be a mechanism of regeneration, particularly if private sector investment can be leveraged into areas of cities that otherwise would not offer attractive property market opportunities (Macintyre 2003). However, Hubbard (2009: 1920) finds that in Loughborough these student-only developments – in some ways akin to 'gated communities' – seem to be deepening the social segregation of students from local communities that is associated with already existing patterns of student-based gentrification. Similarly, Fincher and Shaw (2009) show that the University of Melbourne's reliance on this type of private development to house increasing numbers of new international students in a mainly non-residential area close to the University has the inadvertent effect of separating them from full integration into the city, and also reinforces their cultural distance from Australian students.

This section has reviewed a growing literature on the social effects of students living off-campus as one of the main impacts of the expansion of higher education on cities in the UK and rest of Europe. This problem seems to have arisen in part because of the relative neglect of student housing by universities and governments. More recently, efforts to address the problem have involved private companies in the building of large student accommodation developments, but the wider issue of social segregation between students and local residents remain. We return to the theme of student geographies in the next chapter, where their largely more positive impacts on the economic and cultural life of the city are discussed.

Universities and knowledge-based urban development

This third and final section will cover the impacts of universities' involvement in physical campus development and wider off-campus urban regeneration projects that relate to their new role in supporting the transition to post-industrial local economies based on science, technology and creativity. Hence it follows Madanipour (2011) in emphasising the often overlooked materiality of the knowledge economy and its spatial expression within cities.

The contemporary expansion of university campuses is often related to the internal logic of their growing aspirations in the field of commercialisation and business development, which may require additional scientific and administrative units (for instance, with Marcuse and Potter's (2005) Columbia University study cited above). Van Heur (2010) argues that the design of hybrid higher education buildings, such as business or creative industry incubators, can help facilitate interactions between academics and entrepreneurs or firm employees, and make the campus more permeable to members of the public. This form of expansion may, however, also contribute to the 'spatial fragmentation' of urban universities discussed earlier, as the larger-scale scientific and engineering facilities needed for industry-related research often cannot be accommodated easily in central city locations (van der Wusten 1998: 10). At the same time, universities have also become more heavily involved in local economic development partnerships, where they can act as 'planning animateurs' by mobilising other actors (local governments and planning authorities, private developers, etc.) around specific urban development projects (Benneworth and Hospers 2007a).

The most-established and globally-widespread form of university participation in these types of projects is through off-campus science and technology park developments (Castells and Hall 1994; van Winden *et al.* 2012). Although science parks have a clear economic rationale, in providing space where tenant firms (often including university spin-outs) in high technology intensive sectors can co-locate in geographical proximity to academic or other research institutes, the empirical evidence for their effectiveness in encouraging links between industry and universities or stimulating employment growth in high-technology sectors is inconsistent (e.g. Massey *et al.* 1992; Vedovello 1997; Shearmur and Doloreux 2000; Siegel *et al.* 2003; cf. Phillimore 1999; Löfsten and Lindelöf 2002; Yang *et al.* 2009). Castells and Hall (1994) also conclude that planned 'technopoles' (a concept encompassing technology parks and larger 'science cities') have generally – in varying historical economic and political contexts – been unsuccessful in driving new economic development through technological innovation, whilst many large metropolitan regions have continued to flourish as centres of innovation. Instead, the main significance of science parks is perhaps more often as opportunities for commercial property developments involving universities, but typically led and managed by public sector partners with the goal of attracting private sector investment (Massey *et al.* 1992; Castells and Hall 1994; Shearmur and Doloreux 2000). In the past, science parks have typically been built towards the fringes of the city or town of which the related university is part. More recently, however, van Winden *et al.* (2012) have proposed that the type of 'knowledge spaces' formerly exemplified by large out-of-city science and technology parks are undergoing an 'urban turn' towards sites that are more mixed in function and integrated into the fabric of the city. In their definition, these urban knowledge spaces include science and technology locations often based around universities, but also sites for creative industries activity, such as 'cultural quarters' or 'media hubs' in which higher education participation may be more peripheral and supportive in function (also see Charles 2011). These will be discussed in more detail in Chapter 9. Through the development of these urban sites, universities can contribute more widely to the physical and symbolic regeneration of cities, particularly when this regeneration is seen as part of a move towards a post-industrial knowledge-based economy and society (Yigitcanlar and Velibeyoglu 2008; Johnston 2010).

Physical development projects also offer an arena in which universities can build stronger relationships with both community and business interests in the development of their cities (Russo *et al.* 2007). However, Benneworth *et al.* (2010) show that, while on the surface knowledge-based urban development projects would appear to offer mutual benefits for university and city, in practice their interests often do not perfectly align. The optimal strategy for the expansion of a campus from the university's standpoint may not, in terms of location or function, coincide with projects that have an urban development or regeneration impact targeted to the needs of the city. Equally, the city authorities may have 'unrealistic ambitions' about the impact that university involvement in these projects can have, particularly when these are based on common policy discourses around the growth potential of new industries such as biotechnology (ibid.: 1617). A further problem identified in the literature refers to the longer-term economic development benefits for the city that are related to a university's role as a land developer. In the conclusion to their book of North American case studies, Wiewel and Perry note that:

> In the knowledge economy, universities are more important than ever, but in most of these cases neither the city nor the university appears to have wrestled with what this means for the role of the university and the physical and real estate consequences thereof. Rather projects proceed in a piecemeal fashion, and cities treat the university like any other organization that needs building permits and other municipal services. In most cases contracts are project- and task-orientated and episodic, rather than continuous, comprehensive, and strategic.
>
> (Wiewel and Perry 2005: 310–311)

Similarly, Benneworth and Hospers (2007a) argue that, while universities can take a leading ('animateur') role in development projects to overcome weak or fragmented institutional systems in economically less successful cities or regions, this more often results in the development of *ad hoc* networks or partnerships related only to that specific project, rather than encouraging a more enduring beneficial transformation of governance arrangements.

This brief review of the emerging literature in this area highlights a number of issues that will be developed further in our empirical work and the concluding chapter in the second half of this book. All the cases we feature – whether relating to urban sustainability, public health, or links with the creative sector – include a physical dimension to the relationship between university and city.

Conclusion

This chapter has examined the role of universities (and associated groups such as higher education students) in shaping the built environment and urban social geography of cities. Although this chapter has been framed underneath the rubric of social and economic impacts that inevitably follow from the presence of HEIs in cities (in this case driven by their need to expand and meet extra demands placed upon them in the late twentieth and early twenty-first centuries), the university has to actively manage these impacts through institutional relations with various other organisations and groups. In particular, the chapter has high-lighted the social tensions that can form between universities and local commu-nities around issues of campus expansion and student residents. Hence the community engagement of universities covered here can to a large degree be interpreted as 'enlightened self-interest'. Chapter 5 will return to this theme when it considers the drivers and barriers to academics and institutions becoming more actively engaged in the social development of cities. More specific issues covered in this chapter (e.g. campus development, the link between university building projects and local economic development) will be picked up in different parts of the second half of the book. However, before this, the related economic impacts of the location of universities in cities will be covered in the next chapter.

3 The university in the city II: economic impacts

Introduction

> As a large-scale consumer of inputs (labour, goods, services) and generator of outputs (skills, know-how, local attractiveness) the university cannot fail to be a major factor in metropolitan economic development. Even without a proactive, explicit role in promoting local economic activity, the results of its policies and decisions are likely to impact heavily on the metropolitan economy.
>
> (Felsenstein 1996: 1566)

This second chapter on the impacts of universities located in cities concentrates on the more 'passive' economic benefits that cities and regions gain from the presence of higher education institutions (HEIs). As the quote above highlights, higher education can be an important component of an urban economy even before universities' more active role in supporting innovation (which will be discussed in the next chapter) is considered. This effect has become more widespread with the expansion of national higher education systems and the establishment of universities in places previously unrepresented in the sector. The chapter covers three types of economic impact: those related to university employment and expenditure in local economies; the positive effect of student and academic populations on the city environment as a 'creative' place to live and work; and the human capital effects linked to universities helping to attract and retain graduate workers in regional labour markets.

Economic impact multipliers

As this book will go on to discuss in detail, the teaching and research carried out within universities are vital to the functioning of modern economies in myriad ways. However, the most direct tangible economic benefits that universities have on their surrounding locality are perhaps those that relate to employment and expenditure effects they generate, rather than their main outputs of education services or knowledge produced through research. There are three particular features of universities which ensure that through these employment and expenditure effects alone they will be an integral part of an urban economy. First, they are typically large and labour-intensive organisations (Armstrong *et al.* 1997) which means that they are often one of the biggest single employers within a city or region, alongside local governments, healthcare providers and large private companies (Glasson 2003). The range of jobs they create (including those that relate to management and human resources, administration, technical support, estates and maintenance, on-campus retail and leisure, as well as academic functions) cover different occupations and pay-scales, but include a high proportion of skilled and professional classes. Second, universities will also purchase varied goods and services from local and non-local businesses, ranging in scale from regular expenditure on small items (catering, office supplies, etc.) to larger spends on, for instance, construction projects (Armstrong *et al.* 1997). As the previous chapter showed, universities are institutions in receipt of public and other funding, but typically with the autonomy to spend on large-scale building and land development projects within their city. Third, most universities attract large numbers of domestic, and now increasingly also international, students from outside their region to live within the locality. Students bring money to the university directly through fees and government grants for tuition (the income from which is recycled through university salaries and expenditure), but as discussed in the previous chapter they also create distinctive housing and consumption requirements within a city. The university will only partly meet these needs itself through, for example, on-campus services or providing accommodation to some students, with the remainder producing demand for the local private sector. Universities can also attract large numbers of visitors to their city or region for events such as conferences or graduation ceremonies.

These sorts of 'passive' effects on local economies are represented in the regional development literature on universities through a genre of research known as impact multiplier studies. This methodological approach uses available data on what is referred to as 'direct' economic effects (i.e. the number of people actually employed by the university, its levels of expenditure) and through different modelling techniques reach an estimate of the 'indirect' and 'induced' monetary effects on the local economy at a given geographical scale, for instance, the second-round expenditure of university wages being spent in the surrounding region, or the extra local jobs that are dependent on income from the university as a client. From this modelling (that needs to take into account local contingencies such as the numbers of employers that live in the designated study area and their wage levels), a 'multiplier' value is derived to express the ratio of extra income or employment created from the direct input. The level of multiplier varies considerably between studies, depending not only on the case in question, but also the precise methodology used.

Huggins and Cooke's (1997) study of Cardiff University's impact on its city and regional economy for the year 1994–1995 gives a good illustration of the kind of more credible results that studies of this type can produce. For employment, they estimate that on top of to the 2,747 people directly employed by the University at the time, an additional 604 jobs were supported in the Cardiff area

(3,351 in total) and a further 55 in the slightly larger South East Wales region (3,406 total). This means that the multiplier values derived from their modelling are 1.22 for the city and 1.24 for the wider region. For expenditure, they estimate that the University's direct output in Cardiff of around £64.3 million and in South East Wales of £67.1 million, translated into 'gross local output' (not including deductions for taxes and pension contributions) of £97.2 million and £102.1 million respectively. This gives multipliers of 1.51 for Cardiff and 1.52 for South East Wales. Variations on the Keynesian multiplier model employed by Huggins and Cooke (1997) have been used in a number of other peer-reviewed studies of UK institutions with comparable results (see Bleaney *et al.* 1992; Armstrong *et al.* 1997; Glasson 2003). From a survey of university impact studies in the USA, Siegfried *et al.* (2007: 553) find that the median values for employment and expenditure multipliers are higher at 1.8 and 1.7 respectively.

However, the findings of impact multiplier studies in general should be treated with caution. The majority of these studies are commissioned and published by universities for essentially promotional purposes (i.e. to justify public expenditure on higher education) and are, therefore, prone to exaggeration in terms of the magnitude of multiplier on actual income or employment and the ways in which conclusions are inferred and presented from the results (Beck *et al.* 1995; Siegfried *et al.* 2007). There are also considerable methodological challenges associated with accurately modelling what is in reality an extremely complex system of income flows and interrelationships within local economies. These are discussed by Siegfried *et al.* (2007), who particularly emphasise the problems of specifying an adequate counterfactual; i.e. the true loss to the local economy if the university went out of business or re-located, assuming that, for instance, in this hypothetical situation, some students would move to other institutions in the same city or region (also Beck *et al.* 1995; Blackwell *et al.* 2002). A further set of methodological challenges relate to student expenditure within the local economy because, unlike university expenditure and staff numbers, no official data will be available. Some studies, therefore, carry out supplementary surveys of student spending patterns in the local economy, which include estimation of how many students live in the study area that would not do otherwise if they did not attend the university (e.g. Beck *et al.* 1995; Huggins and Cooke 1997; Steinacker 2005).

The figures for income and employment generated by these impact studies are particular to the time (financial year) and place (university and its local economic context) of the case to which they refer. Hence, as Armstrong *et al.* (1997: 343) argue, the way that economic impacts are conceptualised in these models, in terms of the pathways through which different sources of revenue feed into the local economy, are likely to be of greater general academic interest than the actual results. Impact multiplier studies can also shed light on the geography of these patterns. A fundamental step in the methodology of a study is to define the geographical unit for which the university's impact will be estimated, which may depend either on the scale at which the required data is available and/or the preference of the commissioning party (e.g. the university client). As a general rule, the figure for total income and employment generated will be higher the larger the study area. However, because more of a university's expenditure is likely to remain in its home city or region than move to other individual cities or regions in the same country, this figure will increase at a diminishing rate as the study area expands (Beck *et al.* 1995). Steinacker (2005) demonstrates that employment and expenditure multiplier effects may also be concentrated at the smaller scale of particular neighbourhoods or individual cities within larger metropolitan conurbations. The size and type of place in which the university is located will also make a difference to the patterns of economic impact. Although no systemic research seems to have been done to verify the widespread applicability of this comparison, the various case studies and commentaries within the university economic impact literature do propose several differences between universities in large cities or metropolitan areas and those located in smaller cities or towns. For instance, more of a university's indirect economic impacts are likely to be captured within large cities (i.e. higher multiplier value), because the larger and more diverse local economy will be able to provide a bigger share of the university's required goods and services (Felsenstein 1996). In many cases, a higher proportion of students and staff will also live within a large city. However, the impact related to the presence of a university is likely to represent a bigger share of local economic activity and employment in smaller cities or towns, even if the overall effect is smaller (also Goldstein and Drucker 2006). The paradigmatic case of this may be the American 'college town' mentioned in the previous chapter, where much local economic activity and employment as well as cultural life is related to a large HEI and the students it attracts (Gumprecht 2003). The difference can also frame interpretation of results for UK universities, such as Lancaster or Oxford, away from major metropolitan areas (see Armstrong *et al.* 1997; Glasson 2003). However, larger cities are more likely to have multiple higher education institutions. The implications of this are not often addressed in impact multiplier studies that typically focus on single institutions. As Beck *et al.* (1995: 251) show the economic impacts of an urban or regional 'system' of universities will not simply be equal to the sum of the impacts of its constituent institutions or campuses, because of the interrelationships that exist between them, and chance that in the counterfactual situation of a university disappearing, the remaining institutions would likely absorb some of its students and staff. Finally, several papers suggest that, while the short-term economic impacts of universities related to expenditure and employment may be relatively more important in smaller cities, this is balanced against the likelihood that the 'long-run' economic benefits of universities in terms of contributing to the local labour supply will be higher in large cities because of the greater job opportunities that may encourage students to stay in that region following graduation (Beck *et al.* 1995; Felsenstein 1996; Steinacker 2005). These 'human capital' impacts, which are not normally incorporated within impact multiplier studies (although see Blackwell *et al.* 2002), will be discussed below.

In summary, impact multiplier studies bring notice to the considerable size of employment and expenditure related to universities and their student populations within local economies, and also indicate how this can follow different geographical patterns depending on the location of the university in question. These impacts are of particular importance, because universities are 'anchor' institutions in the local economy; extremely unlikely to move to another city or region, and less prone than most other organisational actors in the economy (e.g. private firms) to stop operating or experience a severe contraction in size caused by an economic downturn, at least in the short term. Hence, universities can increase the 'resilience' of a city or region by providing relatively steady employment and expenditure that buffers against the worst effects of recessions. However, we would advise against placing too much significance on the findings of impact multiplier studies, not only due to the methodological uncertainty that may surround them, but also because of the implication they can carry that the existence of universities can be justified just by the direct and indirect economic effects that are attributable to their size, labour-intensiveness and ability to attract students into the area. In some respects, these studies treat higher education as if it is any other industry, and focus only on those monetary income and employment effects that are quantifiable within an economic model (Kelly *et al.* 2011). By contrast, other outputs to the economy, such as knowledge and skills that are less easily measured, are not typically included in these models.

Academic communities and creative places

The preceding section touched on the economic impact of students and university staff living in a city through the income and employment effects related to their consumption of various goods and services. This section explores arguments about the less tangible economic benefits that these groups may bring through their positive effect on the social and cultural environment of cities. This section does not cover interaction between academics or students with the cultural sector that takes place through university research, teaching and engagement (covered in Chapter 9), but only the more 'passive' effects they have (predominately off-campus) as local populations.

The cultural amenities of a city have taken on an added significance in recent theories of local economic development that emphasise the importance of the wider social attributes of a place in attracting and retaining highly-skilled workers. These arguments are most closely identified with Richard Florida's (2002) influential *Creative Class* thesis. This posits that the competitiveness of cities in the contemporary economy is related to their stock of 'talented' workers in certain 'creative' occupations, who choose to live in a place as much for lifestyle considerations – particularly an open and tolerant social environment – as for the availability of employment opportunities. Florida's (2002) work has drawn numerous statistical correlations between US metropolitan region economic performance (particularly related to high-technology industry), levels of human capital (talent), and proxy values for social tolerance and diversity. Universities fit into this narrative not only through their role in generating human capital (discussed below), but also through the perception that their presence can help foster an appealing cosmopolitan, liberal and creative milieu (Florida 2002; Gertler and Vinodrai 2005;

Florida *et al.* 2006). Academics and those in associated occupations, such as scientists and engineers, artists, designers and architects, are also classified as 'core members' of the Creative Class (Florida 2002: 69). Indeed, one criticism made of Florida is that his definition of creative occupations overlaps too much with groups characterised by higher education attainment (Markusen 2006).

Florida has himself directly addressed this issue with colleagues in the monograph *The University and the Creative Economy*. Here they argue that the previous focus on universities in regional development studies, as agents of technology transfer (whilst still important) has been overemphasised in comparison to 'the university's even more powerful roles in... generating, attracting and mobilizing talent and in establishing a tolerant and diverse social climate' (Florida *et al.* 2006: 20). This claim is supported by empirical work testing the relationships between indicators for higher education and three elements of the Creative Class theory – technology, talent and tolerance – at the level of US metropolitan regions. Relating to 'tolerance', they find a positive correlation between the number of students, and to a lesser extent academic faculty, in a metropolitan region and its score on their 'Tolerance Index' (including measurements for racial integration, foreign born population, artistic and bohemian communities, and gay and lesbian population) (ibid.: 16–17). They also find this relationship is stronger for smaller metropolitan regions with relatively large higher education populations, such as with the 'college towns' mentioned above, where the culture of the place may be 'dominated' by the university (Gumprecht 2003: 51). This leads them to argue that '[b]y creating social environments of openness, self-expression and meritocratic norms, universities help to establish the regional milieu required to attract and retain talent and spur growth in the Creative Economy' (Florida *et al.* 2006: 17). However, it is important to emphasise that the empirical finding cited here only definitely shows that the presence of communities related to higher education in a place has an effect on its social mix. The causal link to economic growth in the region relies on acceptance of Florida's (2002) underlying Creative Class thesis, which has been subject to extensive conceptual, empirical and normative critiques in the economic geography literature (Glaeser 2005a; Peck 2005; Markusen 2006; Storper and Scott 2009; Comunian *et al.* 2010).

Notwithstanding these reservations with Florida's arguments, a wider literature has started to reflect the underlying point that the cultural practices of higher education students can have a favourable effect on the social and economic climate of a city. In contrast to the mainly negative implications of 'studentification' discussed in the previous chapter, students also contribute considerably as both consumers and producers to a varied non-mainstream cultural life within cities, largely (but not entirely) separated from the university. Chatterton (1999, 2000) links this development in the UK to the growth and diversification of higher education participation during the 1990s, with 'nontraditional' students helping to support alternatives in cultural provision to the dominant popular night-time leisure culture associated with young, middle-class students living away from home for the first time. Similarly, Russo and Sans (2009) describe how cultural spaces formed by the student population in Venice are now being used to attract different

types of visitors to the city, as a response to the damaging effects of the local tourism industry being overly concentrated on the city's traditional heritage sites.
More generally, the potential role of domestic or overseas higher education students in building 'Creative Cities' has begun to be recognised internationally by
local policymakers and critically reflected on within the academic literature (see
Russo *et al.* 2007; Atkinson and Easthope 2008; Collins 2010; Shaw and Fincher
2010).

In addition to this cultural contribution, students are also clearly valued by cities and regions as future skilled workers, particularly in less favoured regions
where they may represent opportunities for the upgrading of 'human capital pathways' (Arbo and Benneworth 2006). The next section explores the process
through which higher education students are attracted to a region and retained in
the labour force post-graduation. Although the lifestyle features of a city discussed in this section may have a bearing on the graduate's locational decision,
the following section concentrates on the interplay of factors relating to higher
education and the strength of the regional economy.

Graduate migration and human capital

Perhaps the biggest contribution that HEIs make to national economies is in supplying skilled and knowledgeable graduates for professional labour markets. This
is included in a chapter on 'passive impacts' because, notwithstanding teaching
programmes by many universities that are targeted at specific local employment
needs, at the aggregate level with which the statistical analysis reviewed here is
concerned, the funding arrangements in place that determine numbers and alloca-
tion of higher education places on different courses (whether primarily by government grant or market for fees) are not generally tied directly to regional
labour market demands. Labour markets for graduates operate on a national (if
not international) scale, so the link between the presence of a university and corresponding benefits to its local economy in terms of human capital gains is far
from guaranteed. Graduates are characteristically highly mobile as a group, so
their place of study is only one possible influence on their subsequent place of
work, and this is arguably secondary to demand-side factors relating to the
strength of different regional labour markets. Because of the difficulties of mea-
suring the quantitative human capital impact of graduate labour on a local economy, the academic literature in this area mainly concentrates on understanding
the migration patterns of students and graduates within a country and how this is
linked to economic outcomes in different regions.[1] It was proposed in the section
before last that the long-term human capital contribution to local economies was
greater for universities located in metropolitan areas with labour markets big
enough to absorb a large number of graduates. Correspondingly, studies have
shown that the long-run success of urban economies is strongly related to their
concentration of highly-skilled workers (Glaeser and Saiz 2004; Glaeser 2005b).
However, most of the literature that we review below examines geographical
units equivalent to larger regions and not just their cities.

Some of the best-developed empirical material in this literature on student and graduate mobility comes from the UK, because of the easy availability of fairly comprehensive data. Each year since 1995, the Higher Education Statistics Agency (HESA) has carried out a survey of destinations of HEI leavers, which aims to cover all graduates from UK HEIs. These large datasets have been utilised by academics in a number of recent papers (Faggian and McCann 2006, 2009a, 2009b; Comunian *et al.* 2010; Hoare and Corver 2010). The HESA datasets record information on the respondents 'domicile' region (where they lived upon applying for higher education), the university they attended, and their status and location of employment around six months after leaving higher education. This has allowed researchers to track movement of graduate classes between these three points, and hence combine analysis of the two 'legs' of home to university migration and university to first employment migration, which had hitherto mainly been addressed separately in both the UK and international literature (Hoare and Corver 2010: 481). This is particularly significant in the UK context, because the well-established cultural convention of young people from middle-class backgrounds moving away from home to attend university means that levels of temporary migration associated with higher education students are typically higher than in other countries (Belfield and Morris 1999; Christie 2007; Duke-Williams 2009). This is also linked to high levels of personal geographical mobility in the labour market subsequent to higher education, whether this involves graduates returning to their domicile region or moving to work in a third region (Faggian and McCann 2009a).

The overriding pattern in the UK graduate labour market is the long-observed dominance of the South East and particularly London as a magnet for graduate employment (Johnston 1989; Fielding 1992; Duke-Williams 2009). This 'brain drain' effect through which other regions lose a high proportion of their highly-qualified young workers is amongst the key structural reasons for persistent regional disparities between North and South. Hoare and Corver (2010: 484) show that, for the four graduate cohorts between 1998/1999 and 2001/2002 in the HESA survey, London gains either just over or just under twice as many higher education leavers within its workforce as people from the capital go to university. This is balanced against almost every other English region and Wales and Northern Ireland (but not Scotland) in most years being a net loser of their pre-university resident graduates to provide this surplus for London. Figure 3.1 displays this pattern using Hoare and Corver's (2010) 'gain rate' figures for the graduate cohort 2001/2002, where a score of 100 indicates a perfect balance between undergraduate students nationally from that domicile region and university leavers working in the region shortly after graduation.

Although London does have a large and diverse higher education sector, this pattern is more a reflection of the concentration of the UK's graduate labour opportunities in London. Analysis of the HESA data shows that London is the only UK region that is able to attract large numbers of graduates that neither lived there before university or went to university there (Faggian and McCann 2009a; Hoare and Corver 2010). Taking the UK as a whole, however, it is clear

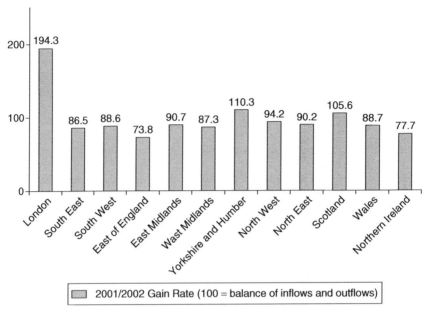

Figure 3.1 Graduate labour recruitment regional 'gain rate' for 2001/2002.

Source: Adapted from figures given by Hoare and Corver (2010: 484).

that university location does have an effect on the subsequent geographical destination of some graduates. Faggian and McCann (2009a: 216) calculate the percentage of graduates (following their first degree) who find employment in the
same region they attended university for the four cohorts between 1996/1997
and 1999/2000. This is unsurprisingly highest for London at upwards of 70 per
cent for all four years. It is also high for the North East of England, Scotland and
Wales (Northern Ireland is not included here) at over 50 per cent for all four
years. Even for the other English regions, however, this is still always just under
or just over 40 per cent. This is also higher for graduates from certain types of
university. The literature shows that the group of 'newer' (former polytechnic)
universities in the UK, that we call Post 1992 universities in this book (Chapter
6), recruit a higher proportion of students locally, who are also more likely to
remain in the region after graduation (Belfield and Morris 1999; Faggian and
McCann 2009a). These universities, therefore, make one of the biggest contributions to upgrading regional labour supplies by creating access opportunities for
local young people who would otherwise be unable or disinclined to participate
in higher education by moving to other regions.

The HESA data allows researchers to distinguish between different migration
'pathways' into regional employment, which vary according to their domicile
region and their place of study (Faggian and McCann 2009a; Hoare and Corver

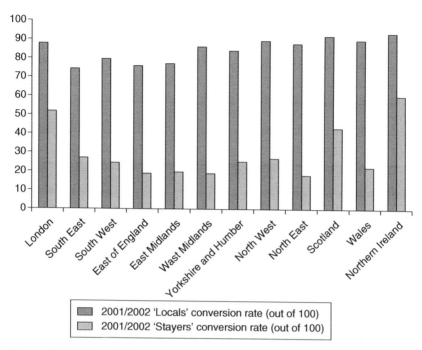

Figure 3.2 Graduate labour recruitment conversion rates for 'locals' and 'stayers' pathways for 2001/2002.

Source: Adapted from figures given by Hoare and Corver (2010: 486).

2010). In Hoare and Corver's (2010) scheme, those who find employment in their region of study are classified as either 'locals' or 'stayers', depending on whether this respectively was or was not also their home region prior to university. The other two pathway categories are 'returners' who move back to their domicile region following university and 'outsiders' who move to a third region for employment. Hoare and Corver (2010: 486) express the results for these four different pathways in terms of their 'conversion rate' of potential students in each category (out of 100) who actually remain or move to that region post-graduation. Figure 3.2 displays these conversion rates for the 'locals' and 'stayers' categories for the graduate cohort of 2001/2002. The 'stayers' category is lower than the 'locals' for all regions (because those who migrate to attend university in a different region are more mobile subsequently), but is significant here because it indicates the proportion of young people attracted to a region by a university who are subsequently retained within the labour market. With the exception of Northern Ireland, the region with the highest conversion rate for 'stayers' is London (52.3), and this drops off dramatically for the other English regions to levels between 17 and 27. This suggests that the size and characteristics of the local labour market is a more important variable than any related to the supply of labour by regional universities (also see Chapter 6). In terms of absolute numbers (and not relative conversion rates), 'stayers' are not the largest of the four groups of graduate employees in any region (for 2001/2002). This is 'outsiders' for London, 'returners' for the other regions in the English South or Midlands, and 'locals' for Northern English regions and the three non-English nations (Hoare and Corver 2010: 487).

Outside the UK, various European studies have examined student and graduate mobility on national and international scales (e.g. see *European Journal of Education* 2000 special issue, Volume 35, issue 2). However, the fullest available comparison to the UK in terms of intra-national migration comes from the USA. The USA does not have a nationwide annual survey of higher education leavers equivalent to that carried out by HESA. However, the migration patterns of college graduates have been effectively studied using other data sources, such as national longitudinal surveys that regularly track a sample of young people on an ongoing basis. For instance, Kodrzycki (2001) uses the National Longitudinal Survey of Youth that has data for 6,000 people between the start point of 1979 (when they were between 14 and 22 years old) and 1996. Unlike the UK HESA data, this survey covers a cross-section of the whole population, and therefore allows comparison between those who attended higher education and those who did not. This allows Kodrzycki to show that the college-educated are significantly more mobile after graduation than those who finished education after high school. Her analysis reveals that the proportion living in a different US state in 1996 from 1979 were '19.2 percent for those completing only high school, but 36.6 percent for those completing four years of college and 45.0 for those with even higher levels of education' (ibid.: 15). Unsurprisingly, this disparity is established early through people leaving their home state for higher education, but is maintained and widened as a life-time pattern by the higher frequency of inter-state moves by college attendees in the ten years following graduation, due to their higher geographical mobility within the national labour market (ibid.: 16).

The level of college graduates in this sample who attended an HEI in a different state from where they went to high school, at 26.8 per cent (Kodrzycki 2001: 15), actually seems low compared to the proportion of young people who move away from home for university in the UK. As well as the obvious differences in geographical scale between these two national cases, this also seems likely to be a product of the different higher education system in the federal USA that includes incentives for young people to enrol in colleges within their home state (Groen and White 2004; Alm and Winters 2009). Groen (2004: 126) evaluates the rationale of these public subsidies by using two longitudinal data sources to assess the effect of 'attending college in a state on the probability of working in the state'. His findings for the whole of the USA are that, 15 years after college graduation '[f]or students who were initially residents of the state, 54 percent of those who attended college in the state ended up working there, compared to 35 percent of those who attended college in another state', where for 'students who were initially non-residents of the state, the corresponding figures are 11 percent and 2 percent' (ibid.: 134–5). This analysis echoes the same four 'pathways' used by Hoare and Corver (2010), although direct comparison of figures is not possible because of the different timeframes post-graduation they refer to (15 years and 6 months respectively). The differences that still occur in Groen's (2004: 134) findings do, however, lead him to conclude that (even in this longer-term) 'college effects are substantial'.

The nationwide geography of graduate migration in the USA has also been covered within this literature. Kodrzycki (2001) observes that the overall pattern for graduate migration in the timeframe covered by her study (1979–1996) has been towards the West and South West of the USA that enjoyed stronger labour markets and more attractive living conditions during this period. In their work on universities mentioned above, Florida *et al.* (2006) also analyse the relative concentration of graduates in different US regions to test the human capital component of their Creative Class theory. They use US census data to construct a 'Brain Drain/Gain index' of net attraction or loss of graduate labour for US metropolitan regions by dividing 'the percent of the population age 25 and over with a bachelor's degree or above' by the 'percent of the population ages 18–34 currently in college or university' (ibid.: 13). This is in some ways equivalent to the 'gain rate' measurement used by Hoare and Corver (2010) for the UK, although it observes students who currently attend college in the region and not those initially from that domicile region. The results also broadly compare with the UK situation where just one region (London) is a big winner at the expense of most other regions. Florida *et al.* (2006: 13) find that only 10 per cent of all 331 US metropolitan regions are 'net attractors of talent', and only ten in total score 1.25 or above on this index. They also find that a high score on this index is strongly correlated to indicators for employment growth, high-technology industry and regional innovation (Florida *et al.* 2006: 14; also see Abel and Dietz 2012). The larger cities that rank in the top 20 on this index include the high-technology centres San Francisco, Seattle, San Jose, Atlanta, Washington DC and Houston (Florida *et al.* 2006: 31).

The relationship between the concentration of graduate labour and levels of innovation within a regional economy has also been examined in the UK context by Faggian and McCann (2006, 2009b) drawing on the HESA data. They find that innovation has a much stronger two-way relationship with the net inflow of graduate labour into a region (measured as the number of students who moved to the region to attend university and stayed there to enter work) than to regional university research performance. This leads them to conclude that there is more evidence in support of the importance of inter-regional graduate flows than there is for the intra-regional knowledge 'spillover' thesis that has received most attention in the literature on university–industry links. Indeed, when the effect of graduate labour is controlled for, they find there is little support left for local academic research and innovation capability independently having a bearing on regional innovation performance; they therefore suggest that its main positive impact is that it indirectly 'augments the existing stock of human capital' (Faggian and McCann 2006: 496). However, because of the imbalance in graduate labour flows within the country, this finding only applies for England and Wales (with

Scotland excluded because of its lower levels of graduate out-migration), and then only when high innovation performing London is included (Faggian and McCann 2009b).

In summary, the overall empirical picture described in this section, drawn from the different contexts of the UK and USA, indicates that, due to high graduate mobility, the pathways between university education and labour markets run along far from bounded regional lines. Demand side factors related to prospective job opportunities in the regional economy – and possibly also the type of lifestyle factors emphasised by Florida – clearly have a large effect on the destination of higher education leavers. However, there is also evidence that a share of students attracted to any region to attend university will remain post-graduation and contribute to the local labour market. In addition, many universities or colleges provide higher education entry for local people who would be less likely to move or commute to other places to access these services.

Conclusion

This chapter has argued that, while universities can have considerable employment and income effects on a city economy, in the long-term these may be exceeded in importance by the other 'passive' impacts of graduate labour retained in the region, and partly related to this, the impact of academic communities (particularly students) in making the city somewhere 'creative' workers want to live. These latter two bodies of literature include a sometimes explicit criticism of the regional development literature's previous focus on the contribution of universities to innovation through forms of knowledge or technology transfer. As Faggian and McCann (2006: 497) argue '[t]he primary role of the university system... appears to be its role as a conduit for bringing high quality human capital into a region'. Whilst this may well be true, the ability of regions to retain former students in its labour market is at the same time reliant on its supply of graduate job opportunities, which is to a large degree determined by its industrial and occupational profile. Therefore, the contribution of universities to innovation, in helping to create new knowledge-intensive economic activities and employment, is still a crucial one in territorial economic development. This is particularly the case in less favoured cities or regions where institutional as well as technological change is required to overcome the problems of industrial path 'lock-in' and low innovative capacity. It is to these issues that we turn now.

4 Universities, innovation and economic development

Introduction

This chapter examines the more active role of universities in supporting innovation in urban and regional economies. Despite suggestions in the preceding chapter that the effect of 'knowledge spillovers' or 'technology transfer' from universities has previously been overemphasised in the regional development literature, these economic relationships remain one of the main ways in which contemporary universities directly engage with their cities or regions. Working with local industry or creating new businesses through spin-offs not only provides universities with new research or revenue generation opportunities, but also allows them to fulfil the public role ascribed in national and regional policies as key assets in the modern-day knowledge economy.

This chapter is divided into two parts. The first focuses on how universities contribute to 'systemic innovation' in regional and metropolitan economies using an evolutionary-based innovation system framework, and advocating a more broadly-conceived 'developmental' role. This section also develops the conceptual argument that universities should be understood as a potential source of 'slack' within a regional innovation system that can add to the long-term adaptability of the economy. We view part of the evolutionary process that this contribution to regional innovation entails as organisational change within universities themselves in order to adapt to an expanded economic or business development mission; an internal dimension that existing work in economic geography has thus far rarely studied in depth. For this reason, the second part of the chapter discusses a literature on the adaptation of loosely-coupled university structures as a form of organisational innovation. The focus is on 'entrepreneurial' university transformations and the development of intermediaries that facilitate engagement in the wider economy. Whilst these sections share a broadly-evolutionary understanding of change in their respective domains (the wider region and the university), the intention is not to integrate them into single analytical framework. Notwithstanding the possibility of co-evolution between these domains, both are distinct systems of interrelationships, and subject to separate dynamics that intersect in complex ways. This points to the need for further work on the articulation between these internal and external factors, and the conclusion to this chapter discusses some of the ways in which the rest of this book addresses this issue.

Universities in regional or metropolitan innovations systems

Since its emergence in the mid- to late-1990s, the regional innovation systems framework (Braczyk *et al.* 1998; Cooke *et al.* 1998; Iammarino 2005; Uyarra 2010) has become one of the main conceptual reference points for economic geographers interested in the contribution of universities to city or regional economic development. Like other systemic perspectives on innovation (Edquist 1997; Etzkowitz and Leydesdorff 2000), this is founded on a fundamentally non-linear and interactive model of innovation as technological and organisational change, which emphasises complex patterns of knowledge diffusion and information feedback across the boundaries of firms and other organisations (including universities). Hence, the focus is shifted away from conceptions of sequential innovation processes internal to the research and development departments of large firms, to collective network-based innovation processes in industrial district environments (Asheim 1996; Cooke and Morgan 1998; Asheim and Cooke 1999). This approach encourages a comprehensive analysis of the various inter-relationships between organisational actors and institutional spheres that are involved in regional innovation. 'Systemic innovation' is seen to occur through the co-evolution of dominant regional technologies, institutions and organisational forms (Cooke *et al.* 1998; Uyarra 2010). In contrast to earlier work that focused on the role of universities in the formation of leading high-technology districts, the Regional Innovation Systems (RIS) framework is equally suited to the study of innovative capabilities or deficiencies in a range of more 'ordinary' regions (Charles 2006; Coenen 2007).

The forerunner to RIS was the National Innovation Systems (NIS) approach, which sought to explain differences in national innovation performance or public and private research and development (R&D) capacity through historically-formed variations in their economic, political and cultural institutions (Lundvall 1992; Nelson 1993; Freeman 1995). The RIS concept adapted this general approach to the recognition that the various institutional resources that collectively influence innovative capabilities in a territory are unevenly distributed at the regional as well as national scale, drawing on then-recent advances in the theoretical understanding of regional economies informed by institutional and evolutionary economics (e.g. Amin and Thrift 1995; Storper 1995; Cooke and Morgan 1998; Gertler 2004). Hence, RIS frameworks typically include formal organisational components relating to production and supporting governance, learning (e.g. universities, R&D capabilities) and finance or enterprise sectors in the region, as well as the cultural or institutional environment of norms, conventions and routines that shape collective economic action (Cooke *et al.* 1998). Fischer *et al.* (2001) have also outlined a 'metropolitan innovation systems' variant by demonstrating the applicability of a systemic innovation approach at the scale of large European city regions (e.g. Vienna, Barcelona, Stockholm).

This non-linear or open model of innovation is on many points analogous to Gibbons *et al.*'s (1994) widely-cited New Production of Knowledge thesis, which poses a challenge to the traditional status of the university as a major standalone site of knowledge production in society. This thesis argues that there has been a shift in the dominant mode of knowledge production within society from knowledge produced in a context governed by the interests of disciplinary scientific communities (mode 1), to one in which knowledge is produced in a context of its application and more oriented to societal and economic needs (mode 2). Hence, mode 2 knowledge is seen to be co-produced by a more distributed range of institutions that supply and use knowledge (e.g. non-academic research institutes, consultancy firms, think tanks, etc.), which suggests a changing if not diminished role for the academy (also Nowotny *et al.* 2001). This parallel raises the question of what, if anything, the distinctive role of universities in RIS is, contra these other types of organisation that comprise the learning infrastructure of a territory.

Charles (2006) provides the beginnings of an answer to this question by highlighting the multi-faceted functions of universities as educational and cultural institutions and not just research bodies. He identifies three forms of value that universities can add to a RIS: knowledge that is directly commodified through spin-offs or licensing of intellectual property; human capital that upgrades skills and knowledge in the regional labour market; and social capital that builds trust and cooperative norms in local economic governance networks. Charles argues that the unique capability of universities lies in effectively linking these different circuits of knowledge transfer together to support wider territorial innovation processes, which in turn depends on them being well integrated with innovation policy and governance mechanisms at national and regional scales. He outlines the implications of this position for thinking about the nature of the university as an institution:

> Universities are only one among many knowledge-based institutions in regions, but their special contribution is their breadth and potential in joined-up governance, and for that some of the traditional characteristics of universities must be reinforced and defended, notably the combination of teaching and research (or scholarship) and multidisciplinarity and autonomy. Successful innovation systems require the integration of research with labour markets, a connection between the research priorities and governance and public debate, and a focus on knowledge that goes beyond narrow technological priorities to include culture and creative activities, management knowledge and support for the public policies and infrastructures that underpin economic development.
>
> (Charles 2006: 128)

Gunasekara (2006) also contributes to an expanded conceptual understanding of this issue by distinguishing between existing approaches in the literature that emphasise universities having either a 'generative' or 'developmental' role in RIS. A generative role, which he cites the triple helix framework as exemplifying (e.g. Etzkowitz and Leydesdorff 2000), views universities as 'key drivers of economic development through a range of boundary-spanning, knowledge-capitalisation mechanisms, such as incubators, new firm formation and science parks, as well as university research centres and participation in the governance of firms' (Gunasekara 2006: 143). A developmental role, which is identified with literature using the terminology of regional engagement (e.g. Chatterton and Goddard 2000), 'while acknowledging the importance of academic entrepreneurial activities in enabling technology transfer and economic growth, points to a broader... role performed by universities through adapting their traditional roles in teaching and research to better support regional knowledge needs' (Gunasekara 2006: 143). Gunasekara discusses the regional engagement approach underlying the developmental role:

> The importance of network knowledge and interactive learning... call for university teaching and research to be more closely connected with local and regional knowledge imperatives.... Further, as the institutions of economic regulation become more regionalised, the historical role of universities in nation-building, through the participation of academic staff in numerous public bodies, must also be adapted. Thus universities, through their resource base of people, skills and knowledge, increasingly play a significant role in regional networking and institutional capacity building.
>
> (Gunasekara 2006: 142)

It seems likely that most universities will have some combination of generative and developmental roles within regional or metropolitan innovation systems, and that these will be connected. Research has shown that generative mechanisms such as spin-off firm formation can have wider cumulative developmental impacts within an industrial cluster by upgrading the knowledge pool and fostering a wider regional culture of cooperation and collective learning (see Keeble *et al.* 1999; Benneworth and Charles 2005; Garnsey and Heffernan 2005). However, here we would like to emphasise the developmental side of this continuum as especially compatible with an evolutionary perspective on systemic regional innovation. Similar to Charles's (2006) conceptualisation, this highlights the university's influence on the political, institutional and network factors that shape regional innovation processes and governance beyond just their input of knowledge capital into local economies (also Benneworth *et al.* 2009). This perspective is especially relevant considering the increasing scepticism expressed in the regional development literature about the ability of universities alone to be agents of transformative change within any regional economy through what may be understood as 'generative' functions related to academic enterprise and commercialisation (see Lawton Smith 2007; Huggins *et al.* 2008; Christopherson and Clark 2010; Harrison and Leitch 2010). This is despite the promotion of academic enterprise and commercialisation having become a standard element of near identikit cluster development strategies as part of a new regional innovation policy orthodoxy in Europe (Tödtling and Trippl 2005). Less successful regions, in particular, will often not have the existing industrial capacity required to assimilate and capitalise on new knowledge or applications stemming from research in proximate universities, and therefore those universities that do generate research with industrial applications are more likely to seek commercialisation opportunities further afield with suitable national or international firms (Huggins and Johnston 2009; Christopherson and Clark 2010). This resonates with wider arguments that innovation is not a territorially-bounded process, but produced through geographically more complex patterns of non-linear interactions between various actors in trans-regional and trans-national networks (Bunnell and Coe 2001; Oinas and Malecki 2002; Amin and Cohendet 2004). Where universities have been cited as having a transformational impact within a regional economy, such as in paradigmatic cases of the Silicon Valley and Cambridge (UK) technology districts, various other favourable economic factors and political circumstances seem to have been in play at the time that are unlikely to be replicated in other regions (see Goddard and Vallance 2011 for a review).

A 'developmental' perspective, by contrast, implies closer attention to existing institutional arrangements and industrial paths. As Charles (2006: 127–8) writes, 'different universities in different national and regional contexts...will need to adopt different combinations [of roles within RIS]....[T]he university role needs to evolve out of these contexts and co-evolve with the regional innovation system itself'. Universities will adopt different levels and forms of 'engagement' within RIS based on characteristics of the institution (e.g. degree of research intensity) and of the region (e.g. industrial profile and number of competing HEIs) (Boucher *et al.* 2003). For instance, Coenen (2007) compares the role of universities in the innovation systems of two former industrial regions seeking to make the transition to a knowledge-based economy. In the North East of England he describes how universities have occupied a leading, entrepreneurial position in regional innovation policies due to the relative underdevelopment of R&D capacity in other sectors of the regional economy. By contrast, in the Scania region of Sweden, that following deindustrialisation had developed wider capabilities in industries such as biotechnology and information and communication technologies, the key role of the region's main research university (Lund) is a largely supportive, networking one in helping to integrate a particular traditional industry (food production) into the RIS. In another paper, Benneworth *et al.* (2009) show how Lund University's role in this RIS had evolved over time from an earlier more 'generative' involvement in a regional science park to a more 'developmental' set of larger-scale interventions in different industrial sectors, through a process involving institutional change within the university.

Recent discussion of technological or organisational innovation in economic geography can be found in efforts to develop theoretical approaches more explicitly based on evolutionary economics (Boschma and Lambooy 1999; MacKinnon *et al.* 2009; Hassink and Klaerding 2011). This work considers economic change in a region as evolving along paths that are contingent upon inherited industrial characteristics, such as dominant technologies, organisational structures, and sets of regional conventions and routines (Martin and Sunley 2006; Mackinnon *et al.*

2009). This concept of path dependency has been used to explain the 'lock-in' of firms in old industrial regions to outmoded technological and industrial paths, in which existing functional relationships, dominant modes of thinking and political interests connected to a regional industrial specialisation prevent adaptation to changing economic circumstances, such as global competition from lower wage-cost countries (Grabher 1993; Hudson 2005; Hassink 2007). The dialectical opposite of this process – more prevalent in regions with greater innovative or adaptive capabilities – is the creation of new development paths, which is seen to be connected to the degree of variety in the regional economy:

> [I]t is clear that two somewhat complementary, if opposed, mechanisms are always at work. On the one hand, mechanisms of convergence to dominant technologies and institutional arrangements, mechanisms of alignment of individual and organizational decisions, and the plethora of increasing returns associated with learning, agglomeration and interrelatedness, tend to impart path dependence and 'lock-in' to the development of the specific places and regions more particularly. Yet, on the other hand, place-specific histories and possibilities of capabilities and competence building, expectation formation, and organizational and institutional creation, produce variety and heterogeneity into the economic landscape, and hence constant pressure for path destruction and opportunities for new path creation.
>
> (Martin and Sunley 2006: 424)

This connection between variety and innovation finds a parallel in a wider economics literature that has recognised the concentration of economic activity in large cities is conducive to knowledge spillovers between firms. Competing viewpoints exist about whether this advantage is more closely linked to industrial specialisation (that encourages knowledge spillovers between similar firms), or following Jane Jacob's (1969) pioneering argument, industrial diversity that allows cross-fertilisation of innovations between firms in different parts of the economy (see Duranton and Puga 2000). Substantial statistical survey and case study empirical evidence exists in favour of the diversity perspective, showing that the long-term economic growth of cities is connected to the degree of variety in their industrial structure (e.g. Glaeser *et al.* 1992; Feldman and Audretsch 1999; Rantisi 2002; Glaeser 2005b). Frenken *et al.* (2007) qualifies these arguments by arguing that it is 'related variety' within the same broad economic sector that supports regional innovation and employment growth,[1] whereas 'unrelated variety' between sectors increases local resilience to falls in employment by ensuring that the economy is not overly-dependent on a small range of industries.

Universities have not featured prominently within this evolutionary economic geography literature. Where processes of regional path generation and selection have not been treated as occurring through random 'historical accidents', agency has mainly been attributed to creative entrepreneurs or adaptive firms (see Martin and Sunley 2006). However, here we want to propose that universities have a role as constituents of regional heterogeneity that is distinctive from market-based actors. Some evolutionary theorists of organisational or regional economic change have argued that the presence of non-productive 'slack' or 'redundant' resources (practices, organisational forms, knowledge) within a system, whilst reducing overall efficiency, provides the variety or adaptive capacity needed to avoid 'lock-in' in the long-term (Grabher and Stark 1997; Grabher 2001, 2003; Staber and Sydow 2002). As institutions partly protected from market pressures by public funds for research and teaching, universities could be viewed as a potential source of this slack at the level of regional or metropolitan innovation systems by virtue of harbouring non-commercial activities (e.g. more basic as well as applied forms of R&D) in diverse knowledge domains that cannot be supported in a region's production system. Hence, the range of decentralised research and innovation capabilities that are housed within large multi-disciplinary universities (see below) may enhance the long-term adaptive capacity of regional economies. In this evolutionary-informed interpretation, the value of the knowledge generated by universities through advanced research should be seen to correspond less to its immediate industrial or commercial applicability than to its long-run capacity to inform alternative future paths for technological development or product innovations, and related 'developmental' changes in the institutional base of the region. This will require universities to be integrated into regional or metropolitan innovation systems, to the extent that mechanisms are available through which these opportunities for new path creation can be identified and developed either by academic entrepreneurs or industrial partners; but this innovative capability is in the first place perhaps also reliant on universities not being too 'tightly-coupled' with the industrial environment (see below).

As well as generating knowledge that can be translated into the creation of new economic sectors, the relative stability and continuity of universities as institutional presences in regions can maintain activity in diverse knowledge domains that are no longer needed (redundant) within the private sector. This process can be seen in case studies of deindustrialised cities or regions, such as Pittsburgh (Treado 2010) or the North East of England (Whitehurst *et al.* 2008; Goddard *et al.* 2012), in which local engineering expertise survives in part through specialist courses taught and research carried out in universities. The regional development potential of these capabilities exist through the opportunity for old sectors to re-emerge in a more technologically advanced (if rarely mass production) form as 'phoenix industries' (Tödtling and Trippl 2004; Christopherson 2009), or for existing capabilities, such as a skilled local workforce and physical assets or infrastructure, to be transferred from a declining sector to an emerging one (e.g. from shipbuilding to offshore wind energy) (Fornahl *et al.* 2012).

In conclusion, the regional or metropolitan innovation system perspective shows that the role of universities is shaped by its systemic relationships with other regional actors and how these change over time. Hence, we support a 'developmental' perspective (Gunasekara 2006) in which the wider engagement role of universities in the institutional development and integration of its region's innovation system is considered as important as the direct commercial valorisation of the scientific and technological knowledge it produces. From an evolutionary

economic geography approach, we have proposed that universities should be considered as a source of 'slack' within territorial innovation systems, with the potential to add to adaptive capacity in the economy through the diverse practices and
knowledge resources it can maintain as a particular organisational form. However,
the work on RIS, and on universities in regional economic development more generally, has not yet extended this perspective to consider how the university itself
evolves internally as an organisation to accommodate this role in regional economic innovation. Despite being a large and heterogeneous organisation, the university itself has, in effect, remained 'black-boxed' in most work in regional
development studies. This is so that talking of the university as a coherent entity
reflects only part of the reality, when most external engagement takes place
through decentralised and semi-independent organisational subunits that operate
according to their own dynamics. The next section discusses the development of
these organisational structures using a broadly-evolutionary conceptual framework taken from studies of university adaptation.

University adaptation and organisational innovation

As a counterbalance to the underconceptualised, 'black-box' view of the university in the regional innovation system literature, this section will examine a literature from organisational and higher education studies on university adaptation.
Here, adaptability is taken to mean 'the capacity of the organization to change in
order to continue to achieve organizational goals when changes in the environment threaten the accomplishment of those goals' (Rubin 1979: 213). According
to Sporn (1999), these changes in the environment may include external societal
dynamics, such as demographic shifts, new information and communication technologies or globalisation, but they most often relate to changes in the funding and
regulation of higher education systems. Within this literature we will concentrate
on adaptations in university structures that help universities fulfil a growing economic or business development function as a form of 'organisational innovation'
(Lam 2005). This particularly focuses on the creation of organisational interfaces
or intermediaries, such as academic research centres and administrative technology transfer offices that facilitate engagement with firms and other economic
actors. This concern with adaptability needs to be balanced against recognition of
the path-dependent nature of entrenched university structures that can be highly
resistant to institutional changes and innovation (Krücken 2003).

The university adaptation literature reflects the organisational complexity of
higher education institutions by considering them as 'loosely-coupled systems'.
This concept refers to organisations that are characterised by multiple, relatively-
independent units with only limited coordination or feedback needed between
their activities, of which universities and other educational institutions are often
cited as exemplars (Weick 1976; Sporn 1999). Rubin (1979: 213) unpacks this
concept by proposing that loosely-coupled relations may exist along three different lines in universities. First, horizontally between functional units, such as
between academic departments with different sets of goals and resources. Second,

vertically between units at different levels of the organisational hierarchy, that are free to make decisions affecting their activities, but have only limited direct influence on other levels. This dimension of 'loose coupling' corresponds with the alternative conception of universities as classically 'professional bureaucracies' marked by decentralised organisation and high levels of autonomy for academics in different disciplinary-based communities (Mintzberg 1980; Lam 2005; Morgan 2006); though, as we discuss below, over the past few decades this culture has been increasingly undermined by the growth of managerialism within higher education (Rhoades and Slaughter 1997; Deem *et al.* 2007). Rubin's (1979: 213) third line of loose coupling is with the external environment, so that changes outside the university do not immediately lead to changes within the university and vice-versa (which links to the 'slack' argument above). In terms of adaptation, while universities are 'open systems' (i.e. intimately related to their external environment) (Morgan 2006), the loosely-coupled structure means that responding to change is easier at the level of individual academic or administrative units than it is for the entire university (Sporn 1999). Similarly Lam (2005: 120) writes of professional bureaucracies that 'individual experts may be highly innovative within a specialist domain, but the difficulties of coordination across functions and disciplines impose severe limits on the innovative capability of the organisation as a whole'. The simultaneous independence and connection of organisational units that the term loosely-coupled system implies has led some analysts to propose that they should be studied through a dialectical framework (Weick 1976; Orton and Weick 1990). Hence, the contradiction in universities between the relative flexibility of individual units and rigidity of the institution as a whole means that organisational change within a university is likely to be a gradual and uneven effect of the interplay of top-down and bottom-up forces. For instance, through a case study of the introduction of a technology transfer office and attempt to inculcate its principles within the institution, Krücken shows that:

> [T]he shift at the discursive and policy level is hardly accompanied by an equally dramatic change at the level of the practice.... In universities, new ideas only slowly diffuse into practice, and the orientation toward historically entrenched concepts play a much stronger role. As a result, one has to take 'two speeds' of change into account.
>
> (Krücken 2003: 317)

Much of the more recent work that examines issues of university adaptation to changes in the higher education environment has taken place under discussion of 'entrepreneurial universities'. This term has featured widely in debates about the changing, more commercial nature of the university and its external relationships in a period of falling relative levels of state expenditure on higher education in many advanced economies. For instance, in regional development it is a concept that Perry and Harloe (2007) use in reference to internal transformations in universities that are connected to them taking a more active role in the knowledge economy. Here we will briefly review three well-known bodies of work that offer distinctive perspectives on an entrepreneurial university model and related adaptations in academic structures or practices. Crucially, each of these commentators identifies the development of business-facing inter- or multi-disciplinary research centres and institutes as a key organisational innovation in the development of entrepreneurial universities. Again, however, this particular organisational change may also exist in tension with the more traditional academic structure represented by discipline-based departments or schools, around which the university's teaching delivery is likely to be organised. Elements of academic research practice are still structured in important ways by mainly discipline-based systems of peer review that are institutionalised through academic journals, university promotion criteria, and assessment regimes such as the UK Research Assessment Exercise (RAE) (Mosey *et al.* 2012). These are issues we will touch upon below, but also will feature as an important theme throughout the empirical chapters of this book.

First, from a higher education management perspective, Burton Clark's work provides a clear account of how universities can respond entrepreneurially to the 'demand overload' that they now face in a mass higher education system, where the responsibilities placed on them – in terms of student numbers and the diverse range of specialised professional training they are expected to supply for national labour markets – exceed the resources they receive from core public funding streams (Clark 1998: 6). Clark's focus on the relationship between changes in the external funding environment and related adaptations in the internal structure of universities means his work is cited as an example of a 'contingency theory' approach (Sporn 1999), although it should be noted that he also emphasises endogenous innovation dynamics in academic organisation that are related to the expansion and diversification of knowledge production through a self-sustaining proliferation of increasingly specialised disciplinary niches (Clark 1996; 1998). Based on case studies of five European universities that were actively pursuing a move to more entrepreneurial orientation during the 1990s, Clark (1998: 8–13) identified five general 'pathways to transformation' that allow universities to address the pressures of 'demand overload':

1   *A strengthened steering core* – capable of forcing through institution-wide change and instilling managerial values within academic faculties.
2   *An enhanced development periphery* – including the establishment of specialised administrative units and research centres that are dedicated to working closely with external organisations including firms. These 'mediating institutions' co-exist with more traditional academic departments to form a dual organisational structure.
3   *A diversified funding base* – undertaking activities that generate additional or discretionary income from a range of non-traditional sources, as an alternative to relying solely on core government funding. Subsequently, Clark (2003) clarified that this did not just mean the university entering into the commercial world through links with private businesses or by attempting to exploit the intellectual property it developed, but could include exploiting a

number of other possible income streams, such as working with governmental agencies in areas apart from higher education (e.g. health, defence, regional economic development), philanthropic foundations (e.g. charities funding medical research) and the university's own surplus-producing revenue sources (e.g. alumni donations, student fees, consultancy services).

4   *A stimulated academic heartland* – referring particularly to departments in areas that have less obvious external revenue-generating potential (e.g. social sciences, humanities) engaging in more applied research and teaching alongside their more traditional academic activities.

5   *An entrepreneurial culture* – formed through an incremental process of the values embodied in the changes described above becoming embedded throughout the university and becoming the basis for a new institutional identity. In later work, Clark (2003) focused on how this entrepreneurial culture becomes sustained and institutionalised in universities. This, he argues, requires a new bureaucracy that supports the institutions external boundary-spanning activities and income diversification strategies.

Second, Slaughter and Leslie's (1997) work on academic capitalism represents a more critical view of the entrepreneurial university from the perspective of how it affects academic labour and work practices. Using a theoretical underpinning from resource dependency theory, they argue that, when faced with dwindling basic resources from the state, members of academic faculty will alter their behaviour to access other sources of money, especially those that allow them to continue pursuing more 'prestigious' research activities. This is linked to the growth of what they term 'academic capitalism': faculty engaging in directly for-profit *market behaviour*, such as attempts to licence intellectual property and form spin-off companies, or engaging in more competitive *marketlike behaviour*, for external funds related to research and teaching (Slaughter and Leslie 1997: 11). The latter encompasses the construction of new performance and assessment regimes (paradigmatically the UK RAE – see Chapter 6) that have introduced more engineered competition into collegiate higher education systems (also Deem *et al.* 2007). In taking up these roles, academics become 'state-subsidized entrepreneurs' (Slaughter and Leslie 1997: 9), and contribute to the transformation of universities as organisational forms that increasingly blur the distinction between public and private (Rhoades and Slaughter 1997). Their research outlines the convergence of these trends between Australia, the UK, the USA, and to a lesser extent Canada, beginning in the 1980s, and driven by changes in national higher education and science policies in response to globalisation. Despite significant variations in the content of these policies related to each country's distinctive political circumstances, Slaughter and Leslie argue that their outcomes were broadly similar moves toward:

> science and technology policies that emphasized academic capitalism at the expense of basic or fundamental research, toward curricula policy that concentrated moneys in science and technology ... toward increased access at

lower government cost per student, and toward organizational policies that
undercut the autonomy of academic institutions and of faculty.

(Slaughter and Leslie 1997: 55)

These resource shifts have had uneven effects within the academy, favouring disciplines that are 'close to the market' (engineering, some sciences and business)
over those that are not (especially in the arts, humanities and social sciences).
This pattern has been reinforced by the strategic prioritisation of science and
engineering departments in institutional restructuring of research universities
(also Rhoades and Slaughter, 1997). In particular, those fields that Slaughter and
Leslie (1997) refer to as 'technoscience' have received a greater share of
research funds from public (as well as private) sources due to their perceived
importance for future national economic competitiveness. The manifest effect of
this within the internal structures of universities has been the growth of specialist
research centres in these fields as 'intermediate organizational forms that enable
faculty to relate directly to external markets', and concentrate on activities that
generate these surplus revenues, whilst having fewer undergraduate teaching or
administrative responsibilities than their counterparts in other disciplinary areas
(Slaughter and Leslie 1997: 173).

Third, Etzkowitz and colleagues (Etzkowitz *et al.* 2000; Etzkowitz 2003,
2004) have written about the development of the entrepreneurial university as an
offshoot of their analysis of 'triple-helix' relations between academia, industry
and government (see Etzkowitz and Leydesdorff 2000). This work represents an
overwhelmingly positive view of the diffusion of entrepreneurial values within
academia and the growing economic involvement of universities through technology transfer or the commercialisation of research that Gunasekara (2006)
referred to as their generative role. This work is framed with the assertion that
the entrepreneurial university is an institutional innovation that represents a 'second academic revolution' marked by universities adding economic development
to teaching and research as part of their core mission (Etzkowitz 2003, 2004).
The driving force for organisational adaptation in this analysis relates less to
changes within national higher education systems than to transformations in the
mode of academic knowledge production as the practice of research occurs
through interaction with industry and government in more disciplinary contexts
(Etzkowitz 2004). Hence, Etzkowitz *et al.*:

explain the emergence of the entrepreneurial university as a response to the
increasing importance of knowledge in national and regional innovation systems and the recognition that the university is a...creative inventor and
transfer agent of both knowledge and technology.

(Etzkowitz *et al.* 2000: 314)

Like Clark (1998) and Slaughter and Leslie (1997), Etzkowitz (2003) discusses
the reconfiguration of (American) research universities to a model of semi-
autonomous centres that interface with external environments. He argues that

these groups which operate in competitive environments for research and other commercial funds (e.g. consultancy) should be considered as 'quasi-firms' with organisational features analogous to private enterprises. However, probably the bigger value of the triple-helix framework here is that it can extend conceptual understanding of the entrepreneurial university to encompass institutional developments outside of the university. 'Intermediaries' in this domain may be external to the formal organisational boundaries of the university (e.g. industrial research and development centres, science parks, city or regional development agencies) as well as internal (e.g. technology transfer offices, business-facing research centres) (Wright *et al.* 2008). For Etzkowitz *et al.* (2000: 316–17), these various hybrid organisational forms represent the development of cross-institutional capabilities between the three parts of the triple helix. They are created when the building of an entrepreneurial culture or structures in universities is matched by the parallel development of interface capacities in the industry and government spheres enabling collaboration. The present-day entrepreneurial university is associated with interactive modes of innovation through research based in collaboration with industry (Etzkowitz 2003, 2004). Here the kind of intermediary or interface organisations mentioned above 'also play a reverse linear role in connecting the university to external problems, sources of knowledge and firms seeking academic resources' (Etzkowitz 2003: 113).

The position of 'external' intermediaries in territorial innovation systems is reflected in a multi-disciplinary literature that is starting to grow on the national and regional roles of non-academic applied R&D or technology and innovation centres (e.g. Van Helleputte and Reid 2004; Clark 2010; Goddard *et al.* 2012). Although many of these centres will reside in a separate institutional sphere to universities (e.g. German Fraunhofer or Max Planck Institutes), there may be strong patterns of interaction between them (Chapter 5). Alternatively, these research institutes may originate from universities. Benneworth and Hospers (2007b) show that in the context of Twente (an old industrial region in the Netherlands), international research strengths in the University formed the basis of a number of research and innovation centres in various industry and technology fields that subsequently moved out into the wider economy. They describe how:

> In the case of Twente, there was initially little regional capacity to build intermediate institutions directly; such organisations have emerged within the university, and then gradually evolved outwards, enrolling regional actors. They have *become* regional institutions, helping to sustain local buzz, but are strongly anchored in the university as key research players. But what have become effective intermediate institutions were not always obvious successes, and required significant support from a range of actors to demonstrate their longer term worth.
>
> (Benneworth and Hospers 2007b: 799; emphasis in original)

Despite exceptions such as these, and a more general recent interest in the role of intermediation in knowledge exchange processes (e.g. Perry and May 2010), understanding of the relationship between universities and different types of external organisational intermediaries is not yet well developed in urban and regional development studies. The second half of this book will build on this issue as a thematic concern. A recent feature of the economic development landscape in UK cities and regions is the presence of intermediary organisations that are set up and funded by universities in partnership with public and sometimes private bodies, but often have independent legal status as companies limited by guarantee, and fulfil the role of 'special purpose delivery vehicles' dedicated to achieving specific goals that the stakeholder organisations in the company themselves are not effectively positioned to fulfil (Chapter 6). For instance, encouraging knowledge-based economic development in a particular region or sector. Chapters 7 to 9 will include several examples that seek to broaden the applicability of this concept beyond just the economic development sphere.

Conclusion

As the brief review of different conceptualisations of the entrepreneurial university above indicates, study of university adaptation provides a potentially-useful theoretical account of how university structures may evolve to meet changing external circumstances and demands, or indeed resist change and remain in stasis. This perspective can supplement established understanding of the position of universities in regional or metropolitan innovation systems discussed in the first half of this chapter, which largely does not delve into issues of internal university organisation. In particular, work on entrepreneurial universities shows that structural developments in universities, such as the growth of inter-disciplinary research centres and other intermediaries such as technology transfer offices, can be a form of organisational innovation within the wider city or region by facilitating new relationships within its innovation system. This chapter has linked these two literatures through their common basis in evolutionary conceptual vocabularies of organisational or institutional change.

As noted in the introduction, however, this does not mean that innovation in the university and city or region should be considered as the same process: they remain distinct objects of study that articulate with each other and possibly co-evolve in complex and fragmentary ways. As Bender writes, reflecting on his edited collection of historical essays, *The University and the City*:

> I propose that we understand the urban university as *semicloistered heterogeneity* in the midst of uncloistered heterogeneity (that is to say, the city . . .). Because of this difference, relations between the two are necessarily tense, and they cannot be assimilated into one another. To do so, either practically or conceptually, is to empty each of its distinctive cultural meaning and to falsify the sociology of each.
>
> (Bender 1988b: 290; emphasis in original)

Just as the regional innovation systems literature neglects detailed discussion of internal university organisation, the university adaptation literature can equally be critiqued for under-specifying the 'external environment' in relation to which the university is seen to evolve. This is often simply taken to be the higher education funding or regulatory environment, without including consideration of other economic and governance spheres that form the wider societal environment in which they engage. In particular, because core higher education funding in most countries still comes from national or state governments, the external environment also implicitly seems to be scaled at this rather than the regional or city level, and therefore remains geographically undifferentiated (although some of the literature does consider the effect of increasing globalisation on national higher education competition, e.g. Slaughter and Leslie 1997). If an understanding of internal transformations within universities are to be combined with a broader territorial innovation systems framework, then any theoretical insights offered by university adaptation approaches need to be attuned to corresponding socio-economic and political factors at local, regional and possibly supra-national scales. The university adaptation literature, and particularly its entrepreneurial university strand, is also concerned predominately with economic drivers, whether financial incentives and pressures in higher education or opportunities for external revenue from working with industry. Therefore they may not capture the factors that shape the broader social and cultural elements of a university's civic mission (also see Subotzky 1999). As the discussion above also suggested, the move to more entrepreneurial, corporate models of the university is connected to the growth of managerialism in higher education. The values of regulation through bureaucratic performance assessment, greater competition, and division of research and teaching that this approach promotes (Deem *et al.* 2007) contradict many of the principles of the civic university (mentioned in the introduction) that can encourage more holistic engagement with cities and society (see Goddard 2009; also Barnett 2007). Moreover, the focus on commercialisation of academic knowledge in some interpretations of the entrepreneurial university also, as the first half of this chapter argued, may not be the most important contribution that universities can make to long-term territorial innovation. In the next chapter we will begin to outline what a more multi-faceted university external environment consists of, as we explore the argument that different sets of higher education and regional development drivers and barriers exist for engagement in the social development of a city or region than for economic development.

5 City social and economic development

Drivers and barriers to university engagement in three European cities[1]

Introduction

As the previous chapter showed, the emerging local development function of universities has largely been founded on the widely-accepted belief that universities are potentially key players in the growth of sub-national 'knowledge economies'. However, the involvement of higher education in the wider development of cities or regions clearly goes beyond the relatively narrow perspective of innovation and technology transfer, academic enterprise and human capital formation that this economic focus entails. This chapter aims to contribute to a broader understanding of this role by considering the societal dimensions of development alongside the more established economic dimensions, with specific reference to higher educational institutions (HEIs) in three European cities and contrasted national higher education systems.

In previous work we have approached this subject through a framework of 'drivers and barriers' that encourage or impede the engagement of HEIs in activity that contributes to regional development (Goddard and Puukka 2008). By framing the issue in these terms, we focused on the changing circumstances that have worked to both bring together and to keep separate these two domains of higher education and territorial development. These underlying factors covered drivers and barriers internal to the higher education system and external drivers and barriers relating to the regional context in which universities engage. However, like most other academic and policy work in this field, our earlier analysis concentrated on those factors that have led to the greater participation by HEIs in regional *economic* development, for instance drivers including: the growing role of universities in regional policy and their incorporation into regional and national innovation systems; the expanded technology transfer function of 'entrepreneurial universities'; the development of external intermediary organisations; and sites such as science parks (also see Chapter 4). The factors that may lead to HEIs being more engaged in societal dimensions of their city or region's development were not discussed in the same detail. In this chapter, we will seek to extend this framework along these lines by considering the drivers and barriers to HEI engagement in social as well as economic development in three European cities drawn from an OECD review programme: Berlin, Jyväskylä (in central Finland) and Rotterdam.

Despite considerable variations between these cities and higher education systems, the overall pattern we find is that where sustained engagement in economic related activities are generally supported by relevant local development policies and 'intermediary' organisations, these are not matched by equivalent drivers for social development. The resultant pattern of *ad hoc* and piecemeal engagement in this domain therefore acts as a barrier to the realisation of a fuller contribution of HEIs to their cities.

The chapter has six further sections. The next section reviews relevant academic literature on more holistic views of regional development and university engagement to provide a wider context for this exercise. The third section explains the OECD review process we draw upon. The fourth section addresses internal 'drivers and barriers' by outlining the regional component in the national higher education systems of the countries in which the three cities are located. The fifth and sixth sections cover the external policy and financial drivers and barriers to HEI engagement in city development through, first, economic innovation and, second, combating social exclusion. The concluding section explains how the distinction between economic and societal dimensions of city development proposed in the chapter informs our research and analysis in the second half of the book.

Universities and modes of urban and regional development

Various strands of loosely-connected thinking in the recent academic literature have explicitly moved from the narrowness of understanding regional development based on economic innovation and competitiveness, towards more multi-faceted frameworks that embrace dimensions such as social equality and cohesion, democratic participation, or environmental sustainability, alongside economic prosperity (Morgan 2004; Moulaert and Nussbaumer 2005; Pike *et al.* 2007; Hudson 2010). For Pike *et al.* (2007), these attempts to reconsider underlying conceptions raise normative questions about how different possible modes of regional development – particularly those focused on promoting economic growth at any cost – have uneven social and geographical effects. In response, they call for a 'holistic, progressive, and sustainable' view of regional development that 'emphasizes the role of the state together with civil society in tackling local and regional disadvantage, inequality and poverty' (ibid.: 1263). Moulaert and Nussbaumer (2005) take a similarly normative position when they outline the concept of 'social innovation' as an alternative dynamic in territorial development to technological innovation in the economy. The definition of social innovation used in this body of work is one that is 'path-dependent and contextual' and 'refers to those changes in agendas, agency and institutions that lead to a better inclusion of excluded groups and individuals in various spheres of society' (Moulaert *et al.* 2005: 1978). Based in the context of the broader range of actors now involved in the governance of European cities, the development of these new forms of non-market and community-based social organisation are seen to arise primarily from the sphere of local civil society and not the state (also Gerometta *et al.* 2005). Hence, the city is seen as a constitutive element of this innovation process, but primarily as a site of community, governance and social reproduction, rather than economic production (Moulaert *et al.* 2005: 1971). These critiques accord with wider arguments that the current emphasis on developing knowledge-based economies is often disconnected – or even in tension – with the social development concerns of cities and regions (see Chapain and Lee 2009). The case has been made that the discourse surrounding *knowledge* and *creativity* can act to obscure and legitimise local development practices with regressive socio-economic impacts for some sections of the population (Collinge and Musterd 2009). Although current approaches to territorial development may stem from a macro-policy environment defined by neoliberalism, we would stop short of conflating economic innovation with social exclusion. Instead, we broadly agree with Morgan (2004: 883; emphasis in original) that innovation should only be treated as 'an *intermediate* indicator of development, a means to an end rather than an end in itself'.

These more holistic frameworks have thus far been discussed with little or no reference to the potential role of universities in city and regional development. This is despite the inherent diversity of expertise residing in HEIs indicating that their potential significance as agents of local development cannot simply be reduced to that of catalysts for knowledge-based economic growth. Different parts of academia are active in shaping various spheres of development beyond the economy (e.g. public services and social welfare systems, environmental sustainability, arts and culture) at a national or trans-national scale, whether through research, professional training, or their intellectual contribution to informing public policy and political debate (see Appendix B). However, the link between this activity and the social development of cities or regions remains little-explored in the territorial development literature. Conversely, much has been written in higher education studies about more local civic engagement or community outreach (Ostrander 2004; McIlrath and Mac Labhrainn 2007; Watson 2007) and increasingly in planning and geography about the potential community regeneration effects of universities through their campus development practices (Chapter 2). Notwithstanding the positive benefits that these activities can have, their wider impact on city development outcomes remain unclear. Community engagement initiatives may be relatively small-scale in terms of resources and geographical scope beyond the campus. The emphasis of this engagement is often not directly on helping to achieve social objectives in the city, but on enhancing core activities within higher education, such as extending the teaching curriculum in the case of 'service learning' (see Lounsbury and Pollack 2001) or enabling the undertaking of social action research. Where the ethos around community development is generally strongest in North America, approaches to addressing social exclusion in Europe are more likely to follow a local partnership model involving various actors from the public and third sectors (Geddes 2000) (also Chapter 6). The embeddedness of HEIs as actors in this social policy and governance sphere (distinct from their bi-lateral relations with, for instance, city governments) does not seem to be widespread, despite universities being typically amongst the largest organisational stakeholders within their localities (also Russo *et al.* 2007).

In this chapter we aim to contribute to a deeper understanding of the relationship between universities and cities by elucidating the drivers and barriers to higher education engagement in the social dimensions of city and region development. These will be defined by creating a clearer analytical separation with the corresponding sets of external drivers and barriers for engagement in economic development, as well as intersecting internal drivers and barriers within the higher education system, in three cities selected from the OECD reviews. Due to limited space, we focus specifically on drivers and barriers related to innovation in the economic development section, and those related to the challenge of social exclusion in the social development section, rather than trying to cover all possible bases of economic (e.g. labour markets dynamics, SME support) and societal (e.g. health, environmental, cultural) development included in these reviews. Before this, the next methodological section will outline and reflect on the use of material from the OECD reviews.

Methodology: the OECD review process

The main section of this chapter will draw on material from the Berlin, Jyväskylä and Rotterdam region reviews from the OECD programme on higher education in city and regional development.[2] The Jyväskylä review is taken from the first round of this programme (undertaken between 2005 and 2007), and the Berlin and Rotterdam reviews from the second (between 2008 and 2010). Both rounds covered fourteen regions from around the world. One of the co-authors of this book was part of the peer review team for the Berlin and Jyväskylä reports, but the three regions were also selected on the basis of several other reasons: that they are all focused on a primarily metropolitan region; that they represent three different types of European city in terms of their size and function within the national and international economy; and that they operate within contrasting higher education and territorial governance systems. This enables us to demonstrate the highly contingent nature of university and city relationships.

Each regional review involves the production of two reports that are published by the OECD. First, a self-evaluation report (SER) is compiled on behalf of the review's commissioning and steering committee drawn from the HEIs and the region (Mukkala *et al.* 2005; City of Rotterdam Regional Steering Committee 2009; Schreiterer and Ulbricht 2009). Second, an international review team of academics, policymakers and OECD representatives prepare their peer review report (PRR) following a visit to the region (Goddard *et al.* 2006; OECD 2010a, 2010b). The contents of the self-evaluation and peer review reports are organised according to broadly the same basic set of chapters topics, which facilitates comparisons between the cases. Following an introduction, both reports have chapters on the socio-economic setting and the key characteristics of the region's higher education sector in the context of its national system, followed by chapters on the contribution of higher education in three areas: innovation in the regional economy; the local labour market and human capital development; and social, cultural and environmental development. A final chapter normally takes the form of a self-assessment of – or set of proposals for building – institutional capacity to support regional engagement and cooperation amongst the HEIs. This standard template encourages the reviews to take a multi-dimensional view of city and regional development. The contribution of HEIs beyond their impact on the local economy is addressed not only in the 'social, cultural and environmental development' chapter, but also in the higher education system and labour market chapters that normally consider issues pertaining to the social development of the city, such as access of different segments of the population to higher education. So while the OECD has arguably been central to the promotion of the global policy discourse around knowledge economies, in its analysis of higher education and regional development it offers a potentially more holistic approach than most specialist-focused academic research in this field.

However, there are also some clear methodological limitations of these reviews when used as a secondary data source. The nature of the review process means there is a danger it can be used (particularly in the SER) to promote the region in question and can also overstate the extent of regional engagement by the HEIs. Hence, in preparing this chapter, we have sought to read these reviews with a critical mindset. We have also tried to cross-reference material between the SER and PRR as much as possible, and wherever suitable also triangulate this against other documentary sources (including academic literature) related to these cities. For the purposes of this chapter, it should also be acknowledged that the non-economic elements of local development are sometimes uneven across these reports, and are generally under-conceptualised compared to the sections on economic innovation or higher education systems, reflecting the current dominant thrust in the literature and public policy. We have tried to address this limitation by selecting three reviews which do have relatively well-developed material relating to social inclusion across different chapters. Notwithstanding these important caveats, and provided that they are used with care, we believe these reports are a potentially useful resource for those seeking to understand the links between HEIs and different dimensions of city and regional development. The next section will introduce the higher education systems of the three territories covered and their internal drivers and barriers to regional engagement.

Background: drivers and barriers in higher education systems

All three city-regions are located in countries with 'binary systems' of higher education, in which a formal division in terms of funding and governance arrangements is maintained between universities and what are referred to here as universities of applied science (UAS).[3] UAS have a stronger focus on the teaching of largely vocational subjects, and are thus typically less research-intensive than universities. What research they do tends to be more user-driven, and their academic staff are often required to have extensive experience outside higher education, for instance, as in the Netherlands' *Lectoren* scheme (OECD 2010b: 72). UAS generally have less autonomy from the state, and some are assigned a specific regional mission to deliver a corporate response to local needs. As a general rule, therefore, the core activities of UAS are more closely orientated towards practical engagement with regional businesses and communities than universities that are focused on national or international research 'excellence', but acting on its own a UAS will often have less overall capacity to draw upon leading research for the purposes of local development.

Although a binary divide is common to all three national systems, the governance and funding arrangements for HEIs varies significantly between them, which has an important effect in setting the parameters for engagement in city and regional development. In the federal German political system, primary responsibility for higher education (HE) is devolved to the level of the *Länder*. Core funding is provided principally by state governments out of the taxation revenue allocated to them by the federal government. This structure means that Germany effectively has '16 idiosyncratic systems of HE...[in which] [r]esources, per capita funding, governance structures, priority areas and programmes differ to a large extent between states and individual HEIs' (Schreiterer and Ulbricht 2009: 15). Despite the scope for determination of HE policy at a sub-national level that this would seem to suggest, funding is provided to HEIs according to formula based on standard academic criteria such as student numbers and research performance that do not directly take into account regional development implications (ibid.: 19). The peer reviewers suggest that this geographical neutrality means '[t]he current extent of regionally relevant activities by Berlin higher education institutions, including industry collaboration, widening access initiatives and entrepreneurship activities, are more the result of bottom-up processes and not fully reflected in higher education policy or institutional set-up' (OECD 2010a: 15). Furthermore, the decentralised structure of HE governance in Germany handicaps the small number of *Länder* that are city-states and have to provide funding for a disproportionately high number of student places due to the concentration of HEIs in their urban centres. This extra burden has been a particular problem in Berlin, where a struggling local economy in the post-reunification period and consequent reductions in overall state spending, has put pressure on the financing of HEIs that are wholly reliant on public sources (ibid.). Some additional strategic resources, such as those that promote international research excellence in leading universities or allow provision for extra student places to meet shortfall against overall national demand, are contributed partly from the federal government (Schreiterer and Ulbricht 2009: 15–16). For example, Berlin universities together host one of the nine federal research 'Excellence Initiatives', which is match-funded by the Senate. However, as the peer review notes '[w]hile initiatives geared to building world class excellence in universities may also help them in their economic development role, such outcomes remain incidental' (OECD 2010a: 165).

Both the Netherlands and Finland have centrally-funded and regulated higher education systems (although some Finnish UAS are 'owned' by their municipality) (also Marginson *et al.* 2008; Davies *et al.* 2009). This means that the relevant level of local government for each city (the municipalities of Rotterdam and the City of Jyväskylä) do not have direct responsibility over higher education policy in their territory, and are therefore largely limited to engaging with HEIs through various partnerships in areas of common concern. Recent higher education policy in the Netherlands has been characterised by deregulation to give HEIs more financial autonomy over their activities. However, the national government has not accompanied this with real incentive structures that would encourage the institutions to become more regionally engaged (OECD 2010b: 35). The Finnish system, in comparison, does involve an unusual degree of system steerage in this area, by adopting a policy that HEIs have a mandatory 'third' mission relating to their societal engagement and impact. This requirement only has an explicit regional dimension for UAS, but limited financial incentives linked to regional engagement do also exist for universities (Goddard *et al.* 2006). The University and Polytechnic in Jyväskylä also have, following a national directive, a joint regional strategy (drawn up in 2002 and renewed in 2005) that underpins close collaboration between these institutions and with other regional organisations in a number of areas, some of which will be discussed below. In contrast, the lack of collaboration between HEIs – especially across the binary divide of universities and UAS with potentially complementary capabilities – is mentioned throughout the Berlin and Rotterdam reviews as a common reason for a lack of city development capacity in the HE sector as a whole. The encouragement of this type of cooperation is not a prominent component of these or many other national higher education systems, where competition between HEIs (including that between universities and UAS) is a corollary of institutional autonomy.

In summary, this short section has highlighted that city or regional engagement is not an inherent component of the higher education systems in these three territories, with the partial exception of Finland. The systems are primarily geared towards more conventional academic drivers related to student numbers and research excellence, even when (as with Berlin) higher education is governed at a sub-national level. This does not mean that all regional engagement is blocked, especially where strong disciplinary drivers for engagement in applied fields (e.g. health, arts, planning) act as a counterweight to institutionalised higher education barriers. However, it does suggest that for extensive engagement on the part of HEIs (and not just small decentralised groups of academics) strong drivers external to the higher education system are needed within these cities. It is to these that we turn now.

Economic innovation

Berlin, Rotterdam and Jyväskylä are three examples of former industrial centres that have undergone a period of structural economic adjustment over the past twenty years and are moving towards a more knowledge-intensive service- and advanced manufacturing-based economy. Each review highlights the presence of at least one innovation strategy that acts as a driver for HEI engagement in this process by mobilising them and other public agencies in the building of industrial clusters. These intended clusters are in targeted sectors where these city-regions are perceived to have an existing or potential advantage in industrial or research capability. They are also supported by organisational intermediaries and physical sites that often have close links to HEIs. The innovation strategies may be formulated primarily at either national or sub-national scales, depending on the particular territorial governance arrangements in place for that country. For this reason, this section will discuss the situation for each city in turn, before reflecting on the drivers and barriers at the end.

Berlin, where the process of deindustrialisation unfolded in the context of a challenging economic adjustment to reunification, ranks behind other German cities such as Frankfurt and Munich as a location for financial and business services, despite the city's international profile and restoration as seat of national government (also Cochrane and Jonas 1999; Gornig and Häusserman 2002; Krätke 2004). However, it does have strengths in other knowledge-intensive sectors that are connected to the city-state's considerable research and development capability and spending, which at the time of the review accounted for a bigger proportion of Berlin's GDP (4.2 per cent) than in any other German *Länder* (Schreiterer and Ulbricht 2009: 33). These sectors are reflected in the city's innovation strategy, which is formulated by the Berlin Senate, and concentrates on supporting six 'competency fields': biotechnology; medical technology; traffic and mobility; IT and media; optics; and power engineering (focusing particularly on renewable energy) (ibid.: 37). This is described in the PRR as a 'science-led strategy' which matches research strengths in the city's universities, but the Senate has also supported some initiatives to encourage industry engagement by UAS, particularly with SMEs (OECD 2010a: 84).

This innovation strategy is underpinned by an exceptionally well-developed set of intermediary organisations, which includes 'an extraordinary density and variety of non-university research institutes' (Schreiterer and Ulbricht 2009: 17), numbering over 70 in total (OECD 2010a: 70). In the German system, these public institutes receive direct research funding from the federal government, ranging from basic science through the Max Planck Society, to applied research through the Fraunhofer Society. This relatively equal footing with universities can result in close relationships with HEIs: the self-evaluation reports about 110 joint appointments of institute directors with Berlin universities, plus extensive research collaboration on national research programmes, staff exchange and co-supervision of doctorates (Schreiterer and Ulbricht 2009: 17–18). The other major innovation assets in Berlin are two science and technology parks (both in the former east of the city), with one (Adlershof) being amongst the fifteen largest in the world (ibid.: 13). Both of these parks house university facilities in either science or medicine alongside their business incubators and tenant firms (OECD 2010a). For instance, Adlershof is home to seventeen academic institutes, including the Science Faculty of Humboldt University (relocated from the city centre in 2003). The park, which is managed by a public/private company supported by the Senate, also has eleven non-university research institutes that are linked together through a formal association (ibid.: 74).

Jyväskylä has historically been a relatively prosperous industrial city and regional centre, but suffered particularly badly during the severe Finnish recession of the early 1990s, when unemployment rose to almost 25 per cent (Mukkala *et al.* 2005: 20). In response to this downturn, the Finnish government adopted a new science- and technology-based economic development strategy (also Schienstock 2004) that the peer reviewers describe as 'possibly the most sophisticated and well funded national innovation policy amongst OECD countries' (Goddard *et al.* 2006: 8). The explicit regional dimension of this innovation systems approach was slower to develop (also see Sotarauta and Kautonen 2007), but the national Centres of Expertise (established 1994 by the Ministry of the Interior) and Regional Centre programme (established 2001) has provided a mechanism for this by combining a focus on sectoral strengths in regional industries with national-level networking and coordination (also OECD 2005). At the time of the review, the Jyväskylä region had branches of Centres of Expertise in papermaking technology (the area's traditional industrial specialisation), energy and environmental technology, information technology, and nanotechnology, and a Regional Centre Programme in wellness technology. The University is reported as not directly playing a leading role in local economic development, partly because of the only limited match between its main research strengths and the sectors prioritised through the Centres of Expertise programme (Goddard *et al.* 2006: 30–1). Instead, most examples of effective local engagement with business in the reviews include a dimension of collaboration between the University and the more applied complementary strengths of the Polytechnic (see below), which can be linked back to the formal agreement between these institutions mentioned in the previous section.

Jyväskylä does not have the same 'density' of innovation-supporting institutions as (much larger) Berlin, but the reviewers do emphasise the importance of the business development function fulfilled by its science park (founded 1987), which acts as a hub for high-technology enterprises and networks in the region (Mukkala *et al.* 2005). The science park has close links with both HEIs and plays host to much of their interaction with firms in the cluster areas mentioned above (Goddard *et al.* 2006). The peer review also suggests that this external intermediary organisation could compensate for a corresponding lack of technology transfer capabilities within the HEIs themselves (ibid.: 32). The city-region's cluster around renewable energy (supported by the Centre of Expertise for Energy Technology) is cited as an example of these different components functioning together – 'a developing system linking University research, Polytechnic R&D, private business, education and training and a particular regional opportunity/ resource with the Jyväskylä Science Park . . . playing a key role as animateur' (ibid.: 29). The HEI involvement in this interdisciplinary field is diverse, covering research and teaching programmes across different faculties of both University and Polytechnic (also Mukkala *et al.* 2005: 53).

Rotterdam has historical strengths in traditional industries based on its Port area which, despite recent decline and migration of activity away from the city, continues to be an important part of the region's economy. Although much of the economic activity that takes place in the Port area is not highly dependent on innovation (OECD 2010b), the reviews identify strong links with the city's HEIs in some areas; for instance, in research on logistics with Erasmus University, and several examples of courses across the different institutions that address specific labour market needs connected to the Port (City of Rotterdam Regional Steering Committee 2009: 69–70). However, there is a strong recognition in economic development policy that Rotterdam needs to diversify its economy away from this traditional specialisation, in particular through upgrading skill levels in the wider labour market and transforming its negative image as an industrial city (also Richards and Wilson 2004; Russo *et al.* 2007; van Winden *et al.* 2007). For the purpose of the national Ministry of Economic Affairs' regional innovation strategy (*Pieken in de Delta*), Rotterdam is classed as part of the *Zuidvleugel* (south-wing) of the Randstad conurbation (which also includes The Hague and Leiden). The four designated cluster areas receiving support in this region include the 'Port and Industrial Complex' and 'Life & Health Sciences' with strong links to the region's research base (City of Rotterdam Regional Steering Committee 2009: 50). The reviews highlight some examples of where these policies have fostered relationships between HEIs and business. For instance, relating to the Life & Health Sciences cluster, the national *Pieken in de Delta* scheme provided part of the funding to create a 'Medical Delta' consortium in 2005, which includes Erasmus University (Medical Centre), DUT, and Leiden University (Medical Centre) with regional industrial partners (ibid.: 55).

However, the Rotterdam review also highlights some barriers to integrating HEIs into an innovation-led economy (also see van Winden *et al.* 2007). The peer reviewers concluded that '[c]ompared to other regions, Rotterdam is less success-ful in aligning the strategies of the stakeholders in higher education with key play-ers in industry ... there is a lack of clear strategy, with shared goals and ambitions' (OECD 2010b: 106). They argue that the metropolitan region displays many char-acteristics of a 'fragmented' innovation system, so that 'while there are many intermediary organisations ... they lack organisational capabilities and their focus is often narrow' (ibid.: 17). This appears to be as much a symptom of the immatur-ity of regional innovation policy at the national level as it does political failings in the city itself. The main regional-level policy in the Netherlands (*Pieken in de Delta*) was only instigated in 2004 and, compared to Berlin and Jyväskylä, mechanisms like science parks or university technology transfer facilities (while present) do not seem as well developed or prominent in the HEI–industry interac-tion discussed in the review. There also appears to be a lack of strong governance mechanisms at a sub-national level, whether that be the municipality or provincial Randstad scale, to deliver an effective and coherent innovation agenda (ibid.).

These barriers (institutional fragmentation, incoherent governance structures) are not exclusive to Rotterdam; similar issues are also mentioned in the Berlin and Jyväskylä reviews. The presence of different institutions in this domain alone clearly does not guarantee their effectiveness. Against this, however, this section has highlighted the clear aspiration in all three cities to engage HEIs in economic development, and the presence of substantial policy and financial drivers working at different governance scales to achieve this interaction. The success of these well-established strategies in Berlin and Jyväskylä is also signalled by the developed links with intermediaries such as public R&D institutes or science parks that can provide an interface for HEIs to engage with firms. This situation will now be contrasted with the territorial drivers and institutional frameworks for HEI involvement in social development.

Social inclusion

All three case study cities face particular challenges around social exclusion and spatial segmentation. In the Berlin and Rotterdam reviews, the most prominent single issue emphasised is the low social mobility and labour market opportunity of those from large (non-western) migrant-background communities, which has a geographical dimension in terms of the concentration of these communities in deprived areas of the cities. In the Jyväskylä review, the biggest issues fall along the lines of social exclusion in the rural municipalities of the sub-region and Central Finland more widely, which are particularly related to long-term unemployment, outward migration to urban areas, and an ageing population. This urban–rural polarisation has become a pressing issue throughout Finland, partly as a result of the shift in national economic development strategy towards prioritising growth in core urban areas, which has largely supplanted an earlier more redistributive regional policy (Goddard *et al.* 2006: 18–19; also OECD 2005). This section will outline the contributions HEIs make to addressing these social problems, and highlight the underlying drivers and barriers. It will focus on, first, their efforts to provide access to higher education for people in these excluded groups and, second, their varied involvement in different types of social development project or programmes.

Higher education is itself one of the institutional spheres through which social exclusion is reproduced, so any action to address this issue on the part of HEIs should start with expanding access to marginalised socio-economic groups. Incentives and targets for widening participation to include excluded groups are well established throughout OECD countries (OECD 2007). Indeed, this motive of widening participation is cited as being behind the establishment of UASs in West Germany during the 1970s (Schreiterer and Ulbricht 2009: 16) and polytechnics in Finland during the early 1990s (Goddard *et al.* 2006: 44). Since reunification in 1990, the Berlin Senate has also supported the establishment or relocation of HEI campuses in more deprived former East Berlin districts as an explicit urban development strategy, including the founding of UAS for Technology and Economy Berlin (Schreiterer and Ulbricht 2009: 32; OECD 2010a: 34).

Even with this expansion of the sector, the reviews note that participation in higher education amongst different socio-economic groups remains uneven. This is particularly the case for those from a migrant background who, according to the best available statistics, are underrepresented in Berlin and Rotterdam's higher education sectors, as well as in the German and Netherlands systems as a whole (see Marginson *et al.* 2008; City of Rotterdam Regional Steering Committee 2009: 38; Schreiterer and Ulbricht 2009: 44). This is largely a product of low levels of secondary education attainment amongst these groups, which determines their pathways into further and higher education (e.g. see OECD 2010b: 29–30). Notwithstanding the deep-rooted socio-cultural causes of the underlying problems, the reviews identify various initiatives to raise participation at the levels of both municipalities and individual institutions. For instance, widening access to higher education is a stated priority for both the Berlin Senate and Rotterdam Municipality (City of Rotterdam Regional Steering Committee 2009: 89; OECD 2010a: 110). However, there do not appear to be the necessary mechanisms available to address this problem comprehensively at a local level. In the case of Berlin, 'no policy tools have been devised to increase the enrolment of pupils with a migrant background having graduated from Berlin secondary schools' (OECD 2010a: 111). Different HEIs in the city have various academic and mentoring programmes that engage with younger members of migrant-background communities, which can have the effect of raising their aspirations and ultimately improving participation rates in higher education (ibid.: 149–50). For instance, a joint masters programme between Technical University of Berlin and the Berlin University of the Arts involves students researching the design of information and communication technologies through collaboration with children and teenagers in neighbourhoods with large migrant-background populations (*Street Lab*) (ibid.: 151). Members of the UAS Alice Salomon Berlin also have a record of using culture-based community engagement as a method in applied social work projects (Schreiterer and Ulbricht 2009: 54–5). However, the PRR notes that, in general, much of 'the concrete action to reach out towards people with immigrant backgrounds ... [is] driven by [academic] individuals and departments without reward or recognition from the higher education leadership' (OECD 2010a: 151–2).

Jyväskylä does not have the same problem of a large socially-excluded migrant population as Berlin or Rotterdam, although the PRR mentions that inequalities in participation between different socio-economic groups do arise when students reach higher education entry age (Goddard *et al.* 2006). As mentioned above, the larger social problems relate to exclusion in the rural municipalities of Jyväskylä as well as the city. Being the only two HEIs in the Central Finland region, both the University and Polytechnic recruit students from this wider catchment area, and have academic programmes relating to rural development (see Mukkala *et al.* 2005: 88–9). Beyond conventional higher education, the region's HEIs (primarily the University and an active Open University) are heavily involved in continuing education throughout the region, which is particularly oriented towards labour market needs of reskilling amongst older people (ibid.).

The second broad way that HEIs contribute to social development is through their involvement (at different levels) in various social development programmes or project activities. These are often connected to applied research and teaching in cognate disciplines such as health and social care, but are also enabled by extra sources of funding or policy initiatives from outside those for core academic activity. For instance, in Jyväskylä several different social, cultural and ecological programmes are discussed that were joint funded from European Regional Development or Social Funds (see Mukkala *et al.* 2005: 161–2). Many of these programmes operate out of either the Central Finland Centre of Expertise in the

Social Field or Regional Centre programme in Wellness Technology (ibid.), which provide an institutional framework for collaboration between key regional stakeholders in these areas, including that between the University and Polytechnic. For instance, the WIRE project, funded by European Social Fund and coordinated by Jyväskylä Polytechnic, aimed to increase social inclusion by helping the long-term unemployed back into work (ibid.: 86). In the field of Wellness Technology, the peer reviewers also highlighted 'the system that was evolving to translate leading edge research in health and physical activity amongst older people into products and services that could benefit an ageing population served by the municipal authorities'. This initiative involved 'applied research in hospitals and community services' by the Polytechnic to access 'the social innovation necessary to facilitate the uptake of technology', alongside basic research in the University and commercial development supported by the Jyväskylä Science Park (Goddard *et al.* 2006: 28). Despite these examples of well-supported and coordinated projects, the Jyväskylä reviews highlighted issues around the impact and sustainability of programmes in non-economic areas of development, including social programmes:

> The diverse project activities of HEIs form the main mechanism for contributing to the social, cultural and environmental development in the Jyväskylä region. Some projects have succeeded in generating continuous development processes that have multidimensional impacts on the (wider) society. Generally speaking, however, the main drawback of these project activities is their incoherence and loose connection to the overall regional development processes. Project funding has been strongly based on the European Regional Development Fund (ERDF) and European Social Fund (ESF). Without careful anticipation and planning, the diminishing resources of the EU structural funds will threaten both the activities that get carried out and the regional development processes launched in the fields of social inclusion, cultural development and the development of environmental sustainability.
>
> (Mukkala *et al.* 2005: 95)

The Berlin and Rotterdam reviews, in addition to the more academic-led outreach programmes mentioned above, highlight municipal partnership-based development programmes for socially- and economically-deprived urban districts, which HEIs participate in as local stakeholders. For instance, Rotterdam's ten-year programme to regenerate its southern districts (*Pact op Zuid*) involves the city's HEIs in various forms. Amongst different applied research, teaching (incorporating work placements), volunteering and community-based cultural development activities, these also include: use of the 'Creative Factory' incubator space to encourage student entrepreneurship in creative industries; a student accommodation development (*Dordtselaan*) that gives subsidised rents to tenants that do community work in the surrounding area; and a university research project to help evaluate and monitor the programme on an ongoing basis (City of Rotterdam Regional Steering Committee 2009: 90–3). An equivalent in Berlin, its extensive Neighbourhood Management Programme (funded by the *Länder*, federal government, and EU

Regional Development Fund) is cited as a possible best practice 'framework for community engagement' for other regions to follow (OECD 2010a: 31–2). However, despite the locational presence of HEIs (UASs) in some of the districts included in this scheme, and possible scope for linking academic programmes to this wider initiative – particularly in relation to its Education and Training strand (ibid.: 154) – the peer reviewers found that:

> To date, the involvement of Berlin [HEIs] in the neighbourhood management activities has been relatively limited and linked to evaluation, student internships and academic events. More could be achieved through collaboration between [HEIs] and by scaling up interventions currently driven by individual academics and departments. This would enable [HEIs] to excel in research about Berlin's immigration experience and public policy in a number of relevant spheres, for example in education, housing and employment.
>
> (OECD 2010a: 32)

In summary, while this section has highlighted the presence of some external funding streams (e.g. EU structural funds) and regional policy initiatives that can support higher education engagement in social development activities, these drivers and mechanisms are not as strong or wide-ranging as those for economic innovation activities. As a result, social development activities are more likely to be characterised by *ad hoc* and short-term funded projects, which will create further barriers in terms of embedding these initiatives back into ongoing academic programmes (also City of Rotterdam Regional Steering Committee 2009: 104). The reviews indicated that much of this piecemeal activity is undertaken at the level of self-motivated individual academics or departments, possibly in spite of the existing dominant drivers for academic work, and not generally supported or coordinated at the institutional level in a way that may enhance its overall impact for the city. An alternative as a possible institutional framework for social development was outlined above in the form of municipal neighbourhood development programmes. However, despite being potentially varied, HEI involvement appears to be largely marginal to these programmes as a whole,[4] so that the intellectual resources that academia possibly offers is not mobilised to play a leading developmental role.

Conclusion

Despite their limitations as a data source, the OECD reviews we have drawn on above enable a preliminary contrast between the drivers and barriers to HEI engagement relating to local economic and social development. The academic literature discussed earlier in the chapter pointed towards the need for more holistic models of city and regional development. The role of HEIs have yet to be discussed in direct relation to these debates, but the diverse intellectual resources contained within universities would suggest that they are well placed to contribute to the various domains involved. However, the three case studies that we featured reveal a marked imbalance in the policy drivers and institutional architecture supporting university engagement with the economic development of cities as compared to that relating to social development. Public policy in all three cities has sought to involve HEIs collectively as vital actors in the building of knowledge economies, which has led to them being embedded (with varying degrees of effect) in metropolitan or regional innovation systems with other public and private agencies. By comparison, the potential role of HEIs in social development partnerships within these cities seems to be less recognised in public policy or governance. An equivalence of the well developed universities, government and business 'triple helix' economic development model does not seem to have developed in the social domain through university relationships with, for example, local government, the third sector and community groups. So while members of individual HEIs are involved in varied projects which have social benefits, these are often piecemeal, so the wider and lasting impacts on the city appear to be relatively limited or highly localised. Hence, in the absence of these strong external drivers, the decentralised or loosely-coupled nature of universities, that the previous chapter suggested could be an asset for the long-term adaptability of regional innovation systems, works against the institution-wide response that is needed to help address large-scale (and interdisciplinary) societal problems and challenges.

As mentioned above, this seeming imbalance could partly be a feature of the OECD review process which, despite including substantive material on social development concerns, still gives pre-eminence to economic dimensions. It is therefore important that future primary research in different territorial contexts examines the deeper structures (drivers and barriers) that underlie HEI engagement with the non-economic dimensions of city and regional development. The second half of this book will aim to contribute to this endeavour through empirical chapters covering the relationships between universities in a selection of English cities and three major areas of academic work and engagement: sustainable urban development; public health and medicine; and the cultural sector.

For the purpose of the argument made in this chapter, the economic and social dimensions of city or regional development have been juxtaposed in the discussion above. However, in practice these two dimensions should not be seen as separated or necessarily in tension. Each of the three broad chapter areas we cover form both part of the societal and economic spheres of territorial development, and in each area organisations in the private, public and third sectors are active. As the economic innovation section of the chapter illustrated, fields relating to the environment or energy, health or medicine, and culture or media are amongst the main sectors prioritised in knowledge-based economic development strategies throughout Europe. Moreover, the engagement of universities in both economic and non-economic spheres may offer the potential for their connection, if public societal concerns are given the same weight as economic concerns. These issues will be explored in the three empirical chapters and the conclusion. Before this, however, the next chapter will discuss the specific context of the UK higher education system and city governance.

Part II
Research: the UK context

6 Higher education and cities in the UK

Introduction to Part II

This opening section outlines the research carried out for this book project and explains the function of the following background chapter on the UK higher education and sub-national territorial governance system. By extension, it therefore also acts as an introduction to the second part of the book as a whole.

To investigate the relationship between universities and cities in the three areas outlined at the end of the previous chapter – sustainable urban development, public health and medicine, and links with the cultural sector – we undertook original research in four major provincial English cities and regional centres, namely Bristol in the South West, Manchester in the North West, Newcastle upon Tyne in the North East, and Sheffield in Yorkshire and the Humber.[1] Three of these cities were selected in part because of their inclusion in another project that preceded this research (see Goddard *et al.* 2010). For all three areas we started doing research in our home city of Newcastle to identify key themes and issues in an environment with which we had some existing familiarity. The three areas were then paired with one of the remaining cities, so that each chapter would be based on empirical material from Newcastle and one other city. For sustainable urban development the second city was Manchester, for health and medicine it was Sheffield, and for links with the creative sector it was Bristol. These pairings were made on the basis of some prior knowledge of initiatives in these second cities that could provide a focus for research relevant to the area in question, but this was with the awareness that the areas we were interested in were general enough to be investigatable in any large city in the UK. All four of these cities are home to two or more universities, and the unit of study in this research is the city and its higher education sector rather than individual institutions. An important theme throughout these chapters, therefore, is the relationship between the different universities in a city. This chapter will provide background to this issue within the context of the UK by introducing a distinction between the two types of higher education institution commonly found together in large UK cities: research-intensive 'old' universities and former polytechnic 'new' universities. We refer to these here as Pre 1992 and Post 1992 respectively, due to their becoming universities either before or after the 1992 government act that abolished the binary distinction within the UK higher education system.

The principal method used for this research was semi-structured, qualitative interviews with key actors from the higher education and other relevant sectors in these cities. In total we did 48 interviews specifically for this book project across the four cities during 2010 and 2011. These were supplemented with relevant interviews from two other projects (see Goddard *et al.* 2010; Goddard *et al.* 2012). The full programme of interviews is outlined in Appendix A. Interviewees were identified and approached through a 'snowball' approach, building on contacts made from earlier interviews. All interviews were recorded, transcribed and coded as part of the analysis. The interview material is supported by relevant secondary documents and other web resources.

During this period we also carried out a survey of academics in six universities in the cities of Bristol, Newcastle and Sheffield, with the aim of exploring the different ways in which individual academics understand their research practice to have an impact (Vallance *et al.* 2011). This piece of research was not explicitly concerned with relationships between universities and cities, but does provide a valuable picture of different patterns of academic engagement with the external world through research, and how this varies between different disciplinary fields and different types of higher education institution. For this reason, we include a summary of results from selected parts of this survey as Appendix B at the end of the book. This is intended to work as a self-contained document for readers interested in this particular topic, but various parts of the appendix are also referred to at points throughout the following four chapters, where the survey results help to ground our analysis in a more nuanced picture of the actual extent of academic practices and external relationships than that promoted by common discourses founded on such reductive dichotomies as academic excellence versus practical relevance. This appendix includes sections that focus in more detail on the chapter areas of sustainability, health and culture.

The original research for this book has been heavily influenced by a wider political and economic context of considerable change and uncertainty. We began work on this book project in October 2008 at the height of the international banking crisis and completed it in July 2012 amidst the ongoing Eurozone sovereign debt crisis. The timespan framed by these twin financial disasters saw a change from a Labour to Conservative-led coalition government in the UK following the general election of May 2010. Against a sluggish economic recovery from recession and rising unemployment, this new government implemented an austerity programme of cuts in public expenditure and associated public sector reforms that involved major institutional and funding overhauls in areas including higher education, regional governance, sustainability, health, and arts and culture. Hence, relationships between universities and cities in each of the areas covered in the following chapters started to be fundamentally reconfigured during this period. This shapes the resulting accounts we offer which, while being largely retrospective studies of developments in the individual cities, also include some prospective discussion of likely future paths for university and city relationships in the areas covered. General issues not constrained to this particular UK context will be drawn out in the concluding chapter (Chapter 10).

The rest of this chapter will provide a general background to these changes by outlining the evolution of both the higher education and sub-national territorial governance systems in the UK (and more specifically England) up to the current time. It will focus predominately on developments relevant to the class of large cities outside London to which the four cities covered belong, and in places make specific reference to these cases. The chapter has two further sections. The next section – the core of the chapter – consists of three sub-sections covering: the funding and governance of the higher education system following the transformation of polytechnics into universities in 1992; the changing position of cities and city-regions in the territorial governance of the UK during roughly the same period; and points of articulation between these largely separate governance spheres, especially focusing on science and innovation policy. This continues the argument introduced in the previous chapter that the territorial development drivers for university engagement are more developed from innovation policy than they are in other governance spheres, including the kinds of local partnerships through which urban social policies are now increasingly delivered. However, it also discusses the limits placed on regional innovation and other economic development strategies by the centralist form of multi-level governance that pervades in the UK context, and discusses how this 'external' context has shaped university engagement. The final section, looking towards the subsequent chapters, briefly introduces and profiles the higher education sectors in the four cities covered in the research.

UK higher education and territorial governance system

The next section discusses changes over the past twenty years in the UK higher education system, territorial governance system, and the intersection between these two largely-independent governance spheres, across three separate sub-sections. It takes a major transformation in the UK higher education system in the early 1990s as the point of departure. The latest reforms in these domains under the new coalition government, that were introduced during the research and writing of this book, are mainly only referred to in passing as a signpost to future developments and are not the main focus of the discussion.

The UK higher education system

A major transformation of UK higher education occurred with the *Further and Higher Education Act* of 1992 that, alongside other reforms, granted university status to the 34 polytechnics that were in operation in England and Wales at this time (many in larger cities with existing universities). In effect, this ended the binary distinction between universities and polytechnics (or universities of applied science) that is still a feature of higher education systems in other European countries today (Chapter 5). The change moved the former polytechnic institutions under the governance of higher education funding councils for England and Wales (which were also a creation of the 1992 government act) and gave them the same degree and higher degree awarding powers as other universities (Pratt

1997). However, this has not led to a full convergence of institutional orientation and capabilities between old universities and former polytechnics. Significant differences between Pre and Post 1992 universities still remain twenty years on, which is testament to the entrenched path dependency of institutional structures and cultures (Chapter 4), reinforced by a funding system that largely preserves the status quo in terms of hierarchical distinctions between different types of universities. Post 1992 universities are characteristically less research intensive than Pre 1992 universities, often have a stronger internal managerial culture and, through their relative priority of vocational training, applied research and recruitment of students from surrounding areas, traditionally have stronger links with their locality.[2] Results from the online research impacts survey, reported in Section 3 of Appendix B, provide broad support for several of these observations regarding the two types of university and the research practice of their employees. However, the results also indicate that some of these differences are in part attributable to variations between the population of academics from Pre 1992 and Post 1992 universities in terms of their disciplinary composition and the number of staff in dedicated research positions. Post 1992 universities, while often having pockets of research excellence in distinct niches that are as strong as anything in their Pre 1992 counterparts, rarely have the same scale of research activity in major scientific and engineering fields (particularly because they typically do not have a medical school). The upshot of this is that the UK still has an institutionally diverse higher education sector (Taylor 2003; Howells *et al.* 2008), although unlike countries such as the USA there are very few fully private universities. According to Universities UK, there are currently 115 universities in the UK (89 in England) and in total 165 HEIs (131 in England) which include other institutional types such as specialist art or medical colleges.[3] The differences between types of university, and the hierarchical stratification through which these are enshrined, are made explicit in formal associations of universities, such as the Russell Group of large research-intensive universities or the University Alliance of business-engaged institutions that includes many of the urban-located Post 1992 universities. The implications for cities of these divisions will be discussed later in this chapter.

This ending of the binary divide – and growth of former polytechnics that it allowed – contributed to a long-term trend towards expansion of the higher education sector that had been encouraged by successive governments (Mayhew *et al.* 2004). This expansion was in terms of numbers of institutions as well as students, with the 1960s in particular being a period of new university formation throughout the country (most in smaller towns or cities outside the major urban centres that already had universities). In terms of students, according to figures collected by Greenaway and Haynes (2003: F150–F152), national numbers rose steadily from a base of around 400,000 in the early 1960s (post the Robbins Report of 1963), but this growth accelerated rapidly at the end of the 1980s and start of the 1990s to surpass two million near the beginning of the 21st century. Table 6.1 shows how student numbers for the whole of the UK have continued to rise between 1995/1996 and 2010/2011, and how this breaks down between

Table 6.1 UK higher education student numbers, 1995/1996–2010/2011[a]

	Students	*By level*		*By attendance*		*By domicile*	
	Total	*UG*	*PG*	*FT*	*PT*	*UK*	*OS*
95/96	1,720,095	1,349,975	370,120	1,107,845	612,250	1,523,750	196,345
10/11	2,501,295	1,912,580	588,715	1,677,345	823,955	2,073,070	428,225
Change	781,200	562,605	218,595	569,500	211,705	549,320	231,880
% change	*45.42*	*41.68*	*59.06*	*51.41*	*34.58*	*36.05*	*118.10*

Source: Adapted from Higher Education Statistics Agency (HESA) Free Online Data Tables – Students by Institution (http://www.hesa.ac.uk/index.php/content/view/1973/239, accessed 16 July 2012).

Note
a Key: FT = full-time, PT = part-time, UK = United Kingdom, OS = overseas, UG = undergraduate, PG = postgraduate. All figures rounded up to nearest multiple of 5.

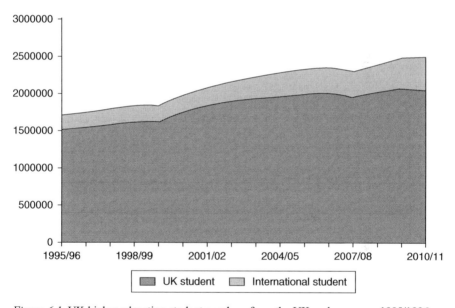

Figure 6.1 UK higher education student numbers from the UK and overseas, 1995/1996–2010/2011.

Source: Adapted from Higher Education Statistics Agency (HESA) Free Online Data Tables – Students by Institution (http://www.hesa.ac.uk/index.php/content/view/1973/239/, accessed 16 July 2012).

increases from categories of undergraduate/postgraduate, full-time/part-time and UK/overseas students. Figure 6.1 charts this overall increase over the fifteen year period from numbers of domestic and overseas students. The number of overseas students – and particularly high fee paying non-European Union students – has increased at a higher rate than UK students (which will in turn have particularly contributed to the increase in numbers of postgraduate and full-time students). However, as Figure 6.1 clearly illustrates, overseas students still account for only a relatively small share of overall student numbers, even with this larger proportional rise in their numbers.

These trends have transformed higher education in the UK from an elite to a mass system with significantly higher participation rates (Greenaway and Haynes 2003; Mayhew *et al.* 2004), although disparities in access between those from richer and poorer backgrounds remain persistent (Blanden and Machin 2004; Galindo-Rueda *et al.* 2004). The increase in even just domestic student numbers, however, has not been matched by rises in expenditure on higher education by the state, leading to falling levels of funding per student. In the past ten years, responses to this challenge of financing higher education have involved a gradual shift in the balance between public and private contribution. Personal tuition fees were only introduced by the Labour government in 1998, initially at the low level of £1,000 per year, before rising to be capped at a maximum of just over £3,000 in England. However, as a concession to those who feared that this move would discriminate against students from disadvantaged backgrounds, the right for universities to introduce these higher fees was linked to them also meeting widening participation targets, regulated by the newly-established Office for Fair Access (OFFA). So, at least until changes by the new coalition government due to come into effect in 2012/2013,[4] teaching has been largely publicly funded, with the Higher Education Funding Council for England (HEFCE) (or its equivalents in Scotland, Wales or Northern Ireland) acting as the client (or 'proxy consumer') by contracting universities (that are institutions autonomous from the state) to take on a certain number of students in different subject areas (Williams 1997).

The funding of research in universities is also still predominately provided for by the state, notwithstanding the important role of private and charitable funders (particularly in fields such as the medical sciences) and also European Structural Funds. The government supports a dual system of funding for individual research projects or programmes and block grants for institutions. Funding for individual research projects primarily occurs through Research Councils in seven fields, including the Engineering and Physical Sciences Research Council (EPSRC), the Medical Research Council (MRC), and the Arts and Humanities Research Council (AHRC). These councils run themed programmes of research as well as open response competitions for other funding applications. There are also six priority areas for cross research council funding, which aim to promote '[n]ovel, multidisciplinary approaches... [to] solve the big research challenges over the next 10 to 20 years'.[5] These areas include Energy, Living with Environmental Change, Lifelong Health and Wellbeing, and Digital Economy. The research councils are funded out of the Department for Business, Innovation and Skills (BIS) administered science budget, but other government departments, such as the Department of Health or the Department for Culture, Media, and Sport, may also fund research infrastructure or commission targeted research projects in their fields through other avenues that will be discussed where appropriate in subsequent chapters. Block grant funding for institutions is allocated by the higher education funding council (so in England HEFCE) on the basis of the Research Assessment Exercise (RAE), which for the next round in 2014 has been renamed the Research Excellence Framework (REF). This is a peer review eva-luation (in the form of appointed panels) of research quality carried out at inter-mittent periods of around five years, which rates the strength of institutions in different subject areas. Since its introduction in 1986, and roll out to the entire higher education sector in 1992, the RAE has, under the banner of promoting the 'excellence' of the system as a whole, been criticised for legitimising the concen-tration of research funding in certain institutions and departments and its with-drawal from others (Willmott 2003). This has reinforced the advantageous position of elite research institutions who continue to gain most from this system (the geographical manifestations of which will be discussed below). The incen-tives established by the RAE have also encouraged the spread of a managerial competitive culture in British universities, which acts as a driver for prioritising publication in high-ranking peer-review journals within academic research prac-tice (Elton 2000; Deem *et al.* 2007). Partly to counter a perceived resulting lack of engagement in more practically-orientated research, a proportion (initially weighted at 20 per cent) of the forthcoming REF will be assessed against the new criteria of social and economic 'impact' (HEFCE 2011). In addition, funding bids to the seven research councils now require the potential impact and beneficiaries of the prospective project to be outlined. The efficacy of these measures in incen-tivising or rewarding research with a genuine public good at its core (as opposed to creating a new set of bureaucratic targets and procedures to be followed) remains to be seen, but this represents a more fundamental effort to establish the principle of external engagement as integral to academic practice across a much wider spectrum of disciplines. Hitherto in the UK higher education funding envi-ronment, this has largely been marginalised as a 'third stream' separate from teaching and research. For instance, HEFCE runs the Higher Education Innovation Fund (HEIF) to support knowledge exchange (covering interaction with both business and community) (see PACEC 2012), but this accounts for only a very small proportion of the total core funding that universities receive (see Table 6.3 below). Since 2008, the Higher Education Funding Councils, Research Councils UK and the Wellcome Trust medical charity have also supported a net-work of six Beacons of Public Engagement across England, Scotland and Wales, which aim to promote cultural change in higher education institutions to increase their public engagement. The Beacons include multi-university partnerships in the North East of England (between Newcastle and Durham universities) and Manchester. The National Coordinating Centre for the Beacon programme is based in Bristol and jointly hosted by the two universities in the city.

Cities and regions in UK territorial governance

This sub-section briefly explains changes in the UK territorial governance sys-tem over the past twenty years, particularly as they relate to the position of cities or city-regions. At the time of the early 1990s, British urban policy under the Conservative government was targeted at reversing the inner city decline that had been one consequence of the widespread deindustrialisation of the 1970s and 1980s. Local elected government in major cities had been left weakened after a politically-motivated decision in 1986 to abolish larger metropolitan county councils in six areas of England (Greater Manchester, Merseyside, South Yorkshire, Tyne and Wear, West Midlands and West Yorkshire) and the Greater London Council in the capital, leaving smaller and fragmented local authorities in their place. The institutional gap at the local level created by this centralisation of power was filled by government policies that promoted a liberalised 'partnership' model of city governance, and created opportunities for private sector investment in urban development projects (Hastings 1996; Tewdwr-Jones and McNeill 2000). The key actors during this period were thirteen Urban Development Corporations (UDCs) established by central government between 1981 and 1992 and focused on areas of varying size in and across cities throughout England and Wales; these included Newcastle (Tyne and Wear UDC), Greater Manchester (Trafford Park and Central Manchester UDCs), Sheffield and Bristol (Imrie and Thomas 1999; Deas *et al.* 2000). In terms of their main economic development function, the UDCs were narrowly focused on the reclamation and physical regeneration of unproductive, former industrial land through property development, exemplified in large prestigious 'flagship' projects (Loftman and Nevin 1995) such as Canary Warf on the London Docklands (Brownill 1999; Minton 2009).[6] For their physical regeneration function, the UDCs were granted powers to operate outside normal planning regulations and hence circumvent local authority influence over their activities (Imrie and Thomas 1999; Deas *et al.* 2000; Minton 2009). According to Cochrane (1999), UDCs were conceived as:

> single-purpose agencies with a proactive entrepreneurial agenda . . . able to overcome the inherent weaknesses associated with the divisions created by the overlapping jurisdiction of local government and other public organisations. In other words, they were intended to be examples of post-bureaucratic (focused, task-orientated and businesslike) organisations with a commitment to market-led solutions. They were expected to solve the perennial problem of co-ordination between a range of different agencies, each with their own 'interests', by integrating them into one organisation.
>
> (Cochrane 1999: 251)

In this way, UDCs represented a particular top-down form of 'partnership' between public and private sector interests that lacked local accountability and community participation (Hastings 1996; Raco 2000).

The period leading up to the election of a Labour government in 1997 saw the beginnings of a re-emergence of a regional tier of governance in the traditionally centralised UK state. The initial impetus for this development did not primarily come from within domestic politics, but from the practical requirement for coordinated political organisation at a regional level in order to qualify for the receipt of

European Union Structural Funds (Garmise 1997; Tewdwr-Jones and McNeill 2000; Musson *et al.* 2005). This led to the formation of Government Offices for the nine (redefined) English regions in 1994. These Offices were functions of central government with responsibilities to administer and coordinate programmes in their region from across various departments (Musson *et al.* 2005). A more political commitment to regional decentralisation was however part of the New Labour project and, upon coming to office, the new government implemented several important territorial reforms. The most significant constitutional changes were the creation of elected assemblies in Wales and Northern Ireland and a parliament in Scotland following positive referendum votes. These new bodies inherited devolved powers in areas including economic development, planning, education and training, environment, health, and arts and culture (Leeke *et al.* 2003). In England, a 'triad' of regional governance was formed with the addition of Regional Development Agencies (RDAs) and Regional Assemblies (or Chambers) to the Government Offices for the Regions (Musson *et al.* 2005; also Tomaney 2002). The Regional Assemblies were non-directly elected bodies (but mostly comprised of local government councillors) created to oversee and hold RDAs accountable (Tomaney 2002; Musson *et al.* 2005; Pearce and Ayres 2007). The RDAs (closed by the Conservative-led coalition government in 2012) were non-departmental public bodies set-up with five objectives in their regions:

1 to further economic development and regeneration;
2 to promote business efficiency, investment and competitiveness;
3 to promote employment;
4 to enhance the development and application of skills relevant to employment;
5 to contribute to the achievement of sustainable development in the United Kingdom (Regional Development Agencies Act 1998).

Under the direct management of the Department for Business, Innovation and Skills (BIS) (or its predecessor departments), the RDAs were funded by a combination of central government departments out of a 'single pot', which was allocated according to a formula-based system that gave more money (per head of population) to those regions with the greatest economic development needs. Therefore, the three northern regions – and above all the North East of England – received the highest per capita investment, allowing them to take a more extensive role in investing in projects with the aim of transforming the industrial base of their region. The approach and priorities for this economic development were set out in a Regional Economic Strategy, which each RDA was required to produce in 2002 and update around every three years thereafter. Despite this active role in policymaking for their region, the constitution of the RDAs meant that they were less independent organisations than delivery vehicles for central government, with constraints on their local autonomy and only limited democratic accountability (Jones 2001). Hence, compared to the devolved powers in Scotland, Wales and Northern Ireland, these English regional institutions constituted a much lesser degree of decentralisation, leaving the UK as a whole with an asymmetrical terri-torial governance system (Goodwin *et al.* 2005). The partial exception to this in England is the capital, where the Greater London Authority was reformulated in 2000 to now consist of an elected mayor and assembly, with powers relating to transport, economic development and the police and fire services in the metropoli-tan region (Travers 2002).

Alongside this re-introduction of a proactive economic development policy tak-ing place at a regional scale, the late 1990s and early 2000s were also marked by an expanding national urban policy (Parkinson *et al.* 2006; Turok 2008). In partic-ular, this was a product of New Labour's efforts to address social and economic polarisation in urban areas, which were constructed around the communitarian discourses of 'social inclusion, neighbourhood renewal and community involve-ment' (Imrie and Raco 2003: 4; also Cochrane 2003; North 2003). This shift from framing the city as a problem of regeneration under the Conservatives to one of community development under New Labour was reflected in a plethora of new urban policies and development initiatives across a range of government depart-ments relating to planning, housing, sustainability, public health, local govern-ance and neighbourhood renewal (Imrie and Raco 2003; Parkinson *et al.* 2006). In terms of institutional capacity, the approach of governance through multi-actor partnerships rather than local government was continued (Whitehead 2007). For instance, the Department of Communities and Local Government made manda-tory the establishment of Local Strategic Partnerships (LSPs) in each local author-ity area to promote an integrated, place-based approach to community development and the delivery of some local services. Although the precise structure of each LSP is decided at the local level, they typically consist of sub-partnerships relating to five core themes (health and wellbeing, children and young people, environment and sustainability, community safety, and economic development and employ-ment) which have board representatives from across various public, private and third sector organisations (including universities). Although LSPs and other similar initiatives brought in under New Labour incorporate a broader set of actors into local governance than in earlier partnership models (e.g. UDCs), reservations have still been raised about the strength of their democratic dimension and their capacity to deliver change in local services (Bailey 2003; Geddes 2006; Whitehead 2007). These issues will be picked up in reference to sustainability and health in the subse-quent two chapters.

Coinciding with this urban policy focus on social inclusion and community development, the period up to the financial crisis of 2008 (throughout which the UK as a whole experienced steady economic growth), was also one of regeneration and comparative prosperity for English cities, including those in the former indus-trial North and Midlands (although the poorest parts of these cities remained largely untouched by this prosperity). During this time, a policy discourse arose that positioned these large provincial cities as 'engines' of national and regional growth (cf. Champion and Townsend 2011 for a sober assessment of their eco-nomic performance from 1984 to 2007 relative to the rest of England). This 'urban renaissance' was championed within central government by the Office for the

Deputy Prime Minister (Urban Task Force 1999; Parkinson *et al.* 2006) and promoted by policy think tanks such as the Work Foundation (Jones *et al.* 2006), NESTA and the Centre for Cities (Athey *et al.* 2007). These emphasised the distinctiveness of knowledge and creative assets concentrated in urban centres, although the economic revitalisation enjoyed at this time was as much down to the growth of routine service employment in the public and private sectors (Champion and Townsend 2011) and a prolonged housing and urban property boom (Pike and Tomaney 2009). A growing confidence based on this new economic identity was reflected in the local authorities for eight of the largest English cities outside London – Bristol, Birmingham, Nottingham, Sheffield, Leeds, Liverpool, Manchester and Newcastle – coming together to form the Core Cities group as a vehicle for collectively promoting their national role and influencing government policy. The role of higher education – and in particular the national Science City network – as part of this new discourse will be discussed in the following section.

The sub-national governance reforms brought in by New Labour also paved the way for the 'reconceptualiz[ation of] urban partnerships and urban governance within new regional institutional and political systems' (Tewdwr-Jones and McNeill 2000: 130). In this context, the concept of city-regions, already established in the academic literature (Deas and Ward 2000; Tewdwr-Jones and McNeill 2000; Scott and Storper 2003; Ward and Jonas 2004), appeared within the territorial policy debate. Initially this was proposed by local government actors as a response to the limited top-down decentralisation represented by the new regional institutions. City-regions were believed to offer an intermediate scale, between too small (often under-bounded) local authorities and too large administrative regions, that corresponded more closely to urban agglomerations and functional economic areas such as travel to work areas or metropolitan labour markets (Deas and Ward 2000; Harrison 2010; Shaw and Greenhalgh 2010). However, following the return of a decisive no vote in a 2004 referendum for an elected assembly in the North East, which ended any short- to medium-term prospect of further English regional devolution, city-regions moved from the margins to the centre of the national discussion around sub-national governance. This notion was particularly supported in the north of England, coinciding with the formation of the pan-regional Northern Way partnership (Harding 2007). A series of policy initiatives were introduced to begin to constitute this new institutional scale, including: Multi-Area Agreements (a framework for coordination of transport, planning and economic development functions across local authority boundaries); City Development Companies (economic development and regeneration vehicles at the level of a city or city-region); and in 2009 the designation of Manchester and Leeds in the north of England as pilot statutory city-regions, with formal responsibility and powers in areas including planning, housing, transport, education and skills, and economic policy across the constituent local authorities (Harrison 2010; also Shaw and Greenhalgh 2010). For Manchester – one of the case cities included in this study – this cemented a long-term collaboration between ten local authorities that have collectively made up the Association of Greater

Manchester Authorities (AGMA) since the dissolution of the Metropolitan County in 1986, and reinforced a strong identity at the city-region scale that existed even when the governance focus was on the region (North West England) (Deas and Ward 2000). In 2011, Manchester graduated from pilot statutory city region status to become the first combined authority of its type in England.

City-regions added to the general 'picture of complexity, experimentation, fragmentation and incoherence in the UK state's rescaling of the governance of economic development' (Pike and Tomaney 2009: 30). Policies and institutional vehicles for different and overlapping economic development and other functions co-exist at several socially-constructed scales of governance: city, city-region, region and (in the case of the Northern Way) pan-regional. The new Conservative-led coalition government has responded to this situation by largely dismantling the regional tier of governance under the banner of 'localism'; although, without any significant devolution of power or resources to localities or communities, this form of rhetorical localism may best be interpreted as little more than an adjunct of renewed centralisation. The Government Offices for the Regions and RDAs have been abolished and, in institutional terms, substituted by around 40 Local Enterprise Partnerships (LEPS) – local authority and business led bodies that are not directly resourced by central government in the same way that RDAs were, but are expected to access funding streams such as the new Regional Growth Fund to support their activities (Shutt *et al.* 2012). LEPs exist at a sub-regional level that in several cases (e.g. Leeds, Liverpool, Manchester, Sheffield) equate with recognised city-regions, and have served to reinforce the presence of this scale in the UK's territorial governance lexicon. At the same time, some cities (including Bristol, Salford and Liverpool) are set to introduce elected mayors at the single local authority level (this option was rejected by other cities including Manchester, Newcastle and Sheffield in referendums held in May 2012). Hence, the multiplicity of scales seems set to continue. The next section considers the implications of these issues for university and city or regional engagement.

Articulation of UK higher education and territorial governance systems

The main elements of UK national higher education policy outlined in the section before last do not include a formal spatial dimension, beyond the devolution of relevant powers to the Scottish Parliament and Welsh and Northern Irish assemblies. This historical state of affairs continues despite the higher education function having moved from the Department of Education and Skills (via the now defunct Department for Innovation, Universities and Skills) into the Department of Business, Innovation and Science (formed in 2009), which has also been the lead government department for regional economic development policies (such as the former RDAs and present Regional Growth Fund).

Higher education funding is related to student numbers and research outputs, with mainly no explicit concern for where those students are taught or the graduates employed, and where the research is undertaken or the associated social or economic impacts occur, so that regional or urban development concerns do not formally enter into decision making. Minor exceptions to this rule are created through regulatory balances built into the system, such as widening participation targets (which universities meet through partnerships with local schools), or by university links with local employers around vocational training (as in the case of links with city and regional health authorities discussed in Chapter 8), but the local engagement here is mainly a result of practical requirements in measures with predominately social or professional development intentions. The geographical element of external engagement drivers such as HEIF or the new research impact agenda is implicit, and the local or regional dimension is not prioritised over the national or international.

The unlevel playing field on which universities compete with each other for state funding in the UK higher education system means that these spatially-blind policies often produce geographically uneven outcomes. For research funding in particular, the approach of directing the majority of expenditure into already high performing institutions, as a way of safeguarding global 'excellence' within the system as a whole, has in particular favoured a few leading universities that are located in the greater south east of England. Table 6.2 shows the leading institutions in England by research funding and the region in which they are located. It uses two measures: the HEFCE total research funding component of their annual recurrent grant for 2011/2012 (the level of which is determined by their performance in the RAE) and figures for all other research income (grants and contracts) from 2009/2010 compiled by the *Times Higher Education* periodical. By both measures, the top of the list is dominated by institutions from London, Oxford and Cambridge, which together form an area colloquially referred to as the 'Golden Triangle' in and around which much of the private and non-university public R&D spending in the UK is also concentrated (Perry 2007). The top four institutions alone accounted for £448,605,000 of funding through HEFCE recurrent research grants in 2010/2011; 28 per cent of the total (of £1,603,000,000) for all 130 English HEIs through this funding stream.[7] The rest of the list is predominately made up of the main research-intensive universities in major cities outside London which, while trailing behind the leading universities in the 'Golden Triangle', still have substantially greater research income than the Post 1992 institutions in their cities (see Table 6.3 on page 83).

The spatial neutrality of the national higher education environment has however been challenged by university involvement in the hybrid economic development sphere of 'science, technology and innovation' policy (see Lundvall and Borrás 2005), which in England developed a limited sub-national dimension through the activities of regional development agencies (Perry 2007). This development reflects the argument of the previous chapter; that drivers for extensive regional engagement by universities are strongest around their incorporation into economic development policy as agents of innovation. In the UK, the emergence of a regional governance context for this regional innovation engagement

Table 6.2 Research funding by institution and region: top 15 institutions in England[a]

Institution (region)	HEFCE total research funding 2010/2011[b]		Other research grants and contracts 2009/2010[c]	
	£000s	Rank	£000s	Rank
University of Oxford (South East)	126,036	1	367,000	1
University of Cambridge (East of England)	117,843	2	267,700	4
University College London (London)	108,978	3	275,061	3
Imperial College London (London)	95,748	4	296,800	2
University of Manchester (North West)	**84,617**	**5**	**194,603**	**5**
King's College London (London)	59,689	6	144,053	6
University of Nottingham (East Midlands)	51,599	7	104,100	10
University of Bristol (South West)	**50,437**	**8**	**101,400**	**11**
University of Leeds (Yorkshire and Humber)	49,873	9	119,319	7
University of Sheffield (Yorkshire and Humber)	**45,977**	**10**	**98,748**	**12**
University of Southampton (South East)	45,397	11	96,323	13
University of Birmingham (West Midlands)	44,619	12	104,811	9
University of Liverpool (North West)	37,619	13	110,800	8
Newcastle University (North East)	**35,483**	**14**	**85,200**	**14**
University of Warwick (West Midlands)	33,317	15	79,802	15

Note

a Numbers rounded to nearest 1,000.

b Source: English HEI HEFCE recurrent grant funding 2010/2011 (http://www.hefce.ac.uk/pubs/ hefce/2010/10_08/, accessed 19 July 2012).

c Source: *Times Higher Education.* Financial Data for UK Higher Education Institutions (http:// www.timeshighereducation.co.uk/story.asp?sectioncode = 26&storycode = 415728&c = 2, accessed 19 July 2012).

coincided with drivers within the higher education system (for instance the intro-duction of HEIF) that encouraged universities to take on a greater economic development role through skill development and knowledge transfer (Goddard and Chatterton 1999; Charles 2003). This led to universities in general forming strong relationships with RDAs; not just individually, but also collectively, as evidenced by joint higher education participation in such regional science and technology governance bodies as Science and Industry Councils or Science Enterprise Centres (Kitagawa 2004; Perry 2007).[8]

Into this category the UK government added Science Cities in 2004, as a 'national endorsement of an urban dimension to the challenges of knowledge-based growth . . . driven by globally-oriented concerns over scientific-technological development' (May and Perry 2011b: 717). Initially, Science City status was granted to three representatives of the northern regions – Manchester (North West), York (Yorkshire and the Humber) and Newcastle (North East) – but a year later was extended to include Bristol (South West), Birmingham (West Midlands) and Nottingham (East Midlands). Although a top-down initiative, the development of a Science City programme to match this designation was left to partnerships formed in each city, which typically included universities, the relevant RDA and other key city or regional actors.

The Science City programme was in many ways shaped by its wider governance context. Although regional agencies gained some scope to form their own science and technology policies during the New Labour era, this domain was still overwhelmingly dominated by concerns related to national competitiveness, which translated into uneven regional public spending on research and development in favour of the greater south east (Charles and Benneworth 2001). Perry (2007) conceptualises this regional science policy in England as a 'minimalist' form of multi-level governance in which local actors are, in practice, restricted to working in frameworks determined at the national level:

> In theory, RDAs had limited power to define their own agendas and distribute resources, but this is minimized by an absence of power over the contours of national policy, resulting in a 'mimicking' at regional level of national priorities. No real arenas exist for the co-production or negotiation of policy with tiers of governance largely parallel rather than strategically joined-up. National reactions to the involvement of RDAs in science policy have been hesitant and reluctant; patterns of interaction are varied across the English regions and responses are ad hoc. The RDAs have thus far failed to significantly reshape science policy from below. In such a minimal system of multi-level governance, the capacity of the English regions to truly develop science regions or cities is limited.
>
> (Perry 2007: 1063)

In line with this type of arrangement, the designation of Science City status by the national government was itself not directly accompanied by extra funding or new powers, but relied on hamstrung local actors mobilising their own existing capabilities or attracting additional resources to support new activities (May and Perry 2011b). This will be discussed in more specific detail in relation to the cases of Newcastle and Manchester science cities in subsequent chapters.

The central role of the RDAs in the Science City programme, meant that they were an example of a nominally urban-scaled initiative in a predominantly regional governance framework. This is partly reflected in the particular configuration of the partnerships in three of the six cases (Manchester, Birmingham and Bristol) being at a city-regional level. For instance, Science City Bristol involves the University of Bath and Bath Spa University in an unofficial sub-region around Bristol referred to as the West of England. However, with the recent abolition of the RDAs and their partial replacement with new institutional formations that often operate at a city-regional scale, the relationship between universities and territorial governance is at present 'unclear' (Kitagawa 2012). This is despite a strong association of city-regions with innovation in the academic and policy literature (e.g. Scott and Storper 2003; Jones *et al.* 2006; Athey *et al.* 2007). Local Enterprise Partnerships do not seem to have the institutional capacity or funds at their disposal to assume the more strategic role in promoting innovation within their regions that the state-backed RDAs could, which (despite its limitations) enabled them to enrol universities in many of their programmes. Innovation policy under the new coalition government has once again become entirely overseen from the centre, and delivered by national agencies such as the Technology Strategy Board. In Greater Manchester, where the evolution towards a metropolitan region model is more advanced than anywhere outside London, the governance of the new AGMA institutional structures that have been created for the statutory city-region and now combined authority – while including some university representation on various boards – is overwhelmingly local authority and private sector dominated. As the next chapter will discuss, in regard to many of the innovation and economic development functions in the city-region, these new structures (e.g. The Commission for the New Economy) have replaced an existing intermediary, Manchester Knowledge Capital, in which the local universities and the regional development agency were key players (also see Kitagawa 2012). The AGMA economic project, as defined in documents such as the Greater Manchester Strategy and the Manchester Independent Economic Review, also does not seem to advance a university-led innovation agenda, preferring instead to emphasise the role of the HEIs in the city-region as attractors of talent (AGMA 2009) or 'social spaces that bring together firms and other parts of the innovation process' (MIER 2009: 50). These issues around different institutional models and territorial governance scales will be elaborated in the following chapters, but before this we will briefly introduce and profile the higher education sectors of the four cities covered in the research.

The case study cities and their higher education sectors

By way of conclusion to this chapter, we will briefly introduce and profile the higher education sectors of the cities covered in this research. As the introduction to this chapter stated, the unit of study for this project is the city and its higher education sector rather than individual institutions. Each of the four cities has a Pre 1992 university and former polytechnic Post 1992 university, which are indicated in bold in Table 6.3 (the Pre 1992 university is listed above the Post 1992 university). We have restricted our attention to these institutions, rather than including those that fall in a wider city-region definition (for instance

Table 6.3 HEI HEFCE recurrent grant funding, 2010/2011: institutions from case study cities and others selected from surrounding region (£000s)[a]

Institution	Research	Teaching		3rd stream	Total
	Research total	Widening participation	Teaching total	HEIF	Recurrent grant
South West (Bristol)					
University of Bristol	**50,437**	**442**	**66,351**	**1,900**	**118,688**
University of Bath	18,134	415	34,148	1,900	54,182
University of the West of England	**5,809**	**1,540**	**65,267**	**1,688**	**72,763**
Bath Spa University	780	434	19,058	347	20,184
North West (Manchester)					
University of Manchester	**84,617**	**1,397**	**100,899**	**1,900**	**187,417**
University of Liverpool	37,619	774	72,698	1,900	112,601
University of Salford	**7,319**	**1,548**	**47,750**	**1,734**	**56,803**
Manchester Metropolitan University	**6,508**	**2,656**	**81,810**	**1,893**	**90,211**
University of Bolton	736	1,362	22,278	454	23,586
North East (Newcastle)					
Newcastle University	**35,483**	**637**	**65,566**	**1,900**	**103,300**
University of Durham	26,177	428	42,106	1,900	70,183
Northumbria University	**3,252**	**2,061**	**60,280**	**1,900**	**65,815**
University of Sunderland	2,595	1,849	36,361	1,724	41,395
University of Teesside	1,332	6,218	61,961	1,467	64,759
Yorkshire and the Humber (Sheffield)					
University of Leeds	49,873	1,157	89,998	1,900	141,771
University of Sheffield	**45,977**	**1,241**	**67,669**	**1,900**	**115,546**
University of York	26,125	487	31,689	1,900	59,715
Sheffield Hallam University	**5,015**	**3,532**	**67,368**	**1,900**	**74,284**

Source: English HEI HEFCE recurrent grant funding 2010/2011 (http://www.hefce.ac.uk/pubs/hefce/2010/10_08/, accessed 19 July 2012).

Note
a Numbers rounded to nearest 1,000.

the University of Sunderland in Tyne and Wear, or the University of Bath in the West of England). The one exception to this is the University of Salford, which is included in Chapter 7 due to its physical closeness to Manchester, the strong identity of the Greater Manchester city-region that Salford forms part of, and the high relevance of parts of this institution to the sustainability area in question. The University of Salford is technically not a post 1992 university, but a former college of advanced technology that became a university in 1967 and expanded through a merger with the independent University College Salford in 1996.[9] The

University of Manchester itself is the product of a 2004 merger between the original civic Victoria University of Manchester and the University of Manchester Institute of Science & Technology. This merger, which was financially supported by the North West RDA, created 'the largest single-site university in the UK'[10] and an institution with more research power than any other in the North of England (see Table 6.2 above).

Table 6.3 shows recurrent HEFCE funding for the universities in these cities and (for comparison) selected others in the same region for the academic year 2010/2011. The institutions are listed in each region by order of their total research funding grant. This shows the large disparities in this income stream between the Pre 1992 and Post 1992 universities, which in part reflects the way the funding is weighted towards established research-intensive institutions as part of the RAE/REF process. Correspondingly, the Post 1992 universities gain a much higher proportion of their recurrent income from core teaching and widening participation funding. HEIF money for third stream activities was capped at £1.9 million per institution (rising to £2.85 million after 2011 (PACEC 2012: 7)) and is therefore more evenly distributed across the institutions, but only represents a small proportion of the Pre 1992 institutions' total grant.

Table 6.4 shows the change in student numbers in these cities for the same fifteen year interval used for Table 6.1 above (1995/1996 – 2010/2011) with the breakdown by Pre 1992/Post 1992 institution, full-time/part-time, and UK/overseas students. For the purposes of this table, the Post 1992 category for Manchester includes students from the University of Salford as well as Manchester Metropolitan University. This table shows that these cities have considerably more students (particularly in the categories of full-time and overseas students) than fifteen years ago, although the overall increase is only around the level for the UK as a whole (45.42 per cent) in Newcastle and Sheffield, and below this in Bristol and Manchester. In terms of institutional type, in all the cities apart from Manchester, the Post 1992 institution(s) gained more students than the Pre 1992 institution, reflecting the effect of expansion following their transformation into universities. The relatively small increases or falls in part-time student numbers in these cities is accounted for by research-intensive Pre 1992 universities largely withdrawing from the provision of adult lifelong learning or continuing professional development courses. As with the national picture discussed above, the largest proportional increase in any category is from overseas students in all four cities which, amongst other impacts, will have added notably to their cultural diversity.

All those that attend these institutions do not necessarily also live in that city, but students make up a significant proportion of the overall population of these cities (albeit lower than smaller towns or cities with universities such as Oxford, Cambridge, Durham or Bath) (see Tight 2007). It therefore seems reasonable to posit that the considerable increase in student numbers (many migrating from other areas) will have contributed to the relative economic 'renaissance' of these and other cities in the UK across the late 1990s and most of the 2000s, predominately by boosting local demand for various services in the local economy, which in turn translates into employment gains (Chapter 3). Further empirical work is

Table 6.4 Student numbers, 1995/1996–2010/2011 for universities in Bristol, Newcastle, Manchester and Sheffield[a]

	Students	By institution		By attendance		By domicile	
	Total	Pre 92	Post 92	FT	PT	UK	OS
Bristol							
95/96	36,290	17,565	18,725	24,145	12,140	33,805	2,480
10/11	50,520	19,990	30,530	37,780	12,740	43,715	6,805
Change	14,230	2,425	11,805	13,635	600	9,910	4,325
% change	*39.21*	*13.81*	*63.04*	*56.47*	*4.94*	*29.32*	*174.40*
Manchester							
95/96[b]	74,725	28,865	45,860	54,370	20,350	65,900	8,825
10/11	96,750	40,410	56,340	79,310	17,445	79,775	16,965
Change	22,025	11,545	10,480	24,940	− 2,905	13,875	8,140
% change	*29.47*	*40.00*	*22.85*	*45.87*	*− 14.28*	*21.05*	*92.24*
Newcastle							
95/96	34,385	15,500	18,885	24,615	9,775	30,435	3,950
10/11	50,365	20,940	29,425	39,980	10,390	41,110	9,265
Change	15,980	5,440	10,540	15,365	615	10,675	5,315
% change	*46.47*	*35.10*	*55.81*	*62.42*	*6.29*	*35.07*	*134.56*
Sheffield							
95/96	43,690	23,625	20,065	31,835	11,855	38,815	4,875
10/11	63,470	26,960	36,510	48,105	15,360	51,830	11,635
Change	19,780	3,335	16,445	16,270	3,505	13,015	6,760
% change	*45.27*	*14.12*	*81.96*	*51.11*	*29.57*	*33.53*	*138.67*

Source: Adapted from Higher Education Statistics Agency (HESA) Free Online Data Tables – Students by Institution (http://www.hesa.ac.uk/index.php/content/view/1973/239/, accessed 16 July 2012).

Notes
a Key: FT = full-time, PT = part-time, UK = United Kingdom, OS = overseas. All figures rounded to nearest multiple of 5.
b Pre 1992 figure for 95/96 is the combined student numbers for the Victoria University of Manchester and the University of Manchester Institute of Science & Technology. The Post 1992 figure for 95/96 includes both the University of Salford and Salford College of Technology.

needed to estimate the economic impact of this rise in student numbers on cities in different parts of the country and the likely effect of any future drops in student numbers or mobility with the increased fee regime introduced by the current coalition government. Other forms of impact (environmental, health and cultural) that students and other groups related to higher education have in these cities will be touched on in the chapters that follow.

As Chapter 3 discussed, in the UK a large number of these students (particularly attending Pre 1992 universities) will have migrated to these cities from other regions, and while a majority are likely to leave the region following graduation, a share of them will (at least in the short-term) remain in the region to work. The relative conversion rates for 'locals' and 'stayers' in the four regions in which these cities are located can be seen in Chapter 3 (Figure 3.2) as part of the discussion of Hoare and Corver's (2010) analysis. One expected effect of expanding student numbers therefore will be a rise in the numbers of graduates in the workforce in these cities and their regions. This picture can be seen in figures from the Office of National Statistics (ONS) on the number of residents of working age (16–64) in an area that have qualifications at National Vocational Qualifications (NVQ) Level 4 or above, which is the level for those with some kind of higher education qualification (including a two-year Higher National Diploma). It therefore offers a reasonable proxy for the number of graduates (or at least university educated) in a labour market. Table 6.5 shows this number and it as a percentage of residents of working age (16–64) for the four cities (local authority level), a corresponding city-region, and their region between 2005 and 2010. Figures for the city-regions are available from ONS at metropolitan county level in the case of Greater Manchester, Tyne and Wear (Newcastle) and South Yorkshire (Sheffield), and at the level of the territory used for the new LEP in the West of England (Bristol). This table shows that the number of residents with NVQ4 level qualification or above has risen – both numerically and as a percentage of the working population – in all areas over this five-year

Table 6.5 Number of residents and percentage of overall population of working age with NVQ4 level qualification or above: 2005 and 2010 for Bristol, Manchester, Newcastle and Sheffield (with corresponding city regions and regions)

		2005		*2010*		*Change*	
		Number	*%*	*Number*	*%*	*Number*	*%*
Local authority:	Bristol	89,600	32.9	114,300	37.1	24,700	4.2
City region:	West of England	212,000	32.2	242,900	33.6	30,900	1.4
Region:	South West	805,700	26.4	1,026,100	31.5	220,400	5.1
Local authority:	Manchester	81,400	27.0	116,300	33.2	34,900	6.2
City region:	Greater Manchester	371,200	23.2	481,400	28.1	110,200	4.9
Region:	North West	1,016,400	24.0	1,271,100	28.7	254,700	4.7
Local authority:	Newcastle upon Tyne	43,100	24.5	55,200	28.0	12,100	3.5
City region:	Tyne and Wear	143,100	21.0	186,100	25.4	43,000	4.4
Region:	North East	335,300	21.3	427,600	25.5	92,300	4.2
Local authority:	Sheffield	84,600	25.2	122,300	33.0	37,700	7.8
City region:	South Yorkshire	159,900	19.9	221,200	25.7	61,300	5.8
Region:	Yorkshire and the Humber	703,400	22.2	904,300	26.4	200,900	4.2
Region:	London	1,695,900	33.8	2,277,200	41.9	581,300	8.1
Nation:	United Kingdom	9,914,300	26.4	12,476,700	31.2	2,562,400	4.8

Source: Office for National Statistics – Nomis official Labour Market Statistics (http://www.nomisweb.co.uk/, accessed 19 July 2012).

period. This general trend reflects a demographic pattern related to long-term increasing national higher education participation: a much lower number of those reaching retirement age during this 2005–2010 period (and therefore leaving this 16–64 age group) will have attended and graduated from university (being in their early twenties during the early to mid 1960s) than younger people gaining higher education qualifications during this same period. However, differences between these cities in terms of the percentage of residents qualified at this level, and the increase over this five year period, will reflect varying patterns of higher education attendance and graduate migration. Because these figures refer to residents and not employees, the city-region level is likely to be a more accurate representation of a local labour market (e.g. closer to a travel to work area) (although in all cases the percentage level is higher for the central city where younger graduates in particular are likely to live). Figure 6.2 shows the 2005 and 2010 percentage levels for these city-regions and those for the UK and London as comparison. The differences between city-regions here reflect the strength of local economies (and therefore different abilities to absorb or attract graduates) with the West of England (Bristol) having a higher percentage of residents qualified at this level (in both 2005 and 2010) than the three city-regions in the North

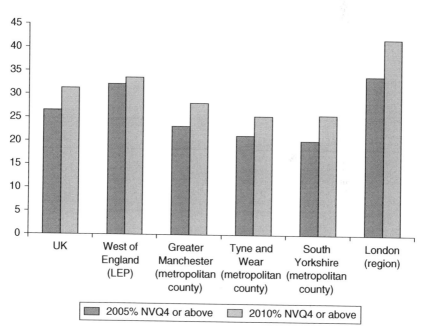

Figure 6.2 Residents of working age with NVQ4 level qualification or above (2005 and 2010) for city regions.

Source: Office for National Statistics – Nomis official Labour Market Statistics (http://www.nomis web.co.uk/, accessed 19th July 2012).

of England. However, this is still substantially below London, which also gained most over the five year period and, due to graduate migration and absorption, is the biggest single winner from the national expansion of higher education numbers.

This brief concluding section has given a general picture of the higher education sectors in the four case cities and some related elements of their local environments. As explained in the introduction to this section, we now move on to three chapters in which the relationship between these cities and their universities is studied in more depth in relation to specific thematic areas. These will, however, draw on the wider context provided by the general discussion of higher education and territorial governance in the middle section of this chapter.

7   Universities, sustainability and urban development

Introduction

Concerns with the environmental sustainability of cities have become central to urban development (Girardet 1999). The growing urbanisation of the global population is associated with greater levels of natural resource use, and yet at the same time the organisation of more environmentally-efficient infrastructure and energy consumption at the level of cities represents a vital dimension of the change required to achieve transition to more sustainable and low carbon societies (Rees and Wackernagel 1996; Bulkeley *et al.* 2010). The complex nature of urban systems has led to this process of moving them to a more sustainable footing being conceptualised as a 'socio-technical transition', often from a multi-level perspective (Bulkeley *et al.* 2010; Hodson and Marvin 2010).

The strategic and operational response of city-level authorities throughout Europe and other parts of the developed and developing world to this challenge has increased over the previous twenty years as green issues have become a core political topic (Bulkeley 2010). However, this local action always takes place in – and is shaped by – some type of multi-level governance system (Bulkeley and Betsill 2005; Bulkeley 2010; Hodson and Marvin 2010). The process of 'eco-state restructuring' has been developed to describe how 'state and parastatal actors mobilise strategic interests and actors around economic development projects and social activities, which ... [they] regard as consistent with very specific and strategic environmental goals and outcomes set at international and national levels' (Jonas *et al.* 2011: 285; also While *et al.* 2010). In England, this restructuring process has led to a range of existing sub-national bodies – including local authorities and regional development agencies – taking on some statutory responsibilities for sustainable development or carbon emission reduction alongside their more customary urban planning and economic development functions, but often without the scope or resources to encourage significant environmental benefits (Gibbs and Jonas 2001; Benneworth *et al.* 2002; Bulkeley and Betsill 2005; Shaw and Theobald 2011). Local sustainable development policies have been criticised for advancing primarily technical or economic fixes that reinforce rather than challenge the priorities of capitalist society that underlie environmental problems (While *et al.* 2004; Bulkeley and Betsill 2005; Hodson and Marvin

2012). In particular, local and regional policymakers have recognised that the transition to a lower carbon society has the potential to create major economic development opportunities in industries such as renewable energy production and energy efficient building construction or retrofitting (Christopherson 2011). By contrast, the 'stronger' ecological sustainability voices and practices of third sector environmental groups or social enterprises, while nominally incorporated into local governance through vehicles such as Local Strategic Partnerships, are often marginalised within dominant policy processes (Chatterton and Style 2001; Kythreotis 2010; Davies and Mullin 2011).

This chapter will examine the contribution of universities to sustainable urban development against this broad context of environmental governance relations. The perspective taken is also informed by the argument outlined in general terms (chapters 5 and 6) that the strongest drivers for substantial external engagement by universities are those that arise from the territorial governance sphere relating to economic development and innovation. The empirical cases featured are of Newcastle upon Tyne and Greater Manchester; two cities/city-regions with track records of active sustainability policy studied in previous work (e.g. Chatterton and Style 2001; While *et al.* 2004; Bulkeley and Betsill 2005; Hodson and Marvin 2012). These cases are used to reveal the developing engagement in sustainable or low-carbon urban development of universities in these cities. An analytical distinction between the university as an institution and as a multi-disciplinary academic community is employed in the discussion. The next section provides a short background by defining these two forms of agency in more detail. The main empirical sections describe how the universities in Newcastle and Greater Manchester have begun to increase their involvement in sustainable urban development. A concluding section reflects on the analysis that the intersection and synergy of these institutional and academic roles creates opportunities for the university to deepen this engagement.

Universities and sustainability

This brief section will define and give background to the institutional and academic modes of interaction between universities and sustainable urban development that frame the empirical material and analysis in this chapter. The university's institutional role in sustainable urban development can take two forms. The first is related to the environmental impact directly tied to the presence and expansion of university estates located in cities. Just as urban universities invariably have significant social and economic impacts on their home cities (chapters 2 and 3), the energy and other resources consumed by their buildings and by their attendant communities (students, staff, etc.) also carry environmental costs and an ecological 'footprint' that corresponds to a geographical area far beyond its campus (see Flint 2001; Venetoulis 2001). Like other types of publicly-funded body, universities in the UK are required, through their funding councils such as HEFCE, to implement carbon reduction strategies in accordance with government targets for the higher education sector as a whole.[1] As well as reducing institutional carbon emissions, efforts to 'green the campus', for example by ensuring new buildings are highly energy efficient or implementing systems for recycling waste onsite, can promote the university as an exemplar of sustainability that appeals to many prospective staff or students (Rappaport 2008). As this chapter will demonstrate, this also extends to university involvement in off-campus urban regeneration projects that may have a strong sustainability focus (e.g. Science Central in Newcastle, the Oxford Road Corridor in Manchester). The second form that this institutional role takes is the role of the university, beyond the campus, as an organisational actor within the set of relationships that collectively form urban environmental governance. In England, this can range from bi-lateral relationships with the local authority around planning issues, through representation on the environment component of such collective fora as Local Strategic Partnerships, to more active involvement as organisational stakeholders in city or region intermediary vehicles. Relating to the latter, Hodson and Marvin (2012) draw on the case of Manchester to show that in the multi-level governance system of environmental regulation in the UK, local sustainability or energy agencies are required to mediate between national state policy and its implementation at the level of cities. However, they also argue that these groups replicate the priorities of their parent governance organisations (in this case the AGMA Environment and New Economy Commissions) which reinforce the configuration of environmental problems as economic opportunities. In addition, the kind of local economic development partnership vehicles discussed in the preceding chapters may prioritise such environment or sustainability sectors as clean energy or transport technologies as strategic growth areas for their cities or regions. It is the second of these forms of intermediary that we primarily concentrate on in this chapter because of their predication on academic scientific strengths. In particular, the empirical sections are particularly focused around the effect that activity connected to three of these organisations are having on sustainable urban development in their cities: Newcastle Science City, Manchester: Knowledge Capital, and Corridor Manchester.

The second way in which the university interacts with sustainable urban development is through the local engagement of its academics. Within the academy, the socio-technical nature of the challenges involved means that environmental sustainability is recognised as a major field for the application of knowledge across different disciplinary fields. Results from the research impacts online survey, outlined in Section 4 of Appendix B, reflect this interdisciplinarity by showing that researchers who see their work as making a contribution to sustainable development or environmental protection are distributed almost equally across disciplines in the natural or applied sciences (e.g. engineering, physical and biological sciences) and the social sciences (e.g. planning, architecture). The survey also provides support for the strength of relationship between research impacts in the area of sustainability and impacts relating to technology and the economy, as well as government and policy at different scales. As a quintessential interdisciplinary societal 'Grand Challenge', in such rhetoric as the Lund Declaration, sustainability-related issues, including energy, living with environmental change and global food security, have been designated as priority areas for funding across the UK research councils (Chapter 6), as well as presented as strategic themes by individual institutions (although see Evans and Marvin 2006; Lowe and Phillipson 2009 for a discussion of the limits to collaboration across scientific 'paradigms'). The applied nature of research that addresses these problems of urban sustainability also means that much of the work is highly grounded in particular local settings. The metaphor of seeing the city as an 'urban laboratory' (or sometimes referred to as a 'living laboratory') has recently been popularised in urban development discourse. This concept positions the city as simultaneously the object of study, the setting or field for the research practice, and as a site for collaborative and interdisciplinary experimentation or intervention (see Evans and Karvonen 2010; Evans 2011; Karvonen and van Heur *forthcoming*). Both cities have adopted some version of this 'urban laboratory' concept, and we will discuss its utility in linking the institutional and academic role of universities in a grounded context.

Newcastle

Table 7.1 shows selected academic units in both of Newcastle's universities that have some specialisation relevant to environmental science, renewable energy, or urban sustainability broadly defined. With a few notable exceptions, such as Northumbria University's Sustainable Cities Research Institute, the most established areas of strength are those that relate to energy generation and use as part of science and engineering faculties or schools. These include the Sir Joseph Swan

Table 7.1 Selected energy, environment and sustainability related university research units in Newcastle

---

Newcastle University

Faculty of Science, Agriculture & Engineering
  Sir Joseph Swan Centre for Energy Research
  Centre for Earth Systems Engineering Research
  Transport Operations Research Group (TORG)
  School of Marine Science and Technology
  Tyndall Centre for Climate Change Research (part of cross-university network)
Faculty of Humanities and Social Sciences
  Global Urban Research Unit (GURU)
Cross Faculty
  Newcastle Institute for Research on Sustainability (NIReS)
  Centre for Research in Environmental Appraisal & Management (CREAM)

Northumbria University

School of Computing, Engineering & Information Sciences
  Energy Systems and Advanced Materials Research Group
  Energy, Design and Manufacturing Research Group
School of the Built & Natural Environment
  Sustainable Cities Research Institute (SCRI)

Centre for Energy Research in Newcastle University and a smaller but leading area of research on solar energy in the Northumbria Photovoltaics Applications Centre (part of the Energy Systems and Advanced Materials Research Group). In addition, nearby Durham University – the other research-intensive university in the North East of England region – has varied and well-established capabilities in different energy fields. In 2001, these academic research strengths in 'offshore and high value-added engineering and energy' were recognised in a mapping exercise commissioned by the newly-established regional development agency (RDA), One NorthEast, in preparation for their first regional economic strategy (Arthur D Little 2001). This led to the RDA establishing the New and Renewable Energy Centre (Narec) on a regenerated site in the coastal town of Blyth in Northumberland (to the North of Newcastle) as one of five Centres of Excellence – large scale investments in sector-specific research and development capacity that were a key part of the regional economic strategy published in 2002. The other four Centres of Excellence set up during this period were the Centre for Process Innovation (CPI), the Centre for Excellence in Life Sciences (Cels), the Centre for Excellence in Nanotechnology, Micro and Photonic Systems (CENAMPS, later to become part of CPI), and Codeworks in the area of digital technologies and media (One NorthEast 2002). These corresponded closely with regional university research strengths because of the lack of private and other public research and development capability in the region. Only the chemical processing sector – and to a lesser extent digital media and software and (through off-shore and marine engineering) new and renewable energy – also had an active industrial base in the region at this time. Narec (since rebranded the National Renewable Energy Centre) has developed substantial working relationships with academics in the three regional universities mentioned above, despite changes in its funding arrangements that have latterly forced it to depend increasingly on commercial income from private and university clients outside the North East of England (for a discussion of these changes and evolution of Narec's relationship with Newcastle University, see Goddard *et al.* 2012). These links are based to a significant degree on the large-scale specialised equipment (e.g. wind turbine blade testing facilities) that, in contrast to universities, Narec has been able to attract funding for and accommodate on its site.

Shortly after the establishment of the regional centres of excellence, Newcastle was designated as the North East's Science City following the 2004 budget (Chapter 6). In Newcastle, this label took shape with the creation of a partnership between Newcastle University, Newcastle City Council and One NorthEast, which was tied to co-investment by these organisations in the purchase of the site of a former brewery (Scottish and Newcastle) in central Newcastle (see Map 7.1 on p. 94), with the intention of transforming this into a mixed-use site with elements of an urban science and technology park. Hence, other prospective participating agencies in Newcastle Science City, such as Northumbria and Durham universities, were not formally included as core members of the partnership. A separate intermediary organisation, Newcastle Science City Ltd, was set-up by the three core partners in 2009 as a company limited by guarantee. This organisation's portfolio

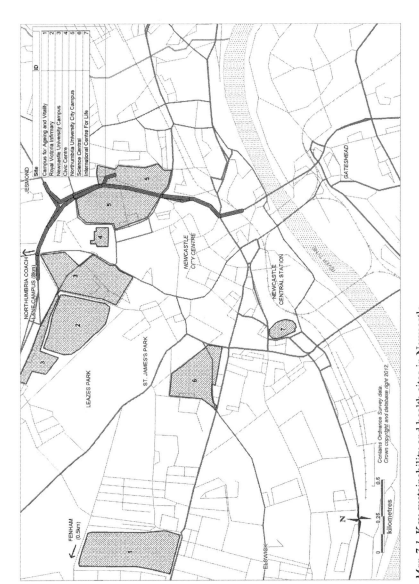

Map 7.1 Key sustainability and health sites in Newcastle.

Source: Contains Ordinance Survey data. © Crown copyright and database right 2012.

includes support for existing businesses, facilitating the creation of new enterprises drawing on scientific capabilities in the region's universities, and a strand of public engagement work with local schools and communities focused particularly on promoting science education in deprived areas. However, responsibility for planning and managing the physical development of the brewery site development, known as Science Central, was separated and given to other organisations; the large consultancy ARUP for the original master-planning and, after its incorporation in 2009, 1NG, the joint city development company (Chapter 6) for Newcastle and Gateshead.

One NorthEast was able to accommodate the Newcastle Science City initiative into its wider regional architecture via the introduction of the new nomenclature of 'innovation connectors' in an updated regional economic strategy published in 2006. The innovation connectors, of which there were seven distributed throughout the region, did not have a common organisational model, but were existing or planned developments with potential to bring local physical regeneration and community benefits to the place in which they were located, as well as supporting regional business innovation relating to their particular sectoral specialisation. Although the seven innovation connectors included original Centres of Excellence Narec and CPI (as part of the Wilton Centre in Teesside), the concept implied a broader role that aligned with the more locally-focused rationale for Newcastle Science City.

> The Centres of Excellence were mainly based on scientific excellence as well as industrial excellence.... But they had no appreciation of the local connectivity, and the local impact; whether it's an economic impact or a social impact. When, if you look at the early days of Science City, it's always been about how we can make sure that, the areas of scientific excellence we have, actually do have an economic and social impact. And the national drivers were, yes there are cities in England that have great areas of science and we recognise this, but it won't be of any use to anybody unless it has an economic and social impact.... The strategy behind [the innovation connectors] is to have a place where you can demonstrate tangibly what the theories are about: so linking industry, and academia, and entrepreneurship, and the local population. And making sure that, in the case of Science Central, all this works together as a kind of extended part of the city, but also a demonstration of what Science City is about.
>
> [*Interviewee, Newcastle Science City Ltd, 08/02/10*]

Four areas of research strength in Newcastle University with commercial potential were selected to become science city priority themes: Energy and Environment; Ageing and Health; Stem Cells and Regenerative Medicine; and Molecular Engineering. Each theme area had an academic leader within the university and an extra appointment created for a 'Professor of Practice', to be filled by an individual with relevant industry experience, who could support enterprise development relating to their theme from a base in the University Business School. The Energy and Environment theme was framed as such to match one of One NorthEast's three science and technology 'pillars' set out in the updated regional economic strategy (One NorthEast 2006). In contrast to the other science city themes, Energy and Environment did not map neatly on to a single existing research department or research institute within Newcastle University. Hence, the theme's activities had to be coordinated by bringing together academics whose interests lay at the intersection of fields relating to energy and the environment; in this case not just from Newcastle but also Northumbria and Durham universities. The inter-institution interaction that took place under this banner preceded a large funding bid to the UK Engineering and Physical Sciences Research Council (EPSRC) and Technology Strategy Board (TSB) by a regional consortium involving the three universities, Narec and CPI, to house a major national R&D centre, the Energy Technologies Institute (ETI), in the region. Although this funding bid was ulti-mately unsuccessful, the activity it catalysed led to the formation of a more perma-nent network, Energy Research North East England (ERNEE), which aims to capitalise on the largely complementary renewable energy strengths of the part-ners by way of strategic positioning and further opportunities for collaborative funding bids.

The mainly regional-level of this collaboration does, however, point to some of the ambiguity of Newcastle Science City as an appropriately-scaled vehicle for engagement around the theme of Energy and Environment. While many interventions to improve energy efficiency and reduce consumption clearly must to be concentrated on densely-populated cities (e.g. transportation), and notwith-standing the potential for small-scale renewable energy technologies (for instance solar panels on buildings) to provide some local energy self-reliance within urban areas (Haughton 1997; Girardet 1999), efforts to provide low-carbon and renew-able electricity or heating on the industrial scale required to meet the needs of energy-dependent large cities (and the economic development opportunities that becoming a leading region for the supply of this energy represent) are likely to be focused on the rolling out of technologies (wind, tidal, solar, etc.) in either rural or off-shore locations. The following quotes give an indication of the ten-sions experienced by key academics who were involved with the Energy and Environment theme:

> From the original contacts about Science City, and then through to what we've been doing with ETI and ERNEE, it's clear to me that the region has a big capability in energy. And quite a lot of the work that goes on in the different universities is complementary...which means that I think as a team, it's possible to address a lot of the issues....So I think we've done some things [that contribute to the city, but] I think we could do more....I guess my biggest problem with Science City is understanding the scope, and understanding where it starts and stops in terms of the interaction with the city. Because if you look at energy, you go all the way from cutting-edge research, where you're trying to invent new things or new processes, with a view to someone in the region picking that up from a commercial point of

view...through the problem solving aspect, which is taking existing technologies, putting them all together, seeing how they interact...down to the straightforward infrastructure development and demonstration.

[Interviewee, Northumbria University, 01/06/10]

By [Science] City I've always assumed it to be this city and its immediate hinterland and all of the ripples out from that.... You don't tend to put big manufacturing and energy-intensive companies right in the heart of the city.... If you box yourself in and say we're trying to create something in the city, then you start to think small spin-outs.... So I'm always encouraging people to think about the broader picture; where do we get our electricity from, where do we get our heat from, where do we get our transport fuels from, and where we are locating the facilities that generate all that for us. And how do we grow all of those, to the prosperity of the city, rather than looking for energy businesses that you could set up within Newcastle.

[Interviewee, Newcastle University, 11/04/10]

This mismatch between activity and scale was addressed in 2009 when this Science City theme was changed to Sustainability; which although being an even broader concept than Energy and Environment, has a more direct link to urban development, and also to the priorities of the City Council as one of the core partners in Newcastle Science City. This reformulation was part of a rationalisation of the Science City themes, in which molecular engineering was dropped (where relevant to be absorbed into the other themes) and the three remaining themes were matched with a particular site in the city: Science Central for Sustainability, the International Centre for Life for Stem Cells and Regenerative Medicine, and the Campus for Ageing and Vitality for Ageing and Health (the latter two of which will be discussed in the next chapter). This strategy provided the Science Central development with a clearer focus on plans to attract environment-related businesses to the site and to relocate university facilities related to sustainability from the main campus. This vision for Science Central and the other two sites, as 'knowledge hubs' creating critical mass in selected fields, was written into a joint Newcastle and Gateshead economic and spatial strategy produced by city development company 1NG (1NG 2010). The change in Science City theme also coincided with the establishment of the Newcastle Institute for Research on Sustainability (NIReS) – a 'soft' institute within Newcastle University that aimed to create an organisational framework in which to bring together diverse research on natural environment, technological and human dimensions of sustainability across the institution's three faculties. The connection of Sustainability with an actual site in Science Central may also have contributed to academics finding this theme more amenable to doing work that is oriented towards the city.

The Energy and Environment area, what you had really was a disparate set of activities; you know where individual academics are engaged with relevant private and public sector players for their specialism, but not a lot of integration really. And the integration is still something of a holy grail. But I think, actually, having the development site on Science Central offers us the opportunity to finally do some of that for real. And some of it is [already] happening, at the level of for instance, having ARUP [the big civil engineering consultancy] involved in the technical aspects of the master-planning now. I feel we're genuinely in a situation where there's two-way learning going on with ARUP, because we're able to use Science Central as a conversation piece.

[Interviewee, Newcastle University, 05/03/10]

The commercial development of Science Central has been delayed by the collapse of the local property market following the financial crisis of 2008 and subsequent UK recession; so at the time of writing the site still remains under construction. Progress has been further complicated by the widely anticipated and then confirmed closure of One NorthEast, after which Newcastle University and City Council purchased the RDA's share at a near market rate set by the new coalition government, in order to secure the future of the project (Warburton 2011). The two partners subsequently received £6million of funding for the site from the new UK Government's Regional Growth Fund. However, these delays have had the upside of extending the opportunity for alternative energy uses for the site to be explored by academics at Newcastle University as part of the wider development plans to use Science Central as a hub and exemplar of sustainable development. Most notably, in a project that has gained national media coverage, a borehole has been drilled to successfully access deep geothermal energy from hot groundwater located 2,000 metres beneath the site (e.g. see Wainwright 2011; Wilkinson 2011). This represents an unusual instance of low-carbon and renewable energy provided from within the city, that it is hoped will be able to meet the future heating needs of not just the Science Central site, but other parts of central Newcastle as well. The potential of this approach was articulated in an interview relatively early on in these proceedings with a key figure in the scheme:

It's beginning to get embedded in the planning. And I think the view that we now share with the City [Council] is that, the phrase I use for it is Science City can be a beachhead of sustainability.... from where you can gradually expand the principle. Once you've established the principle of shared services, of renewable energy driving district heating and local generation of power, you know that principle can be extended, we can bring it onto this campus, share it with the Civic Centre, share it with Northumbria [University]... the whole civic boulevard that we're thinking about developing here.

[Interviewee, Newcastle University, 05/03/10]

The stronger relationship between Newcastle University and the City Council around sustainability has also recently extended beyond their mutual interest in the Science Central development through increasing commitment at an institutional strategic level to shared services (involving the estates and services side of the University) and collaboration in research and knowledge sharing (involving academics). Relating to the latter, NIReS has adopted the notion of a 'Living Lab' focused on Newcastle as a core part of the institutes' work. This is still a developing model within Newcastle University, but potentially encompasses a range of existing applied research and teaching on sustainability that involve study of and practical solutions for the city or wider region. For instance: a joint project with Newcastle City Council developed a 'carbon routemap' strategy to reduce greenhouse gas emissions in the city; the Transport Operations Research Group in the University has done a range of work on managing traffic pollution levels and testing the use of electric vehicles based in Newcastle and surrounding areas; and a project with multiple partners (including the City Council, Northumbria University's Sustainable Cities Institute and local housing cooperatives and tenant associations) engaged with local communities to co-produce plans for developing low-carbon neighbourhoods (see Genus and Armstrong 2011).

This section has outlined how predominately energy-focused academics in Newcastle University, and to a lesser extent also Northumbria University, have become more engaged with local urban sustainability issues through Newcastle Science City and other regional initiatives. It provides an illustration of the interaction of institutional and academic engagement with sustainability outlined above. Newcastle Science City has always existed in the two forms of the science-based economic development partnership represented by the company limited by guarantee and the former brewery site Science Central property development. Both of these strands have developed a focus on sustainability that has attempted to mobilise the distributed academic capabilities on this theme in Newcastle and (more selectively) Northumbria universities: the intermediary company in the form of the theme that has evolved from Energy and Environment to Sustainability, and the property development through its identification as a planned site for sustainable development. Although these two parts of Newcastle Science City have largely developed independently of each other (and a tension has existed over the perceived priority given by the partners to the commercial development of Science Central), there is a potential for them, in the future, to be joined up through the Science Central site becoming a focal point for sustainability-related research and business development, and latterly an extension of this principle to the city with the adoption of a 'Living Lab' concept.

Manchester

The three Greater Manchester universities included in this case (not including the University of Bolton) each has particular research strengths in fields relating to environmental science, renewable energy, or urban sustainability broadly defined. Selected research units within these three universities are shown in Table 7.2.

Table 7.2 Selected energy, environment and sustainability related university research
units in Greater Manchester

The University of Manchester

Faculty of Engineering and Physical Sciences
   Dalton Nuclear Institute
   The Joule Centre for Energy Research & Development (partnership of North West
      universities)
   Tyndall Centre for Climate Change Research (part of cross-university network)
Faculty of Humanities
   Centre for Urban Regional Ecology (CURE) (School of Environment and
      Development)
   Manchester Architecture Research Centre (MARC) (School of Environment and
      Development)
   Global Urban Research Centre (GURC) (School of Environment and Development)
   Society and Environment Research Group (School of Environment and Development)
Cross Faculty
   Sustainable Consumption Institute

Manchester Metropolitan University

Faculty of Science & Engineering
   Centre for Earth & Ecosystem Responses to Environmental Change (CEEREC)
   Centre for Air Transport and the Environment (CATE)
Faculty of Art & Design
   Manchester School of Architecture (MSA) (joint architecture school with the
      University of Manchester School of Environment and Development)

The University of Salford

College of Science & Technology
   Centre for Sustainable Urban and Regional Futures (SURF) (School of Built
      Environment)
   Salford Centre for Research and Innovation (SCRI) (School of Built Environment)
   Urban Quality Research Centre (UQRC) (School of Built Environment)
   Centre for Environmental Systems and Wildlife Research
   Research Centre for Urban Change

The University of Manchester, the most research-intensive university in the city-
region, has wide-ranging areas of scientific and social scientific expertise relevant
to sustainability, including substantial capabilities in renewable and nuclear
energy. The largest strengths of Manchester Metropolitan University (MMU, the
former polytechnic Post 1992 university within the city) are in relation to environmental impacts on a global scale. One of its principal research units is the Centre
for Air Transport and the Environment (CATE), which is connected to the city
through close links with Manchester Airport (owned by the ten Greater Manchester local authorities that comprise AGMA). The University of Salford has one of
the leading Schools of Built Environment in the country, with a number of

research centres that cover technical fields in the construction industry and also social science with a strong urban policy and sustainability dimension.

These three universities have an ongoing history of collaboration at the institutional level (pre-dating the merger of Victoria University and UMIST to form Manchester University) through a largely informal partnership arrangement (CONTACT) that is primarily focused on identifying opportunities for joint funding bids and promotion of their shared strengths. The collective relationship with the city was put on a more formal basis through the creation of Manchester: Knowledge Capital (M:KC) in 2003. This occurred during a period of growing economic aspiration within the city, influenced by the promotion of the Core Cities by the Labour government of the time (Chapter 6), and policy discourses such as the Work Foundation's concept of Ideopolis (also May and Perry 2006).

In governance terms, M:KC started as a wider partnership housed in other organisations, including Manchester Enterprises (the predecessor to the Commission for the New Economy), but subsequently became an independent company limited by guarantee with the three universities and Manchester and Salford City Councils as the core members, and additional funding support from the North West RDA (NWDA) and the Manchester Airport group. As an intermediary vehicle, Knowledge Capital's main function was described to us in terms of connecting suitable university, local government and private or third sector partners within the city-region on a project-by-project basis, and then supporting the resulting initiatives until a time when they were ready to move out on their own or into another delivery organisation:

> We've been a catalyst and a kind of incubator for Greater Manchester.... If we start running things we get bogged down in the delivery.... So we've always operated around orchestration rather than delivery.
>
> [*Interviewee, Manchester: Knowledge Capital, 07/07/10*]

This position led to M:KC taking on the coordination of a major city-regional initiative on climate change, branded Manchester is my Planet, in 2005; hence broadening the organisation's portfolio beyond the knowledge economy emphasis found in its original prospectus (Manchester Knowledge Capital Partnership 2003) to also include environmental concerns. The first phase of the Manchester is my Planet programme (up to 2008) was focused on building widespread commitment to reducing carbon emissions amongst city public agencies (local authorities, health, schools and universities, etc.), the private sector and the general public, through a 'pledge' scheme and various smaller-scale carbon reduction projects targeted at specific sites in the city-region. Following completion of the original programme, M:KC maintained a strand of work on sustainability by managing two European Union projects on behalf of the city-region, while plans for a separate city Climate Change Agency (currently absorbed in the AGMA Environment Commission) were put on hold. On one of these projects, M:KC worked with the consultancy firm ARUP to develop a Sustainable Energy Action Plan for Greater Manchester, that drew on widespread knowledge and intelligence in the region, including from the University of Manchester (through the Joule Centre for Energy Research) and the University of Salford (ARUP and Manchester: Knowledge Capital 2010).

When Manchester was awarded Science City status in 2004, the decision was made to place this in the already-existing M:KC as a programme of work, rather than establish it as a separate institutional entity as Newcastle had done. Although this prevented organisational duplication, it did not fully avoid problems of external confusion between the two brands (Knowledge Capital and Science City) in Manchester which were acknowledged by interviewees. The designation of Science City in Manchester did, however, give a renewed focus to Knowledge Capital's economic development and public engagement activities:

> The very positive thing that it did was to allow a kind of refreshing of the whole agenda. . . . It was a slightly narrower focus and it had . . . a much stronger innovation edge to it than the original [M:KC] prospectus which was very broad indeed.
>
> [*Interviewee, Manchester: Knowledge Capital, 07/07/10*]

To give Manchester Science City substance, six Innovation Partnerships were set up in areas where it was believed that universities in the city had academic research capabilities that matched global market demand (Manchester: Knowledge Capital 2005). Three of these Innovation Partnerships were in areas related to sustainability, corresponding to major research strengths in each of the three universities: Nuclear Futures (The University of Manchester), Clean Aviation (MMU) and Design for Sustainability (The University of Salford). In general, interviewees acknowledged that these Innovation Partnerships did not have significant impacts in terms of creating new activity or relationships. Because of the lack of extra external resources attached to the partnerships, and the Science City programme more widely, they were largely a vehicle for repackaging already-established areas of academic work in a form that emphasised their potential economic benefit for or engagement with the city. The partial exception to this was the Design for Sustainability partnership, which was based on the University of Salford's strengths in the built environment, but attracted interest from a wider cohort. The partnership chair was the chief executive of a property developer (Allied London), and also included participation from senior management in the University of Salford, the consultancy ARUP, a third sector consultancy (National Centre for Business and Sustainability), and some involvement from academics in other universities in Greater Manchester. The resulting network and meetings led to plans being made – including proposals for Manchester to sponsor national and international prizes in sustainable design – but due to a lack of resources this thinking was not translated into action. Despite frustration with the direct outcomes, participants interviewed for this study expressed the belief that the Design for Sustainability partnership, and other initiatives such as Manchester is my Planet, helped to support the mainstreaming of sustainability and climate change concerns into Manchester urban policy, which are now being addressed through the city-region infrastructure of AGMA's Environment Commission.

It was a very exciting, stimulating time ... [but] the team suffered from lack of resource, either people or money. ... And that was a shame. But actually they stimulated a lot of good ideas. And a lot of those ideas, are maybe not still being carried forward by Knowledge Capital, but that's where they began. And they've moved off, and maybe morphed into other things.

[Interviewee, ARUP consultancy, 12/05/10]

I think Design for Sustainability was subsumed within the Commission and other things. ... [The chief executive of Manchester City Council] is now being advised by all the people we work with and I actually think that the Environment Commission partly came out of that. The thinking that we did wasn't lost. ... You have to change the politics to get the biggest return on the investment and I felt that Design for Sustainability was out on its own. It was probably a pioneer, but people didn't know how they could take possession of it. But they have taken possession of it through the Commission.

[Interviewee, the University of Salford, 26/05/10]

If you wanted to coin a phrase, they are momentum initiatives. ... I would like to think that the Environment Commission is the direct result of a whole series of these kind of initiatives that kept the pot boiling and kept people talking, that raised the profile where politically it would be easy to forget about it, and with the RDA in control ... that it didn't allow pure economic driven policy to dominate.

[Interviewee, the University of Salford, 01/04/11]

As these quotes allude to, the establishment of AGMA Commissions for the New Economy and the Environment amongst others created alternative institutional vehicles in a similar space to that occupied by M:KC. Preceded by the merger of its board with the innovation board of the Commission for the New Economy, and the announcement that much of its core funding would be withdrawn with the winding down of NWDA, M:KC was closed in early 2011 and its remaining functions transferred to the Commission for the New Economy.

Even before the closure of M:KC, the priorities of Manchester University and MMU had shifted to another city intermediary vehicle, which has economic development, environmental sustainability and community engagement goals. Corridor Manchester is a partnership between these two universities, Manchester City Council and Central Manchester University Hospitals NHS Foundation Trust, with a very specific geographic focus on the development of the 'corridor' around Oxford Road – a main transport thoroughfare to the south of the City Centre along which the main campuses of both universities and the hospital are located. Map 7.2 shows the locations of this and other relevant organisations and sites on the corridor. An earlier version of the corridor concept ('the Arc of Opportunity'), which extended beyond Manchester to connect with the main University of Salford campus, was included in the original Knowledge City prospectus as an organising principle for spatial planning in this part of the

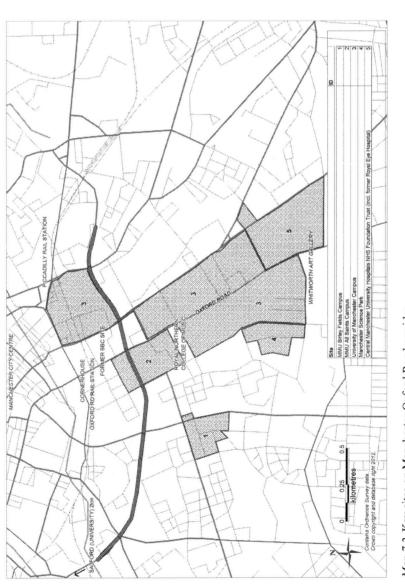

Map 7.2 Key sites on Manchester Oxford Road corridor.

Source: Contains Ordinance Survey data. © Crown copyright and database right 2012.

city-region (Manchester Knowledge Capital Partnership 2003). However, it was not until 2008 that the present Corridor Manchester partnership was formalised,[2] following the decision to base a major re-location of national British Broadcasting Corporation (BBC) facilities in a new development (MediaCityUK) in Salford, rather than in a redeveloped existing BBC site on Oxford Road in Manchester that was the subject of a rival bid. The concentration of research organisations in this part of the city, including a large urban science park as well as the universities and hospital, means that it is recognised as the strategic centre for knowledge-based economic development in the city. Over the past ten years, the partners have been successful, both individually and jointly, in attracting funding for various development projects on the Corridor. In particular, NWDA invested in a number of innovation and infrastructure related projects in the area, including campus developments by both universities, the conversion of the former home of the Royal Eye Hospital into a new biomedical centre (on the hospital site), and the installation of new generation broadband across the area. However, perhaps the largest benefit that the universities in particular are set to gain from this partnership is from collective efforts to improve the environment of the corridor. Oxford Road is an extremely busy bus route, with the associated problems of noise and air pollution that significantly detract from the attractiveness of the university campus settings. One of the core initiatives of the Corridor partnership (working with the Greater Manchester transport authority) has been to reduce traffic flows by closing part of Oxford Road to private vehicles and to introduce new buses that meet better emission standards. This will be accompanied by public realm improvements, such as the widening of pavements as the number of traffic lanes is also cut. These moves will also contribute to the universities reducing their carbon footprints, because students and staff from both institutions who live in and commute from surrounding areas are major users of transport on the corridor.

The Corridor Manchester vehicle itself is a company limited by guarantee, with a chief executive and small team that are funded by the four core members. The size of this organisation means that it concentrates on brokering funding for joint projects to be delivered by the partners. The Corridor board includes senior figures from the core members, but also representatives from other organisations located along, or with interests in, the Corridor; these include Manchester Science Park, ARUP, the commercial property developers Bruntwood, Cornerhouse (an independent cinema and arts complex) and, up to its dissolution, NWDA. Although campus developments are presented as part of the Corridor's portfolio of activities (such as MMU's new Birley Fields campus in the poorer area of Hulme), the universities and other partners retain full independent control over their Estate strategies. The Corridor does, however, provide a forum in which the partners can coordinate these developments, as well as work on infrastructure projects of common benefit such as the traffic improvements mentioned above. One of five themes that the Corridor uses to organise its work is 'Sense of Place', which is based on the principle of the area having a strong identity as an integrated and well-connected whole. The other four themes are Transport, Environment and Infrastructure, Research and Innovation, and Employment, Business and Skills (Corridor Manchester 2010).

A significant extra facet of the environmental strand of the Corridor's work has started to emerge more recently with its adoption of an urban laboratory approach (also Evans and Karvonen 2010). This has primarily taken place within the framework of Greater Manchester's status as Low Carbon Economic Area (LCEA) for the Built Environment.[3] The LCEA in Manchester, despite having little extra funding attached to it, has a clear lead agency in the city-region in the form of AGMA's Environment Commission supported by the Commissions for the New Economy and Planning and Housing (Hodson and Marvin 2012). The urban *laboratory* label seems to have more applicability to this setting than in many other examples of its use, due to a number of features: the Corridor's relatively well-defined geographical focus; the existing commitment of key institutions such as the universities and City Council to the Corridor programme; and in particular the unusual opportunity to monitor environmental and climatic changes in a semi-controlled way afforded by the significant traffic and environment improvement plans described above.

> One of the central pieces [in the LCEA] is this low-carbon laboratory, where we will be recognising and exploiting the fact that we have two universities, a health trust and a city council, plus a number of private sector partners, all in the same vicinity, all working together. And so what we're very keen to create there is an evidence base approach to a lot of work that's coming forward, using the intellect that is in the universities, and using technology; to capture what's going on now, to capture it during the change, and to capture it again post the change.
>
> *[Interviewee, ARUP consultancy, 12/05/10]*

Corridor Manchester has been identified as a work programme for the LCEA in a Joint Delivery Plan published in 2010, and is the only one of nine programmes that is focused on a particular geographical area of the city-region (AGMA 2010). This document describes the Laboratory concept along the following lines:

> The bedrock of the LCEA in the Corridor will be the comprehensive network of sensors and monitoring devices that will gather real-time data relating to environmental, social and climatic parameters. This socio-ecological information will be correlated with economic and spatial data, to provide a robust evidence base. In conjunction with the Observatory and research facilities and capabilities embedded in the stakeholder organisations, the evidence will underpin analysis that will withstand peer review and professional scrutiny, and which will be transferable to low carbon communities elsewhere. The sensor network, data observatory and research capabilities will collectively comprise the **Manchester Low Carbon Laboratory**.
>
> (AGMA 2010: 70)

As this excerpt implies, part of the plans for the Low Carbon Laboratory is to make the various datasets generated available to researchers in Greater Manchester universities (AGMA 2010: 71). More generally, the framing of the Corridor as an urban laboratory creates opportunities for academics to be involved in an initiative that had hitherto mainly been restricted to the senior management and estate director level of their institutions. This has intersected with a pre-existing research programme in the University of Manchester's School of Environment and Development called EcoCities, which focuses on adaptation to climate change (rather than its mitigation). This programme was established in 2009 with core funding via sponsorship from the property company Bruntwood, which is active in office-space development in the Oxford Road area of Manchester and whose chief executive sits on the Corridor board. EcoCities includes a range of different projects supported by Bruntwood or external research funding bodies, and mainly led by staff in either the Manchester Architecture Research Centre (MARC) or Centre for Urban and Regional Ecology (CURE). Several of these research projects are based in Greater Manchester and the environment around the university campus and Oxford Road. The main overall output at the end of the initial EcoCities programme was a climate change adaptation plan for Greater Manchester (EcoCities 2011). The programme has already included one project (also funded by Manchester City Council and MMU) that has focused on monitoring climate changes in and around the Oxford Road corridor (i-trees) and another two based on examining energy and heating in local Bruntwood buildings (CaRB and SETS).[4] Interviewees involved with the programme talked about extending it beyond the current initial phase and strengthening the link into the Corridor Manchester initiative:

> There is some interest, I think, in the way... the EcoCities brand, which is gaining some purchase around the region, now could actually provide a larger context for the Corridor work.... I'm potentially really excited about it because I think this idea of the Laboratory, provides us with a real spatial focus. It gives a kind of material context to those relationships. I mean everyone's got an interest in what happens on Oxford Road, so it gives you a reason to come together.
>
> *[Interviewee, The University of Manchester, 18/08/10]*

Collaboration in the Low Carbon Laboratory has prospective advantages for both the Corridor partners, who can potentially access academic research monies as a source of continuing funding for Corridor activity in a post RDA era, and for academics, who with the new 'impact' criteria for research funding are now looking for ways to demonstrate the real-world grounding and applicability of their work. At the time of our research, however, we found few signs that this involvement had yet spread to other universities. The main research strengths of MMU in environmental impacts (e.g. in clean aviation) do not seem to map as easily on to the Corridor agenda. The University of Salford, through its School of Built Environment, does have significant expertise in areas salient to Corridor projects, as well as some points of connection into the Greater Manchester policy community, but the institution is not engaged in Corridor Manchester either as a formal organisational partner or by having an interest in the project through a physical campus presence in the Oxford Road area of Manchester.

In conclusion, Corridor Manchester has proved to be a vehicle through which the two universities within central Manchester have become more engaged with the sustainable development of the city; initially at an institutional level but also seemingly now at an academic level as well. The basis of this partnership within a practical context related to its physical setting, and building and infrastructure projects connected to this, has granted participation a clear rationale for the institutions.

> We saw the Corridor as much more important to us than Knowledge Capital, because the Corridor was on our doorstep, was tangible, and would deliver real physical benefits to the environment that the university operates in. And possibly actually, in the long-run deliver more additional sources of public funding for projects that were material.
>
> [*Interviewee, The University of Manchester, 12/05/10*]

The physical development dimensions of the Corridor has also helped to form the opportunity for future academic benefits represented by the 'urban laboratory', although the presence of the LCEA for the Built Environment and the EcoCities research programme have also been important to its configuration.

Conclusion

There are clear differences in context between the two cases covered in this chapter; for instance, in terms of territorial governance (with the city-region institutional structure of AGMA in Greater Manchester), the strength of the local property market (which has been more fragile in Newcastle), and patterns of institutional interaction between universities and with other partners (which seem more established in Manchester). However, the two cases also show parallels in the ways that universities have developed their engagement in sustainable urban development. In both cases diverse interdisciplinary research strengths relating to energy and sustainability have begun to be mobilised for local societal and economic benefit through their institution's participation in city partnerships (Newcastle Science City, Manchester: Knowledge Capital and Corridor Manchester). This engagement has had a physical dimension in the two cities through off-campus developments with a sustainability dimension on the Newcastle Science Central and Manchester Oxford Road corridor sites. The framing of these (and connected) spaces as 'living' or 'urban laboratories' has provided a mechanism for academics as well as institutions to become more involved with sustainable development projects in their localities, providing them with new opportunities for research and acting as a vehicle for transferring knowledge within the city. The Corridor Manchester partnership and the adoption of a joint 'Living Lab' model in Newcastle have also cemented a collaborative relationship between one or more universities and the two city councils around this sustainability agenda. This is of potential future significance for the universities (especially in a post RDA period) in moving the focus of this local sustainability engagement beyond a predominately economic development concern with developing energy or sustainability-related businesses, as pushed by national-level drivers reproduced through local initiatives such as the LCEA in Manchester or Newcastle Science City, and connecting more strongly with a wider set of socio-technical challenges (e.g. urban planning, transport) that are the responsibility of local authorities.

8 Universities and health

Institutional relationships in the city

Introduction

Large parts of universities of varied types are dedicated to teaching and research in the field of medical and health sciences. These activities involve close institutional links with medical facilities, such as hospitals in the same city or region, and other parts of the complex public and private systems that have evolved to provide and support healthcare in developed countries. Together these different organisations form what van den Berg and Klink (1996) call local 'medical complexes' with related healthcare, research and educational functions.

The size of these medical complexes and the high value of the services they provide means that they are recognised as a cornerstone of local economies. Large hospitals are often, with universities, one of the single biggest employers in a city, and their size creates many of the same types of employment and expenditure economic impacts that were discussed in Chapter 3 of this book (Adams 2003). Publicly-funded universities and healthcare facilities can also together form the hub of what Markusen (1996) calls 'state-anchored industrial districts' by attracting private firms in related medical or life science industries, such as pharmaceuticals or medical technologies, which may benefit from proximity to academic or clinical institutions that generate local knowledge spillovers or provide a client base for their products (van den Berg and Klink 1996; Simmie 1998; Llobrera *et al.* 2000). In particular, extensive research in economic geography on biotechnology, as a paradigmatic new knowledge-intensive sector with a high propensity for clustering, has supported this link to the local medical science base in the form of universities, although it seems the presence of large multinational pharmaceutical companies and other extra-local networks seem at least as crucial in the successful formation of a cluster (Zeller 2004; Gertler and Levitte 2005; Birch 2008). These factors have led American researchers to talk about 'Eds and Meds' as potential developmental assets in urban economies (Adams 2003; Bartik and Erickcek 2007), echoing an emergent narrative about the post-industrial renewal of cities such as Pittsburgh, in which large healthcare facilities are positioned alongside universities as key knowledge economy actors (e.g. Smaglik 2010).

Less direct attention has been paid in the mainstream of city and regional development studies to the impact of this medical and healthcare system on the actual

health of local populations, even within recent more broadly social conceptualisations that propose wellbeing as a constitutive element of local development (e.g.
Pike *et al.* 2007). This is despite the presence of stark health inequalities within
and between cities and regions, which are studied by geographers as well as epide-
miologists as one of the clearest and most persistent spatial expressions of socio-
economic disparities between different class- and ethnic-based groups (e.g.
Wilkinson 1996; Shaw *et al.* 1999; Wilkinson and Pickett 2009). This also contrasts with understandings of international development in the Global South,
where health factors such as life expectancy, infant mortality rates, the prevalence
of diseases, levels of sanitation, nutrition and access to decent healthcare figure as
core elements and measures, rather than corollaries, of social and economic development (e.g. Sen 1999; Sachs 2004; Vlahov *et al.* 2007). This situation is, in part,
a reflection of institutionalised distinctions between professional fields and related
academic disciplines. The modern field of urban planning originated partly in
response to infectious diseases caused by poor living and working conditions in
the industrialised cities of nineteenth century Britain and the USA, but the equivalent present day concerns with aspects of the urban environment, such as housing,
traffic and public infrastructure, have developed into a separate domain largely
unconnected with public health (Corburn 2004). This is despite the recognition
that, notwithstanding improvements in the general environment of cities in the
developed world, these material aspects of urban planning can have an impact on
factors such as lifestyle or social networks that are key determinants of physical
and mental health (de Hollander and Staatsen 2003; Jackson 2003; Vlahov *et al.*
2007). Over the course of the twentieth century, the field of public health itself
became increasingly segmented from the more powerful discipline of medicine,
with its focus on the treatment of individuals rather than the population as a whole,
and a biomedical rather than a social model of disease (Brandt and Gardner 2000).

   This chapter will examine the different ways in which universities in Sheffield
and Newcastle upon Tyne engage with their cities through the considerable teaching and research they do in the areas of health and medicine. Reflecting the focus
of our research on particular academic strengths in the two cities, these sections
have slightly varying foci: the Sheffield case concentrates on health research and
teaching, and the institutional relationships between the two universities, healthcare providers and city council; the Newcastle case concentrates on how medical
science strengths have been mobilised for city development (including economic
development and regeneration) as well as health purposes by a wider set of organisational actors. The common thread throughout both of these sections is the centrality to this engagement of the relationship between the universities and the main
healthcare provider in the UK – the publicly-funded National Health Service
(NHS). The next section will outline the main features of this relationship (and
other related institutional links) as background to the rest of the chapter. Following
the Sheffield and Newcastle cases, a concluding section reflects on the way university health and medical engagement with the city is shaped by these different
disciplinary concerns and institutional relationships.

Universities and the NHS

In the UK, university health and medical engagement with the city and wider society is mediated by a series of institutional relationships, principal amongst which is that with the NHS. Results from the research impacts survey, outlined in Section 5 of Appendix B, show that respondents who have an impact in the area of 'healthcare or public health and wellbeing' are highly likely to view 'healthcare services' (in this context predominately the NHS) as one of the main beneficiaries of their research, compared to a much lower proportion for other types of organisation active in this domain, such as local authorities or third sector bodies. This axis between higher education institutions and the NHS is a longstanding one that works through mutual dependence and common understanding of respective requirements. Two quotes from interviewees on either side of the relationship in Newcastle summarise this bond.

> Our single biggest engagement programme, bar none, is our clinical engagement programme with the NHS.... It dominates numerically and financially every other thing that we do.... There's huge understanding inside the relevant parts of the academy about what makes them tick, what's likely to go down well with them, and what won't go down well with them.
> *[Interviewee, Newcastle University, 19/05/09 (2nd interviewee)]*

> The relationship is more than just partnership; it's inextricably linked. Without a range of key academics, who, if they don't deliver on their side of the fence, our business suffers. If we don't deliver for some of the academic objectives, and research objectives that are set by the University . . . they suffer too. We're joined at the hip . . . because we're in the research and innovation game together, we're in the training and education game together. . . . You can't pick and choose on the relationship.
> *[Interviewee, Newcastle upon Tyne Hospitals*
> *NHS Foundation Trust, 26/06/09]*

The NHS is a complex multi-level organisation, and universities engage in different ways with these different levels. At the time of the research, the NHS was operating with a three tier structure that had been reached by the Labour government in 2006 following the latest of the many reorganisations in the service's history. (For a recent guide to these changes and the structure of the NHS see Ham 2009.) At the national scale, NHS policy is set by the Department of Health as part of central government. The Department of Health also has a research commissioning and innovation arm (separate from the UKRC Medical Research Council) in the form of the National Institute for Health Research (NIHR), through which in recent years it has helped promote the principle of translational medical and health research (see below). Since 2006, the regional scale had been represented in the NHS structure through ten Strategic Health Authorities (SHAs) in England, which correspond to the nine Government Office regions (see Chapter 6), save for the division of the South East into two SHAs. (The model varies for post-devolution Scotland, Wales and Northern Ireland.) Much like the Government Offices were, the SHAs are administrative bodies in effect responsible for the implementation of national Department of Health policy, and the monitoring and managing of performance of NHS trusts in their regions (Ham 2009: 209). At the sub-regional scale, the actual provision of healthcare services is managed directly by NHS trusts for: primary, community-based care (primary care trusts); secondary, typically hospital-based acute care (acute trusts); mental health; and ambulance services. These NHS trusts vary in size of the population covered, but for large cities their boundaries are roughly commensurate with those of local authorities. So there are primary care trusts (PCTs) and acute hospital trusts at the city-level for Sheffield and Newcastle upon Tyne, and neighbouring trusts in other parts of their wider city-regions. Since 2004, most acute trusts have obtained foundation trust status to become locally-governed public benefit corporations that are still accountable to – but outside of direct control by – the Department of Health (Ham 2009). In practice, this degree of local autonomy gives foundation trusts more leeway to raise income, by retaining surpluses or borrowing money, and invest in land development projects or commercial ventures (Pollock *et al.* 2003; Allen 2006; Ham 2009).

Although higher education and the health service are in separate governance domains, they are joined together by many types of common organisational and personal inter-linkage of a formal and informal character. Areas of shared activity often operate according to a nonfinancial transaction-based quid pro quo type agreement known colloquially as 'knock-for-knock'. Many members of staff within university medical faculties are clinical academics and have joint (honorary) appointments with NHS trusts where they practice part-time as doctors, nurses or other health professionals. Higher education in health and medical fields follow a work-based learning model in which students spend a large proportion of their courses on placements in local hospitals; which means that at any time there a large number of university students working in the health service as trainee doctors, nurses and other health professionals. For medicine and dentistry, undergraduate training is funded by a combination of HEFCE and the NHS, whilst for nursing, midwifery and allied health professionals it is funded by the regional SHAs on a contract basis. Extensive linkages also exist between university and NHS staff around medical, public health and health services research, reflecting the inherently practical nature of research that is concerned with clinical applications or health interventions (see Appendix B). In British cities, university campuses and hospitals are frequently located next to each other and, as the Newcastle case in this chapter particularly illustrates, the two bodies will often have agreements for conjoint or shared facilities where clinical and research activities can take place side-by-side.

The areas of training and research typically covered by Pre and Post 1992 universities in a city – and therefore their relationships with different types of NHS trust – do however vary. This normally results in a clear division of functions for their sub-region. Research-intensive Pre 1992 universities in large cities and regional centres normally house a medical school in which biomedical scientific research is carried out and students are trained in medicine and dentistry. Post 1992 universities, which may also carry out health or medical research but on a lesser scale, typically train nurses and allied health professionals, with a strong local dimension in terms of the home regions of a large proportion of their students and their future place of employment. These differences will be elaborated below, particularly in the Sheffield case.

The election of a Conservative-led coalition government in 2010 ushered in yet another major restructuring of the NHS, which was justified on the basis of reducing bureaucracy and increasing local patient choice and clinician power. These plans (see Secretary of State for Health 2010a) included the abolition of both PCTs and SHAs, with their key role in the commissioning of health services being given to doctor-led (general practitioner) groups. Although few of these changes were implemented at the time of the research (and during the period that this chapter was written – early 2012 – their progression still faced considerable political, professional and public opposition) these proposals for the future were prominent in the thoughts of interviewees for this study. Of particular significance to the discussion that follows are the changes pertaining to public health. With the closure of PCTs, responsibility for leading local health improvement will be shifted into local authorities, working with other bodies (including the NHS) through statutory health and wellbeing boards (Secretary of State for Health 2010b). Local authorities have been part of the local partnership model through which public health was approached in the UK under the preceding Labour government (Perkins *et al.* 2010), and already have responsibilities for potentially-related functions such as social services, environmental health, sport and leisure, and planning and transport, but this move has significant implications for public health, and particularly for the role of universities in this field, that we will discuss in the following Sheffield case.

Sheffield

Both universities in Sheffield have large units dedicated to health-based teaching and research as well as more disparate pockets of work in other parts of the institution that have broad relevance to public health. In both universities, organisational mechanisms have been developed to coordinate these health and wellbeing capabilities and encourage inter-disciplinary collaboration.

In the Pre 1992 University of Sheffield, the Faculty of Medicine, Dentistry and Health contains a specialist School of Health and Related Research (ScHARR). The origins of ScHARR go back to the early 1990s when the University invested in establishing a small health services research centre within the medical faculty. Since this time ScHARR has expanded considerably through external research and consultancy funds to become a leading national and international centre of health research and, in terms of university structures, a school in its own right. Academic work in ScHARR is now organised into three Sections: Health Economics and Decision Science; Public Health; and Health Services Research.

ScHARR is predominately a research-focused school, but has developed some postgraduate teaching, including a Masters in Public Health (MPH) programme since 2004. Collaboration between members of ScHARR and colleagues elsewhere in the University interested in the social science aspects of health (including geographical disparities) have resulted in the establishment of a 'soft' cross-faculty research unit, the Centre for Health and Wellbeing in Public Policy (CWiPP), to facilitate joint funding bids and workshops. This formalised network is focused around the specific issues of considering 'how people's health and well-being can be defined, measured and improved in ways that help policy-makers determine the best use of scarce resources, and to investigate the determinants of well-being insofar as these are relevant to policy formulation'.[1]

Sheffield Hallam, like other Post 1992 universities, has a faculty with a business model primarily oriented towards supplying professional training in different health and applied health fields under contract from NHS regional SHAs and other public bodies, in particular meeting demand from local areas. It's Faculty of Health and Wellbeing has a portfolio that includes nursing and midwifery, paramedics, radiotherapy and oncology, physiotherapy, occupational therapy, and social work, as well as the associated subject areas of biosciences and sports and active lifestyles. The size of the faculty has increased significantly since 2006, following its attainment of the contract for pre-registration nurse training in South Yorkshire (which had previously been held by the University of Sheffield). More unusually for a Post 1992 institution, Sheffield Hallam has some post-registration training courses in medicine and dentistry. Its postgraduate programme also includes a Masters in Public Health (MA) course, which was described to us as having a greater emphasis on the social elements of health improvement compared to the more medically-based focus on epidemiology as a science in the corresponding University of Sheffield MPH. The research profile of this faculty too has grown over the past five years under the banner of the Centre for Health and Social Care Research (CHSCR). Although smaller in research numbers than ScHARR, this centre also addresses a number of different aspects of health relating to: the social causes of disease; the use of evidence-based approaches to inform new health interventions; and measures to improve health service delivery. Perhaps even more than in the University of Sheffield, however, health-related research in Sheffield Hallam is marked by concerns with wider scientific/technological, organisational/management, or social/environmental elements that are not confined to a single faculty in the University. To link together these distributed capabilities, the institution has created a formal organisational infrastructure, the Public Health Hub. In comparison to the more bottom-up academic network of CWiPP in the University of Sheffield, the Public Health Hub is a university administrative centre, with staff representatives contributed from all four faculties as public health leads on a part-time basis. The Public Health Hub also has an outward-facing dimension as a virtual front-end portal for the University through which external organisations seeking public health consultancy, applied research or training services can be put in contact with a relevant set of expertise inside the institution to address their needs.

The universality of the health conditions and problems addressed in these two universities means that their research is targeted towards a national and international audience. This has not precluded some work in either institution drawing on the context provided by Sheffield for some of their research projects; whether in the form of evaluations with local health organisations, epidemiological studies that use local populations as subjects, or selection of research topics that are informed by the significant health inequalities and chronic conditions that are endemic in this former industrial city (see Thomas *et al.* 2009). The respective university faculties do, however, seem to be more fundamentally embedded in their surrounding locality of Sheffield and neighbouring parts of South Yorkshire and the East Midlands through their health teaching than through their health research. As with other universities throughout the UK, an integral part of medical and nursing courses are training placements in local hospitals. Sheffield Hallam University, in particular, works closely on ensuring their courses are tailored to the specific and changing workforce requirements of the local NHS trusts that will subsequently employ a large proportion of their students on nursing and allied health professional courses.

> We're continually revising our curriculum, in partnership with our stakeholders – the strategic health authorities, the acute trusts, the PCTs – in order to be that one step ahead in terms of anticipating the need. ... We are very much wedded to work-based learning delivery, and particularly when you're talking about some of these groups – part-time, postgraduate [students] – our unique selling point is around that you come here to learn, but actually you learn by using your day-job, and so the assignments are actually around projects that will take your organisation forward as well as yourself forward in there.
>
> *[Interviewee, Sheffield Hallam University, 21/07/10b]*

> What we try to do here is map the educational requirements to the workforce developments. If the workforce requirements aren't mapped and achieved, that will impact on the health of the city and the local community, you could argue. ... Because [public health issues such as obesity, smoking and teenage pregnancy] are prevalent in Sheffield, we tend to have those as a focal point for our students who develop the skills. ... Because we have health inequalities, very starkly, within the city, I think most of the health services target those areas, as does the local authority. So you get [those links] almost automatically and if we didn't adhere to that we wouldn't really be meeting the needs of our communities.
>
> *[Interviewee, Sheffield Hallam University, 18/05/10 (2nd interviewee)]*

In the University of Sheffield, the MPH delivered by ScHARR since 2004 has a large cohort of former students who now hold key positions in local health organisations, such as directors of public health in primary care trusts, and who have helped to cement the School's place within the public health professional community throughout the region.

The local link with the health service through research practice has, however, been strengthened in recent years by the joint involvement of these two universities and a number NHS trusts from across the Sheffield city-region (including four PCTs) in a Collaboration for Leadership in Applied Health Research and Care (CLAHRC) centre. This centre, one of nine across England, is an initiative from the National Institute for Health Research (NIHR) with match funding from the partners. The CLAHRC programme is part of a national agenda, following the Cooksey (2006) review, to improve the translation of medical and health research into clinical practice or products. It aims to provide an infrastructure to 'address the evaluation and identification of those new interventions that are effective and appropriate for everyday use in the NHS and the process of their implementation into routine clinical practice' and 'the need for the NHS to harness better the capacity of higher education to support initiatives to enhance the effectiveness and efficiency of clinical care' (NIHR 2012: 1). The South Yorkshire CLAHRC is specialised on the overarching concept of 'self-management and self-care of long term conditions', which is a common element of research areas in both ScHARR in the University of Sheffield and CHSCR in Sheffield Hallam. These existing research strengths are reflected in a number of themes for implementing the CLAHRC, which are led by academics from either or both of the universities. These include 'chronic conditions', such as obesity or depression, types of health technology, such as 'telehealth and care technologies', and issues for 'achieving translation', such as health inequalities, intelligent commissioning, and user-centred healthcare design.[2] The funding provided by the CLAHRC has enabled researchers from the two institutions to dedicate more time and resource to implementation-based work with their health service partners that – in the context of the dominant drivers for research funding and evaluation – may otherwise not be justified by the strength of academic output alone. As part of its aim to increase research capacity in South Yorkshire, the CLAHRC has also encouraged more links between health researchers in the two university partners. This process builds on good existing relationships, based on the mainly complementary and not directly competitive nature of their respective specialisations, and also several recent cases of key staff moving between the two institutions.

The CLAHRC programme is focused on interventions specifically within the NHS, but a much broader range of organisations in Sheffield form the wider health sector for the city. The City Council's Public Health Improvement Team works closely with the public health directorate in Sheffield PCT to address concerns such as health inequalities (see NHS Sheffield and Sheffield City Council 2010). Like Newcastle, Sheffield has, under the sponsorship of the City Council, been a long-term holder of World Health Organisation Healthy City status and participant in its associated network of (mainly European) cities for knowledge exchange and research collaborations around urban health. Both universities have been involved with research- or evaluation-based studies in partnership with, or commissioned by, the City Council (often jointly with the Primary Care Trust) that concern public health interventions within the city around issues such as lifestyle and physical activity. The city also has a sizable number of voluntary, community and charitable health organisations; many of which have grouped together to form the Sheffield Well-being Consortium as a way of increasing their collective ability to secure contracts from the health service and local authorities. Representatives from this third sector – along with those from the NHS and the universities – have sat on the local authority coordinated Health and Wellbeing sub-partnership of the Local Strategic Partnership (Sheffield First), which has acted as a more collective forum for discussion of health policy in the city.

The importance of this non-NHS local health architecture is set to increase in the future when the government's plans to abolish PCTs and shift responsibility for public health completely into local authorities (and health and wellbeing boards) come into effect. For better or for worse, this change carries the possibility of a reformulation of the public health paradigm in the UK from one based in a professionalised discipline that evolved separately from urban planning (Corburn 2004) to a wider interdisciplinary field that more centrally encompasses concerns related to lifestyle and the urban environment. At present, this shift would seem to fit more easily with the slightly broader and more social-based understanding of public health applied in Sheffield Hallam. The more specialised disciplinary-based understanding of public health practiced in ScHARR, on the other hand, notwithstanding their relationships with social scientists through CWiPP, has developed primarily through very close institutional links with the NHS.

> There's a huge amount of research that goes on across the University which, you know, you might define as public health research in the sense that it has impact on health in a similar way that you would define a lot of the City Council's responsibilities as being about public health. But I think there is a distinction between public health research in that broadest sense, which is done by, yes, by architects and planners and geographers...and public health as a speciality, where essentially we're interested more in, I guess the aspects of public health around epidemiology, inequalities, and more specifically the interface between public health and the NHS.
>
> [*Interviewee, University of Sheffield, 28/07/11*]

Regardless of differences in emphasis between different types of institution, any change to responsibility for public health being based in local authorities will create challenges for all universities. Links will already exist between universities and local authorities around health, but this side of the triangular relationship completed by the health service is not currently as well developed in most cases. To avoid being 'locked-in' to their existing relationships, they will have to adapt to changes in language and working norms between the evidence-based practices dominant in the NHS and an approach in local authorities that is more likely to be influenced by wider policy concerns.

Newcastle

This Newcastle case extends the perspective of the chapter to consider the local engagement of university health and medical faculties in societal and economic areas beyond those that relate just to the provision of healthcare or health improvement in the surrounding population. This wider city development role particularly reflects the perceived value of the life and medical sciences in regional economic development and their incorporation into local innovation strategies by agencies outside of the tri-lateral relationship with the NHS and local authorities discussed above (also see Chapter 5). Hence, the disciplinary focus here is also broadened to include those working in more of a medical sciences context as well as the health sciences concentrated on above. Social engagement with the local populations is still an important component, and in this Newcastle case takes place in and through certain physical off-campus sites within the city to which academic units are attached.

Newcastle University has a large Faculty of Medical Sciences that, uniquely for England, is the only full university medical school in its region. This means its medical students do clinical training in teaching hospitals throughout the region and not just in the surrounding area of Tyneside. For historical reasons, Durham University (the other Pre 1992 institution in the North East of England) no longer has its own medical faculty.[3] Durham University is, however, active in this broad field of research, with a particular focus on health policy that is not replicated in Newcastle University. This activity takes place in the inter-disciplinary Wolfson Research Institute, located on Durham University's second campus in Stockton-on-Tees further south in the region. Since 2001, through its School of Medicine and Health, Durham University has also begun to offer the first two years of an undergraduate medical degree based at the Stockton campus, before students transfer to Newcastle University for the remaining three years of their training. In Newcastle, the Post 1992 institution, Northumbria University, fulfils a similar set of inter-professional education functions within the northern part of the North East region as Sheffield Hallam does for South Yorkshire. The largest of its main academic units, the School of Health, Community and Education Studies, has a business model based primarily on undergraduate and postgraduate teaching for workforce needs across a number of health and non-health related fields, including nursing, physiotherapy, occupational therapy and social work, as well as education. The clear identity of this School is reinforced by it being located on a separate campus several kilometres from Northumbria's main city-centre base (see Map 7.1 in the previous chapter). The school also has a research capability that has been concentrated into one main research unit, the Community, Health and Education Studies Research Centre (CHESsRC).

Similarly to the energy-related fields discussed in the previous chapter, broad complementarities between the North East's universities have been conducive to regional collaboration in the public health domain. All five universities in the region (including the other Post 1992 institutions Sunderland and Teesside) share one of five national Public Health Research Centres of Excellence, which in the North East is branded as Fuse, the Centre for Translational Research in Public Health, and funded by a combination of the Economic & Social Research Council, the Medical Research Council, the NIHR and two large charitable organisations (the British Heart Foundation and Cancer Research UK), in their role as members of the UK Clinical Research Collaboration (UKCRC). The Public Health Research Centres of Excellence were established with the strategic aim to 'increase infrastructure, build academic capacity and encourage multi-disciplinary working in public health research in the UK' in response to a recognised underdevelopment of this field (as distinct from medical research) (UKCRC 2008: 2). The inclusive regional basis of the North East partnership (the four other centres of excellence are not primarily constituted along geographical lines in the same way) in part came out of pre-existing discussions between the five universities about working together on public health, encouraged by the regional SHA. Although focused on a national agenda, and with an expectation to produce international academic outputs, much of the research carried out under the auspices of Fuse involve public health studies, interventions or knowledge exchange based in the North East of England. The Newcastle University component of the centre, in particular, builds on a tradition of work on the local population, including epidemiology-based studies of conditions such as cardiovascular disease and longitudinal analysis of medical records in areas such as maternal and perinatal health. The latter work, in particular, is dependent on a close relationship with the relevant local NHS services:

> We are absolutely reliant on the clinicians to get good data on every birth in the region, every pregnancy, every outcome. Without meticulous attention to detail by doctors and midwives, you wouldn't have a dataset worth analysing. . . . So we're reliant on them, but they also get regular data fed back to them on their outcomes, and that is gold dust to them, in terms of clinical audit. So it's a two-way relationship; they're reliant on us, we're reliant on them, and it's mutually beneficial.
>
> [*Interviewee, Newcastle University, 03/03/10*]

In organisational terms, this activity takes place in the University's Institute of Health and Society, which is now the main home for more interdisciplinary and social-based applied health research in an otherwise predominately biomedical focused Faculty. This is one of seven 'hard' research institutes that, since 2006, have been the principal units around which the Faculty of Medical Sciences is structured. In this model there are four schools in the Faculty with administrative responsibility for delivering undergraduate and postgraduate teaching, but most research active members of staff are based in one of these resource-holding institutes. This approach to building critical mass in strategic areas of medical research has arguably contributed to individual institutes developing an external engagement role that goes beyond standard involvement in clinical research and training. In addition to the Institute of Health and Society, which has a research portfolio that is the equivalent for Newcastle of that of ScHARR in the University of Sheffield, these include two institutes, Genetic Medicine and Ageing and Health, which from a primarily biomedical science basis, have built more extensive links within Newcastle and the North East. This role reflects their position as the focus for two of the three themes for Newcastle Science City (see previous chapter), but also encompasses a broader range of agencies in the city and region that have sought to mobilise these academic capabilities for local development purposes. The NHS (which is not a formal part of the Newcastle Science City partnership) also remains a key structuring relationship for these institutes. The physical presence of both institutes in locations within the city but away from the main campus of Newcastle University, has also been a vital interface for their engagement with the health service, business, and the community. The rest of this section will outline these two cases in more detail.

For the Institute of Genetic Medicine (IGM, formerly know as the Institute of Human Genetics) the key partner in the city has been the International Centre for Life (ICFL) – a multi-use science complex built on a then-derelict site next to the main train station in central Newcastle (see Map 7.1 on p. 94) and opened in 2000. The ICFL hosts a unique mix of activities onsite: a major science-themed public visitor attraction and educational exhibition space; a bioscience centre encompassing research laboratories occupied by Newcastle University, NHS clinical facilities, and incubator space for start-up companies; and more generic commercial income streams such as conference facilities, retail units for bars and restaurants, and a multi-floor car park next to the centre. This initiative was led by the chief executive of the Urban Development Corporation (Chapter 6) for Tyne and Wear up to its closure in 1998. The ICFL was established with a combination of funders, including the Millennium Commission (a UK charitable body set up to distribute National Lottery funds to a range of public projects) and European Regional Development Fund, which have helped shape its varied portfolio of social and economic development functions.

The laboratories tenanted by Newcastle University in the bioscience centre have been an off-campus home for the IGM since the opening of the ICFL, and has helped it form an ever closer, near-symbiotic relationship with co-located parts of the NHS. The Institute itself houses the Northern Genetic Service, which provides 'comprehensive, fully integrated, high quality clinical and laboratory services that help reduce morbidity associated with genetic disease' for NHS patients from across the North East region.[4] It (and other parts of the medical school) also have very close links with the other NHS acute hospitals trust facility based in the ICFL, the Newcastle Fertility Centre; including a significant overlap of key staff who hold clinical academic positions and carry out research that incorporates clinical trials with patients. These synergies between academic research and clinical functions have particularly helped the IGM to become a leading centre in the emerging field of stem cell research. In this area, Newcastle University is part of a regional partnership, the North East of England Stem Cell Institute (NESCI), with Durham University and the NHS, which has its main hub at the ICFL and has also received substantial investment from the RDA, One NorthEast. The ethical issues around stem cell research have also been addressed in research and the wider public sphere by the activities of a social science-based research centre, Policy Ethics and Life Sciences (PEALS), which is now wholly within Newcastle University but was originally also a joint centre with Durham University.

The ICFL project predates the RDA era, and has played a significant role in the North East region by pioneering the approach of mobilising science – and more specifically the genetics and stem cells capabilities in Newcastle and Durham universities – for the purposes of city economic regeneration and development. Since the establishment of One NorthEast, however, other regional development programmes have sought to draw on this same resource. Most notable amongst these are the Centres of Excellence and Newcastle Science City initiatives that were introduced in the previous chapter. Relating to the former, the 2001 consultancy mapping exercise that preceded One NorthEast's first regional economic strategy particularly emphasised the medical or bioscience focus of the dominant public sector research base in the region (Arthur D Little 2001: 33). The report advised that, despite the high level of international competition in the bioscience sector and lack of existing firms or academic–industry links in the region, 'there are emerging areas where there are real chances for the North East to establish a leading position in the UK, and potentially internationally', including both Stem Cells and Ageing (ibid.: 126). This led to One NorthEast setting up The Centre of Excellence for Life Sciences (Cels, based in Newcastle), with a remit to 'work with the life science community in the North East of England to help companies and industry stakeholders grow a competitive cluster of national and international importance'.[5] Healthcare and Health Sciences was later included in the updated regional economic strategy of 2006 as one of three science and technology pillars (with Energy and Environment and Process Industries) (One NorthEast 2006). Stem Cells and Regenerative Medicine was also chosen, along with Ageing and Health (see below), as one of four (later three) Science City themes based on scientific strengths in Newcastle University alone. The ICFL has longstanding links with Cels (through cross membership of each other's boards) and is incorporated into Newcastle Science City as the designated site for the Stem Cells and Regenerative Medicine theme (largely by virtue of housing the IGM). However, because of its establishment with national and European funding sources, and subsequent high level of financial independence and sustainability, the ICFL has not otherwise been closely integrated into the wider regional or city organisational architecture supported by One NorthEast and Newcastle City Council (both partners in Newcastle Science City). The presence of these three intermediaries in overlapping domains has, therefore, undoubtedly led to some institutional duplication and fragmentation within the healthcare innovation system of the region. More fundamentally, the aspirations for economic development in the region based on the growth of medical or bioscience clusters have yet to materialise on any significant scale in terms of new firms or employment created, notwithstanding a small number of successful biotechnology and pharmaceutical spin-outs from Newcastle University.[6] Compared to other regions in the UK, this part of the North East's economy remains centred on pharmaceutical manufacturing (concentrated in the Teesside area) rather than private sector R&D activity (see Department for Business, Innovation and Skills 2011). This is despite the scientific advances made in the region's universities, supporting the argument made in

Chapter 4 that in most cases – and particularly in less successful regions – the economic development potential of models of innovation based on the commercialisation of academic research are likely to be limited (also see Appendix B). In the absence of other public or private R&D capabilities in the region, it also points to the overleveraging of the university medical research base as part of recent economic development strategy in the North East of England (also Hudson 2011).

The second research institute in Newcastle University's Faculty of Medical Sciences that has developed a strong grounding in the setting of its city and region is the Institute for Ageing and Health (IAH). This was the first formally-recognised research institute in Newcastle University, set up in 1994 as a non-resource holding 'soft' institute with the aim of enabling collaboration across existing departmental boundaries. The IAH carried on an established tradition of biomedical research in the University on conditions associated with ageing such as Alzheimer's disease and dementia, but coincided with a broadening of focus on this subject to also encompass the science of ageing and its social context.

> Right from the start the institute was set up with three main topic areas; to understand the biological determinants, the clinical manifestations, and the social implications of the ageing process.
>
> [*Interviewee, Newcastle University, 29/01/10 (2nd interviewee)*]

The success and durability of the social part of this portfolio as the IAH has grown is demonstrated at an institutional level by the designation of Changing Age as the first of three 'Societal Challenge' themes within Newcastle University. This is a strategy introduced by the University management to encourage institution-wide engagement with particular contemporary issues that coincide with existing research themes in each of its three academic faculties. (The second challenge theme is Sustainability, coinciding with the establishment of the Newcastle Institute for Research on Sustainability mentioned in the previous chapter.) The Changing Age programme, which is delivered by the Faculty of Medical Sciences rather than the IAH, has helped work on ageing in the University to continue being cross-faculty, as the IAH itself has moved to a more independent 'hard institute' model in line with the rest of the Faculty.

The social strand of the IAH's work has developed in conjunction with a growing public engagement of older people in the North East of England. In particular, the Institute has been closely involved with Years Ahead, an association of regional or national organisations and charities founded in 2005, which acts as a forum for discussion of social issues related to the ageing population, and with a particular mission to 'represent the views of older people in the development of regional policy and strategy'.[7] The IAH later extended this by setting up a user panel called VOICENorth (Valuing our Intellectual Capital and Experience North), working in partnership with organisations from Years Ahead to recruit members of the public from the North East. VOICENorth acts as a resource for the IAH, not only by providing easy access to large numbers of people willing to participate in studies, but also by allowing public feedback on projects that informs the outcomes and future research agendas as part of a developing co-production of knowledge culture in the Institute.

> We've always wanted VOICENorth to be a vocal critical friend if you like.... So the academics or researchers have been looking at them as being subjects, but they've come along and said... 'you're asking me the wrong question' or, you know, 'you're showing me technology for the sake of it' ... and that's beginning to shape the thinking of the researchers within that programme.
>
> *[Interviewee, Newcastle University, 19/07/11]*

The IAH has also formed good relationships with Newcastle Science City around the common purpose created with Ageing and Health being designated as one of its thematic areas. Initially, the significance of Science City to the IAH was mainly about 'creating a favourable climate for certain types of conversation to take place' *[Interviewee, Newcastle University, 29/01/10 (1st interviewee)]* that coincided with the growing local dimension in the Institute's work.

> I suppose any clinical academics working within, the kind of NHS framework work with the local population, because they form the public and patients with whom the clinicians work and they also provide a kind of research context for some of their studies.... But in terms of an agenda with the city, consciously for the health of the regional population, that has come really much more recently. I think the Science City partnership, you know, has made it more explicit that the University has to have a partnership with the City Council. But also I think some of the new programmes of research that we've initiated over the last five years have really been in recognition of the need and opportunity to do things with the local population.
>
> *[Interviewee, Newcastle University, 29/01/10 (1st interviewee)]*

In particular, the Professor of Practice (see previous chapter) for the Ageing and Health theme, a managing director of a health technologies company (based in Sheffield), is seen as having had an impact in building capacity for working with industry in Newcastle University and also strengthening links with ageing-related researchers in Northumbria University. More recently, the relationship has taken on a more concrete nature as the intermediary company side of the Science City programme came into being and introduced relevant business development initiatives, such as the Innovation Machine which supports the matching of academic expertise with commercial partners and support.

A key driver of this relationship is linked to the planned development of the site where most of the IAH is physically based into a multi-purpose Campus for Ageing and Vitality. This location, in a relatively disadvantaged area of the west of the city (see Map 7.1 on p. 94) had been home to the Newcastle General Hospital, but was largely vacated by the NHS by 2010 with the bulk of its facilities re-located to the two other existing hospitals in the city (including the Royal Victoria Infirmary next to the main Newcastle University campus). The Newcastle upon Tyne Hospitals NHS Foundation Trust remains the main land-owner, however, and has entered a partnership with Newcastle University to redevelop the site for functions related to Ageing and Vitality; adopting a similar model of regeneration around a particular knowledge-based theme as used for the ICFL and Science Central sites in the city. A third main partner in this scheme is the supermarket chain Tesco, who propose using the front of the site for a store with specialist facilities adapted for ease of use by older people. Hence, the plans for the Campus involve distinct but overlapping zones on the site for academic, healthcare, business and retail quarters. These plans were first proposed in 2008 but, due to a protracted planning permission process (amidst local opposition to the building of the Tesco store), go-ahead was only granted by the City Council in early 2011. The major developmental challenge for this project is perhaps in attracting science or technology firms with an ageing-link to populate the middle zone that is designated for business functions: the aca-demic and clinical parts of the site are already well inhabited with existing Newcastle University and NHS activity. The IAH has itself entered a phase of needing to attract private sector businesses to the campus. One of its major new buildings, the Biomedical Research Building, carries an explicit commitment to bring academic, clinical and business activities together in the same facility. The imperative to fill this space by attracting companies in the ageing field has helped drive expanding business engagement by the IAH (through a new ERDF-supported Changing Age for Business initiative) and strengthened already exist-ing links with Newcastle Science City. While this may prove challenging in the short-term, especially in the current economic downturn, the demographic trend towards an ageing population will inevitably create major future opportunities for social and business innovation in areas like assistive technologies, which the North East of England may be in a stronger position to capitalise on due to the present strategic investment in the Campus for Ageing and Vitality.

Conclusion

This chapter has aimed to show that university health and medical faculty engage-ment with the city and wider society is shaped by their key mediating institutional relationships. The starting point for this chapter has been the extremely well-established organisational relationships between large academic units in both Pre and Post 1992 universities and the National Health Service (NHS). This link, an important component of the national system of healthcare provision and develop-ment throughout the UK, facilitates university activity in the areas of medical or public health training, academic clinical practice, scientific research, and contact with local populations. These different functions intersect and feed into each other, as the examples of research through clinical and public engagement in Newcastle University's Institutes of Genetic Medicine and of Ageing and Health discussed above particularly illustrate. The Department of Health (through the

NIHR) has sought to support these kinds of links by promoting the translation of research into clinical treatments or health interventions through initiatives, jointly with other national or local bodies, such as the Collaboration for Leadership in Applied Health Research and Care Centre or Public Health Research Centres of Excellence, as the examples in respectively South Yorkshire and the North East of England discussed above show. These inter-institution centres also have the positive effect of encouraging greater collaboration between largely complementary health strengths from the Pre and Post 1992 universities in the cities of Sheffield and Newcastle (in this case also with those in the wider North East region).

The city (or equivalent sub-regional) geographical coverage of individual NHS trusts, as part of the multi-level structured organisation of the Service as a whole, means that urban university medical and health faculties are to some extent embedded in their locality through these links around teaching, research and engagement. These links can take on an extra dimension in the case of public health research and teaching, in which the urban populations and environment of the city figure as subjects of research, particularly in former industrial cities such as Sheffield and Newcastle where chronic health conditions and socio-economic related health inequalities remain entrenched. The nature of local engagement in this particular field is set to change with its institutional environment in the near future, as principal responsibility for the public health function shifts from the NHS into local authorities (with associated partnership vehicle Health and Wellbeing Boards). This could have important implications for the approach to public health in the UK that may favour a more broad urban-based interpretation, but it may also mean that universities have to adapt to the different working norms and practices in local authorities as opposed to NHS trusts. A further set of organisational relationships – by now well established for medical science units in universities throughout Europe – are with local firms (often themselves university spin-outs) and local economic development agencies. In the research that underpinned this chapter, this issue was covered through discussion of several overlapping organisations active in the North East of England: Newcastle Science City, the International Centre for Life, and the Centre for Excellence in Life Sciences (Cels). Despite strong relationships between these institutions and sections of Newcastle University's Faculty of Medical Sciences, which have helped develop its external engagement around business development, the large-scale impact on the North East economy of the policies driving these links has as yet remained unproven.

9 Universities and the cultural sector of cities

Introduction

This chapter examines university relationships with the cultural sector of cities. We take a broad view of the cultural sector to include the arts, the media and creative industries. This reflects a changed, expanded view of the significance of culture to urban development in the context of more entrepreneurial modes of city governance (see Harvey 1989; Hall and Hubbard 1996). From the 1980s onwards, European cultural policies have shifted from an emphasis on social and political priorities – such as 'personal and community development, participation, egalitarianism, the democratisation of urban space and revitalisation of public social life' – to economic development and urban regeneration investment (Bianchini 1993: 13). This instrumentation of culture encompasses the city's status as a centre of both cultural industry production and consumption (Zukin 1995; Scott 1997). Cultural consumption, in relation to economic drivers such as tourism, leisure services, and above all property development, has in particular grown in importance as part of the economic base of post-industrial cities. Investment in large cultural assets (e.g. art museums, opera or concert halls) has been widely adopted as an economic and physical regeneration strategy in former industrial cities as well as more recognised centres of art and commerce, as much as for the symbolic effects it is hoped that these developments (complete with iconic architecture) will have in transforming the marketable image and external perception of the place, as for the direct economic returns from people visiting these facilities. In the UK this form of regeneration underwent a relative boom after 1997 with significantly increased public spending on the arts and culture under New Labour (Hesmondhalgh 2005), although this has retreated over the past few years in the retrenchment of public spending following the 2008 financial crisis and change of government. This approach of using cultural policy as an urban development vehicle has also been criticised for doing little to address underlying problems of social exclusion and economic inequality in cities (e.g. Oakley 2006).

The diversity of the cultural sector in cities is mirrored in the diversity of creative and artistic disciplines taught, researched and practiced in universities. These disciplines occupy distinctive positions within the organisational structures of higher education institutions and within the spectrum of academic practice. In the UK, many art and design schools originated in the nineteenth or twentieth centuries as freestanding civic institutions, before becoming incorporated within universities or (as in the case of the University of the Arts London) retaining their semi-autonomous institutional status within a collegiate model. Even when they have become part of the school or faculty structure of multi-disciplinary urban universities, as is the case with the institutions we discuss here in Bristol and Newcastle, these art schools and their constituent communities of students and staff have a strong identity and connection to metropolitan cultural life (Hilton 1991). The provision of cultural and art education, formerly being the preserve of both traditional universities and polytechnics, also spans the divide between Pre and Post 1992 universities. The division of these creative fields between universities within a city is determined by a combination of particular historical circumstances and more recent institutional strategies that we will discuss in relation to the two cases below. Indeed, culture is a field where the hierarchy in research capability between Pre and Post 1992 universities observed in other parts of the academy (Chapter 6) largely disappears: the mode of practice-led research and teaching used in art, design, media and related subjects is one that fits comfortably into the inherited remit and wider institutional norms of Post 1992 universities. Many features of these distinctive forms of practice are reflected in the relevant findings of our online survey (see Section 6 of Appendix B). From another much larger survey of academic knowledge exchange in the UK (Abreu *et al.* 2009), Abreu and Grinevich (2011) drew out a broadly complementary set of findings on how academics from the 'creative arts' differ from members of other disciplines: the connection of their research to practice; the orientation of their external links towards teaching and student placements; the greater likelihood of these external links being with small firms or third sector partners; and of being local or regional in terms of geography (also see Hughes *et al.* 2011).

In this chapter our focus is relationships between universities and cultural organisations or venues in the city that come from active engagement on the part of academics or the university as an institution. This cultural engagement may be primarily social or economic in purpose, and in many cases effectively bridges the two. We do not directly address here the kinds of impacts of university-related communities (e.g. students) on the creative environment of the city and the wider economic benefits that Florida and others have argued this brings, which we discussed in Chapter 3. Nor are we directly concerned with the local economic impacts of graduates from creative fields and their personal outcomes in regional labour markets (for this Ball *et al.* 2010; Comunian *et al.* 2010). Instead the main perspective we take, extending wider themes in the book, is to highlight the role of cultural spaces (e.g. museums and galleries, performance venues such as theatres or concert halls, media labs or studios, creative quarters or districts) within cities as a constitutive element of the cultural strategies of universities and practices of academics. In particular, we explore the distinction between the use of cultural spaces that are on-campus and off-campus. The main body of the chapter is divided into two parts. The first introduces this specific spatial perspective and develops it through an overview of the main cultural activity and local engagement of the two universities in Newcastle and Bristol. The second part focuses on a single area of cultural engagement: the developing interdisciplinary field of creative digital technologies. This is comprised of mini case studies of 'media lab' type facilities connected to universities in both cities: Culture Lab on the campus of Newcastle University and The Pervasive Media Studio, part of the Watershed Media Centre in Bristol that now hosts members from both the universities in this city.

Placing universities in the cultural spaces of cities

The creative activity and image that is now viewed as a vital element of urban development policy is tied to specific places or landmarks within the city – cultural venues and museums, creative/cultural quarters or districts, public art and monuments (Zukin 1995; Miles 1997; Rykwert 2000). These places are defined not just by their functional use by groups such as artists or cultural audiences, but also by the meanings with which they and surrounding areas of the city are ascribed by different public and private interests and, in turn, the way that this space is used by different parts of the urban population. As Zukin (1995) argues, at the heart of what she calls the new 'symbolic economy' are the dual processes of the production of symbols and the production of space (also see Harvey 2012 for a discussion of 'collective symbolic capital' and 'the right to the city'). For instance, flagship cultural regeneration projects are typically designed to transform derelict former industrial parts of cities (such as waterfront docks) into revitalised sites of cultural consumption and tourism. Just as common in European cultural policy is identification of a particular part of the city as a creative or cultural 'quarter', archetypically combining workspace for creative industries with related leisure and residential functions (van Winden *et al.* 2012). This type of space has become an especially common feature of English cities such as Manchester, Sheffield, Birmingham, Leicester and Nottingham (Brown *et al.* 2000; Shorthose 2004; Porter and Barber 2007). Some cultural quarters develop in a largely organic way through artist-led gentrification (Matthews 2010) and the clustering together of small creative and media businesses in areas with suitable and affordable workspace (see Hutton 2006; Rantisi and Leslie 2010), but others are planned by local authorities as a conscious economic development strategy and anchored around public investment in one or more significant cultural facilities (Brown *et al.* 2000; Shorthose 2004). A more decentralised approach to supporting urban economic development and liveability through 'creative placemaking' is outlined by Markusen and Gadwa (2010), which focuses on neighbourhood renewal around a number of smaller community and independent producer-based art spaces.

University campuses may also be important sites of cultural activity within cities, particularly when the institution in question contains an art school or faculty with a large community of creative students and staff. Campuses themselves are often home to cultural venues – museums, theatres, art galleries, concert halls, media labs – whether these are managed directly by the university or just located within its vicinity. While these spaces are unlikely to be large 'flagship' facilities with a national or international profile around which a city can develop economic development or regeneration strategies, they are often notable civic institutions and longstanding fixtures in the cultural ecology of the city or region. They can also help the university to access alternative sources of cultural funding (e.g. Arts Council England) for capital investment projects that more conventional academic teaching and research funders (e.g. AHRC) do not directly support (although HEFCE does have a Museums, Galleries and Collections Fund) (see Oakley and Selwood 2010). More fundamentally, these cultural facilities represent tangible opportunities to link practice to education and research in corresponding departments of the university (e.g. galleries with fine art departments, theatres with drama departments, etc.). Students and staff can act as important constituencies supporting these venues as exhibitors or performers, curators or directors, and as a readymade audience.

These on-campus venues may not however be sufficient for all the practical needs of academic creative arts departments. They therefore benefit from engagement with external cultural organisations and venues for the purposes of collaborative research, student placements, and reaching a wider audience for events such as student performances or art degree shows. In some cases, where on-campus space or facilities are limited, this external engagement will take the extra step of re-locating university teaching or research into off-campus facilities within or close to the buildings of these cultural organisations, hence creating new forms of spatial relationships between the university and the cultural sector of the city. The rest of this section outlines these varying sets of relationships, and their underlying urban and institutional dynamics, for the universities in Newcastle and Bristol.

Newcastle

Over the past fifteen years Newcastle has come to be recognised as one of the leading exemplars of culture-led regeneration in the UK (Minton 2003; Bailey *et al.* 2004; Chapain and Comunian 2010). This reputation is largely based on two major developments on the previously deindustrialised Quayside: the Baltic Centre for Contemporary Art, housed in a renovated former flour mill and opened in 2002; and the Sage Gateshead, a large concert venue and music facility in a striking new building (designed by Foster and Partners architectural practice) that opened in 2004. These venues are on the Gateshead side of the River Tyne (outside but facing the city of Newcastle upon Tyne – see Map 9.1), with Gateshead Council taking a lead as local authority partner in the development of both projects (Minton 2003). During the same period of relative abundance of public funding for the arts, Newcastle City Council also supported a number of less high-profile projects to create or refurbish cultural venues on their side of the river; including theatres, museums and centres for dance and children's literature. To capitalise on their shared cultural assets, the two councils work together to promote the area

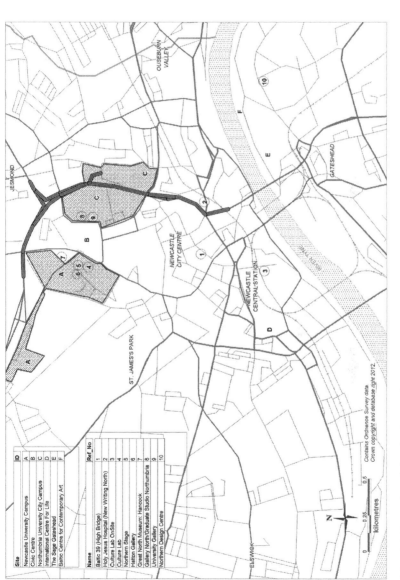

Site	ID
Newcastle University Campus	A
Civic Centre	B
Northumbria University City Campus	C
International Centre For Life	D
The Sage Gateshead	E
Baltic Centre for Contemporary Art	F

Name	Ref_No
Baltic 39 (High Bridge)	1
Holy Jesus Hospital (New Writing North)	2
Culture Lab OnSite	3
Culture Lab	4
Northern Stage	5
Hatton Gallery	6
Great North Museum: Hancock	7
Gallery North/Graduate Studio Northumbria	8
University Gallery	9
Northern Design Centre	10

Map 9.1 Key cultural sites in Newcastle.

Source: Contains Ordinance Survey data. © Crown copyright and database right 2012.

under the amalgamated place brand of 'NewcastleGateshead'. A key phase in this partnership between Newcastle and Gateshead was a joint bid to be the UK's representative as European Capital of Culture for 2008.[1] During this competition NewcastleGateshead was perceived as a frontrunner, and although it eventually missed out to Liverpool (see Griffiths 2006), the energy and collaborative activity it stimulated, along with a legacy of actual and planned investments linked to the bid, is recognised as having had a lasting effect on the cultural domain in the city and wider region.

This effect of the Capital of Culture bid was especially profound on the role of Newcastle University as an actor in the creative life of the city. Prior to this, cultural links with the city largely did not extend far beyond the engagement activities of members of individual departments such as Music, English or Fine Arts. Institutionally, the university did not consider local cultural engagement a strategic priority, despite its campus – centrally located within the city – being home to several significant arts and culture venues: a large natural history museum (the Hancock) run on behalf of the university by Tyne & Wear Archives & Museums; an important regional theatre (Newcastle Playhouse) in a building owned by the university but managed by its resident Northern Stage theatre company; and the Hatton Galley attached to the department of art (Map 9.1). This detached stance began to change with the wider cultural regeneration in the city-region. The University established early collaborations with the major new cultural organisations off-campus: with the Baltic Centre for Contemporary Art through the appointment of a practicing artist as a jointly-funded professor; and with the Sage Gateshead through the location of a new degree in folk and traditional music in this complex (although later, for practical reasons, this transferred back on to campus). As part of the Capital of Culture bid, however, more ambitious plans were made for Newcastle University's campus to become a 'cultural quarter' alongside other areas in the city-region sharing this broad label, such as the Quayside and the Ouseburn Valley (Cross and Pickering 2008). The University, with support from a range of funders, undertook a major capital project to redevelop the Hancock Museum, which was completed in 2009. The museum now also houses the University's antiquities collection, and has been renamed (with the Hatton Gallery) as the Great North Museum. This development was preceded by a refurbishment of the theatre on-campus (now known as Northern Stage) led by its company with funding from Arts Council England and Newcastle City Council. A new on-campus facility for creative technologies, Culture Lab, was also developed at this time with investment by the University (see below). A further project for a writers centre on campus was planned in partnership with the North East region's creative writing development agency, New Writing North – an intermediary organisation that 'specialise[s] in the development of talent and act[s] as a dynamic broker between writers, agents and producers across the creative industries'.[2] This was intended to give literature (that has a distinctive heritage in the North East of England) a physical presence within the city to match other branches of the arts that had recently developed or renovated facilities, and to provide a more permanent home for New Writing North, who at the time were temporarily based on the University's campus (in the Culture Lab building). However, the launch of fundraising efforts for this centre coincided with the beginnings of the late 2000s financial crisis and collapse of the national and regional arts funding environment,[3] which ultimately led to the project being abandoned. In the wake of this, Newcastle University's School of English Literature, Language and Linguistics established a new research centre, the Newcastle Centre for the Literary Arts, to continue its public engagement work in the region and public events programme of readings and lectures in other venues. New Writing North in the meantime has re-located to a building within the city (Holy Jesus Hospital) that now belongs to Northumbria University. Although these plans to transform its campus into a 'cultural quarter' may not have been fully realised, these capital developments have together had an effect on Newcastle University and its relationships in the city around culture. The Great North Museum project in particular has since its re-opening been successful in attracting large numbers of visitors on to the campus, providing the university with a flagship example of large-scale public engagement to support its aspirations of being a 'civic university' (also Oakley and Selwood 2010).

Northumbria University has a cultural offer as diverse and strong as that of Newcastle University. The city's independent College of Art & Industrial Design (which itself had roots in different institutions going back to the nineteenth century) became one of the three constituent parts of Newcastle Polytechnic (the predecessor of Northumbria University) when this was founded in 1969. This college was constrained to offering a curriculum of commercial and technical arts (including industrial design and related trades); fine art higher education courses in the city were taught only by Armstrong and King's colleges of Durham University (the foundations of the present day Newcastle University) until Newcastle Polytechnic came into existence and also began to develop courses in this area (Allen and Buswell 2005). The legacy of this today is that Northumbria University has a separate School of Design and School of Arts & Social Sciences. The School of Design, in particular, is a leading national and international establishment for teaching and research across a range of 3D (e.g. industrial or product), 2D (e.g. graphic and interactive media) and fashion design disciplines. The national profile of the School is reflected in its recent opening of a branch in London, the centre of the UK's design economy, from where a small number of enterprise-focused postgraduate courses are delivered. This perhaps represents a response to the peripherality of the North East economy as a centre for creative industry professionals (see Swords and Wray 2010). However, the school also has links with regional industry, particularly around student placements, graduate enterprises, and the research and consultancy activities channelled through its dedicated intermediary unit, the Centre for Design Research. These regional links are set to be enhanced with the belated opening of the (now defunct) Regional Development Agency backed Northern Design Centre in Gateshead, that will support this sector of the North East economy. The School of Arts & Social Sciences is one of the largest schools in the University, with departments in Art, Media and Humanities as well as Social Sciences. As part of a new more ambitious research strategy for the University, members of these schools and others (such as architects from the School of Built Environment) have begun to explore collaborations under the cross-cutting research theme Design, Creativity and Digital Media (one of four such interdisciplinary priority areas adopted by the institution).

Together these strengths mean that Northumbria University has a wide range of links into the creative sector of the city and region. These have predominately taken the form of relationships developed around the research and teaching practice of individual creative academics or departments rather than formal strategic partnerships on the part of the institution.

> Northumbria had a pretty rich connection to the cultural life of the city and region, perhaps not particularly led by the institution but through individuals... casual interaction between students and teachers and their individual research and professional interests.... Northumbria I think still produces a fantastic range of cultural graduates and their research programmes are very very good.
>
> [*Interviewee, Newcastle City Council, 18/02/10*]

> At their inception none of [these partnerships] are formalised in the sense of they will exist beyond the people that are there.... They very much come from the individual professional links or they have been formed out of research strategies, and they've met with a receptive non-research organisation interest in what people are trying to do because they're project based.... I mean, if it's a relationship based on experience and trust, that's great; you don't need to formalise it at that point. Again, I think when you do formalise these things, if you're working with creative organisations particularly, it kills it a bit. You prefer to work in a much more flexible way.... The point of formalising it is, I would say, to be able to build on it and to announce that to the world.
>
> [*Interviewee, Northumbria University, 22/11/11*]

> There's a lot going on around the School [of Arts & Social Sciences], but I think in the end, at an executive level of the school, the decision is very much around, look, we'll just let these thousand flowers bloom as they are, because trying to stop it is impossible. Something may come from them, but in fact if we're going to do anything we'll do a few big things. I think ideally it would be each department having one good strategic partnership.
>
> [*Interviewee, Northumbria University, 23/11/11 (1st interviewee)*]

This prevailing decentralisation perhaps explains why Northumbria University was less markedly affected than Newcastle University by the wider developments in the cultural sector of the city in the period leading up to the Capital of Culture bid. More recently, however, top-down changes throughout the institution, including the introduction of a Pro Vice-Chancellor for the Region, Engagement and Partnerships, with a related management structure at the school level, have helped orientate departments towards the possibilities of more strategic relationships with large cultural organisations in the region. The leading current example is that between the School of Arts & Social Sciences and the Baltic Centre for Contemporary Art. This builds on an established collaboration between these two organisations in the form of a joint MA Fine Art and Education course, which is targeted towards existing art teachers studying part-time to improve the Fine Art component of their curriculum and practice. In the previous couple of years the relationship has deepened into a more extensive formal partnership. As part of this new arrangement, the University has gained a visual presence in the Baltic through one of its large exhibition spaces being renamed on a permanent basis as the Northumbria Gallery. In turn, the University has appointed a renowned practicing artist as Baltic Professor, who will act as director of a new BxNU Institute of Contemporary Art. In 2012 the two organisations opened a significant new off-campus facility in the middle of Newcastle City Centre (Baltic 39) to house this Institute, using a building leased by Newcastle City Council (formerly the Waygood Gallery) and additional funding from Arts Council England. As well including substantial studio space for local artists not connected to the University and a public gallery on the top floor, this new facility provides downtown teaching and practice space for the University's third year undergraduate and postgraduate students. A member of the School described a key objective for this new venture:

> I think what we are attempting to do is to try and crack that nut that a lot of fine art departments have to crack, which is how do you work in a professional practice environment that's recognised by students and postgraduates, but also works to the needs of a research culture.... What kinds of resources do you need?... Really the model you want to put forward is a sort of relationship of art and the city; so very metropolitan, very urban. It's not on campus, its right in the middle of town.
>
> [*Interviewee, Northumbria University, 22/11/11*]

Baltic 39 will complement the School's existing gallery space on-campus (Gallery North), which is managed and curated by staff members and hosts exhibitions that are open to the public as well as a teaching resource.[4] Alongside Gallery North, the School of Arts & Social Sciences also provides studio space for a number of their recent graduates on very low cost basis (Graduate Studios Northumbria), partly with the intention of attracting students and encouraging them to stay in the region after graduation.

Bristol

Within the context of UK cities, Bristol also has a prominent cultural sector, but with a different character to Newcastle and Gateshead. The city authorities have not pursued a culture-led regeneration strategy on the same scale as those in many other large cities throughout the UK and Europe. The partial exception to this was the redevelopment of the Harbourside area near to the City Centre during the 1990s and 2000s which, while being property-driven in commercial terms, involved investment in its cultural infrastructure (Griffiths *et al.* 1999). This area already included three of the city's major cultural venues: the Watershed Media Centre (see below); the Arnolfini arts and performance centre; and the Bristol Old Vic Theatre. The cultural side of this regeneration project was coordinated by an intermediary, the Bristol Cultural Development Partnership (BCDP), established by Bristol City Council, South West Arts (now part of Arts Council England) and an association of chambers of commerce for the West of England sub-region, GWE Business West. The BCDP has subsequently been a key actor in leading or organising other cultural projects in Bristol, such as the city's bid to be European Capital of Culture in 2008 (that, like NewcastleGateshead's, was unsuccessful) and the annual Bristol Festival of Ideas (which, through its arts and science programme, has gained a national profile). Both universities in Bristol have links to the BCDP and are closely involved with the Festival of Ideas. Bristol does have a major public sector cultural presence in the form of the British Broadcasting Corporation (BBC), which has production facilities for some national as well as regional programming located in the city. Of particular note is the BBC's renowned Natural History Unit based in Bristol since 1957, which has been the hub of a wider network of independent nature-film production companies and providers of related specialist services in the city (Bassett *et al.* 2002).[5] In addition to those firms connected to the BBC, the rest of Bristol's media and creative industry private sector is amongst the strongest in the UK outside London, with distinct areas of specialisation such as animation (Chapain *et al.* 2010). Away from this more formal side of the city's cultural sector, Bristol has a reputation for cultural diversity and vibrancy in alternative or underground areas such as electronic music, street art and performance that some interviewees commented the two universities contributed to by helping to attract a 'critical mass' of creative young people, who as discussed in Chapter 3 are active as producers and audience in the cultural life of the city outside of their studies (also Chatterton 1999, 2000).

In terms of institutional and academic relationships, Bristol's two universities plug into this cultural sector in different ways due to their varying coverage of artistic and cultural disciplines and geographical position in the city. The Pre and Post 1992 universities in Bristol seem to have a clearer division of cultural education and research fields than in Newcastle (although both institutions teach English and Drama). The University of Bristol largely covers a more traditional set of cultural roles in the city (Chatterton 2000). Its Faculty of Arts has a strong humanities focus on subjects such as History (including the History of Art), Philosophy and English, but also has two performing arts departments in Music and Drama: Theatre, Film and Television. Both of these departments are attached to notable cultural venues in the city that they use as rehearsal and public performance spaces as well as for more conventional teaching and research purposes.

The Department of Music is based in the Victoria Rooms, a significant nineteenth century civic building including a large auditorium for concerts and other public events, which has passed into ownership of the University of Bristol. Amongst the Department of Drama: Theatre, Film and Television's facilities is the Wickham Theatre, which hosts productions by student groups as well as professional touring companies in its public programme. As its title indicates, this department combines study of drama on screen and on stage, and collaborates with other performance- and media-based cultural venues off-campus, such as Arnolfini and Watershed. Research in this department has included a particular focus on the subject of using practice as a research approach in performance-based disciplines (e.g. drama, music, dance) around which it has recently completed a major AHRC-funded research programme.[6] The Victoria Rooms and Wickham Theatre are based inside or close to the 'precinct' of buildings that forms the hub of the University of Bristol's example of a relatively dispersed and integrated urban campus (Chapter 2), in this case located between the central city and the affluent Clifton area (see Map 9.2). Because the public that attends events at these two venues provides a wider audience for their performances, 'inevitably there is that sense of public engagement built into the School' to which both of these departments belong [*Interviewee, University of Bristol, 17/05/11b*].

In contrast to the University of Bristol, the University of West of England (UWE) is geographically distributed across a number of separate campuses and non-campus environments in and around the city. The University's largest campus and administrative centre, Frenchay, is located on the northern outskirts of Bristol. However, what was the Faculty of Art, Media and Design, and following a university re-organisation in 2010, is now the Department of Creative Industries (in an expanded Faculty of Arts, Creative Industries and Education), based predominately at the Bower Ashton campus to the west of the city (Map 9.2). Under this department heading of Creative Industries – reflecting the institution's desire to position engagement with this sector of the economy as central to its outlook – the subjects collected together include fine art, graphic design, animation, photography, journalism and media, and a specialist centre for Fine Print Research. The Department of Arts in this faculty (which covers English, Drama and Film Studies, as well as several of the humanities) is mainly based at another campus, St Matthias that, like Frenchay, is north of the city.[7] Furthermore, over the past decade the university has pursued a strategy to partner with key cultural organisations in the city to enhance its research practice and teaching offer for students. This strategy was described to us as following a three-pronged approach of joint projects, joint appointments, and the leasing of space in the premises of these cultural organisations [*Interviewee, UWE, 17/05/11*]. These off-campus tenancy arrangements have involved UWE taking significant space in Arnolfini, Watershed/Pervasive Media Studio (see below), and the Spike Island contemporary art centre (also in the Harbourside area) on an ongoing basis. This gives the University a presence in the city centre close to key cultural activities, but also provides them with access to extra space and the kind of workshop or studio environments that teaching delivery and research practice in art- and design-based disciplines require. Another link with a major cultural

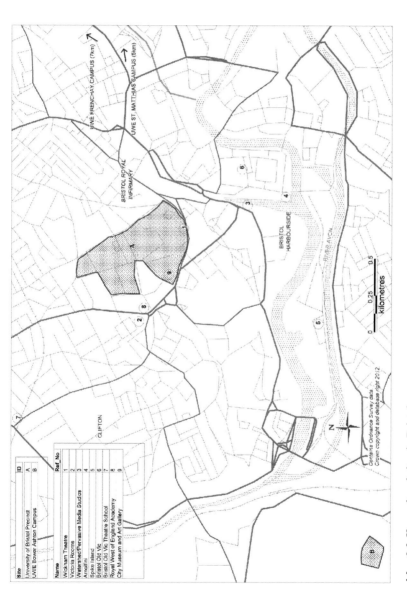

Site	ID
University of Bristol Precinct	A
UWE Bower Ashton Campus	B

Name	Ref_No
Wickham Theatre	1
Victoria Rooms	2
Watershed/Pervasive Media Studios	3
Arnolfini	4
Spike Island	5
Bristol Old Vic	6
Bristol Old Vic Theatre School	7
Royal West of England Academy	8
City Museum and Art Gallery	9

Map 9.2 Key cultural sites in Bristol.

Source: Contains Ordinance Survey data. © Crown copyright and database right 2012.

current in the city exists through the university's decision to establish the Bristol School of Animation, that provides short courses tailored for the local workforce as well as an undergraduate degree within the Department of Creative Industries. This focus on links with the city's creative industries, in disciplines largely not included in the University of Bristol's cultural provision, has helped UWE to establish a distinctive position. More recently, however, the two institutions have begun to converge and collaborate around the growing field of creative digital technologies that will be the focus of the section below. The themes around on-campus and off-campus spaces introduced in this section will be discussed in the chapter conclusion.

Creative and digital media practice

This section extends the discussion above by focusing on university activity in one particular cultural field: artistic or creative practice in the interdisciplinary context of digital technologies and media. The identity of this new field has developed in part through its association with a new type of organisational space – 'Media Labs' (often within universities or large corporations) where creative research and experimentation into the development and applications of new technologies is carried out (see Frost 2011 for these in the UK). In this section we concentrate on examples of such institutes in both cities: Newcastle University's Culture Lab and the Watershed's Pervasive Media Studio in Bristol. These two centres have contrasting relationships to universities: Culture Lab is an on-campus research facility for a single university, while The Pervasive Media Studio is a part of an independent arts organisation that nevertheless has close links with the two universities in Bristol and now houses members from both.

In both cities activity connected to these labs/studios have been invested in as areas of strategic importance by one of the universities. This can be interpreted in part as a response to the wider academic funding environment: digital economy is one of the RCUK's six cross-council priority areas (Chapter 6) – 'supporting research to rapidly realise the transformational impact of digital technologies on aspects of community life, cultural experiences, future society, and the economy'.[8] The two examples we discuss have been successful in accessing research funding through this and related channels (such as the AHRC-led Connected Communities programme).

As this field has developed, a key dynamic has been the move towards media delivered on mobile or wireless platforms (such as smartphones or tablet computers) and the related spread of 'ubiquitous' or 'pervasive' computing into the spaces of our everyday lives (Thrift and French 2002; Galloway 2004). This decentralisation of access to advanced computing technologies has strengthened a focus on its users and encouraged its designers into dialogues with social scientists as well as artists. For 'Media Lab' institutions, this more distributed environment has prompted the objects of their work to expand into an urban laboratory of research and engagement beyond their building. Notwithstanding this process, the two labs/studios that we discuss here remain vital physical hubs for the situated practices of their associated community of researchers and as venue spaces for university and wider civic audiences.

Culture Lab (Newcastle)

Newcastle University is a relative latecomer to the field of creative technologies amongst higher education institutions in the North East of England. Both Teesside and Sunderland universities are central to digital and interactive media-related business development initiatives based in their home cities; respectively Digital City and Software City. These have been supported by one of the Centres of Excellence (Codeworks) set up by the regional development agency One NorthEast in 2002 (Chapter 7), in this case relating to digital innovation. Designing for digital interactive media is also developing into an increasingly important focus of research and teaching in Northumbria University's School of Design. While building links with these other regional actors, Culture Lab (opened in 2006) was established by Newcastle University with a distinctive set of strategic aims around providing a physical space and specialist equipment to encourage interdisciplinary creative technology collaboration inside the institution.

> Culture Lab was created because in a number of different areas, not least music, fine art, and creative writing, the creative artists were interested in improving their facilities for that kind of [digital media] work, alongside the computer scientists and engineers wanting opportunities to develop wider uses of some of their scientific techniques.
>
> [*Interviewee, Newcastle University, 08/02/10*]

On the institution's website, Culture Lab is described as 'the focal point for creative arts practice at Newcastle University, supporting the work of researchers and students involved in high level, experimental and multi-disciplinary creative arts projects in a technologically rich and custom designed environment'.[9] Another interviewee emphasised the dual position of Culture Lab as a research facility that could become part of an international network of academic and corporate 'media labs' (such as MIT Media Lab or Ars Electronica Futurelab), but also as a 'cultural and technology centre that could be inscribed in a local context and that could be a member of the cultural quarter' that at the time was planned for the University campus [*Interviewee, Newcastle University, 14/07/11*].

This new centre is based in a University-owned nineteenth century building, the now heritage protection listed Grand Assembly Rooms, which were converted and equipped for their present use with a capital grant from the HEFCE Science Research Investment Fund (SRIF). In terms of the institution's structures, Culture Lab is a cross-departmental research facility in the Faculty of Humanities, Arts and Social Sciences (HASS), but it is managed as a resource that can be used by academics from any faculty with an interest in the development or application of the kind of creative technologies in which it specialises. Indeed, one of the largest constituencies that is housed in Culture Lab's main open-plan office space on an ongoing basis is an established Digital Interaction Group from the School of Computing Science. This group does have an interdisciplinary focus on the social and health benefits from the adoption of interactive digital technologies by non-standard user groups in everyday settings. For instance, they have collaborated with members of the University's Institutes of Health and Society and Ageing and Health (Chapter 8) on projects to develop and demonstrate assistive technologies embedded in the homes of older people with cognitive impairments such as dementia.[10] The strand of Culture Lab's work enabled by the presence of this group has been strengthened with it becoming the physical hub for a major RCUK-funded research project on Social Inclusion through the Digital Economy (SIDE) that involves researchers from across Newcastle University (in partnership with the University of Dundee).

In line with its founding aims (see above), Culture Lab has been home to technologically-versed academic researchers who are also practicing artists in fields such as music, film or visual art, and who incorporate experimental use of digital technologies into their performance or exhibitions. This cultural area has developed more recently through teaching activity in the centre as much as research. The School of Arts and Cultures delivers two postgraduate courses from Culture Lab: an MA in Creative Arts Practice (that takes students from across artistic disciplines) and a research-based MRes in Digital Media. Creative artists and designers are also represented amongst the substantial community of PhD students from across the University that are based in Culture Lab in order to make use of the specialist facilities it houses in their projects. Again, the Culture Lab building itself acts as a facilitator of interdisciplinary work involving the creative artists that cuts across other organisational boundaries within the University:

> To have a physical space is everything, and we use the space to bring people together, to carry out research projects.... The fact that we have a beautiful space that's historically listed but has 21st century technology in it,... and by using this space to bring together researchers from different disciplines... this mix of arts students and computer science students is unique.
>
> *[Interviewee, Newcastle University, 14/07/11]*

Culture Lab also has a large event space on its first floor that is used by different departments within the University for public lectures, readings and other performances. For instance, the Newcastle Centre for the Literary Arts (see above) is a regular user of the venue. In this way the artistic component of Culture Lab is connected to its public engagement work and civic role in the city. This is also represented in the SIDE project through a Creative Industries strand of activity that focuses on using the creative arts to engage with socially-marginalised young people. In 2011, following a series of 'open days' in which local schoolchildren were invited into the on-campus facility to view demonstrations of the projects and technology developed in the centre, members of Culture Lab extended this engagement by temporarily leasing an unoccupied building in the city (see

Map 9.1) and setting up a project, exhibition and event space (Culture Lab OnSite) that was open to the public. Although this venue only functioned for around six months, it illustrates the aspiration to re-locate activities off-campus, away from the Culture Lab building (which despite its external orientation is a university research facility), as a strategy for opening up the work of the centre to the wider public of the city. This practice is reflected in the Bristol case of an off-campus collaborative university centre to which we turn now.

The Pervasive Media Studio (Bristol)

The Pervasive Media Studio differs from Culture Lab not just in its off-campus location, but also in its parent body being not a university but an arts organisation. Watershed (see above) is one of the major cultural venues in Bristol. It began in 1982 as a media centre focusing on film and photography housed in derelict warehouses on the Bristol Harbourside. The building is still physically based around an independent cinema and connected recreation and event spaces, but over the course of its history the organisation has developed into a leading promoter of multimedia digital practice in Bristol and the South West of England. Although Watershed had started to explore digital media during the early 1990s, a key phase in accelerating the diversification of its activities occurred in 1999 with the centre's participation in a project, run by a computer scientist from the University of Bristol, to explore how media organisations would use the greatly-expanded broadband capacities that were then becoming available.[11] This new capability to support online sound and images led to Watershed assuming a wider 'brokerage' role (see Oakley and Selwood 2010) as a commissioner, curator and archivist of digital creative content in the city.[12] As well as beginning an ongoing collaboration with computer science at the University of Bristol, this helped forge new inter-personal relationships with creative practitioners within local universities, particularly those in UWE's Faculty of Art, Media and Design. From the early 2000s onwards (preceding The Pervasive Media Studio) a feature of some of the larger projects through which these relationships were taken forward (e.g. NESTA Futurelab, Mobile Bristol) has been universities taking space in the Watershed building.

The Pervasive Media Studio was established in 2008 as part of the iShed subsidiary of Watershed, and was supported with funding from the regional development agency for the South West of England. The studio aimed to provide an organisational framework and physical hub in which collaborative work could be sustained on a more permanent footing:

> We were constantly doing these great projects with the universities, and then we'd stop. And then we'd do another one and then we'd stop. And each time, we'd build community and a bit of it would hang on. But we realised that if we had a physical location, then we'd get a lot more of the energy flowing forward.
>
> [*Interviewee, Watershed/The Pervasive Media Studio,*
> *24/10/11 (1st interviewee)*]

The Pervasive Media Studio was located in a separate building close to the Watershed centre and supplied with a full-time director and small team to curate its collaborative activities. Building on the earlier Mobile Bristol project, the studio takes its name from a focus on 'pervasive' forms of digital media that are sensitive and respond to the real-world situations in which they are used. Accordingly several projects attached to the studio have involved developing and testing applications in the setting of Bristol.

The initial partners of Watershed in The Pervasive Media Studio were the South West Regional Development Agency and Hewlett Packard (HP) Labs, the research division of the multinational technology corporation who have a base just outside Bristol and had collaborated with Watershed and university partners on previous projects (including Mobile Bristol). UWE joined as a core partner after one year. The entry of UWE into this venture followed the institutional leadership establishing a new unit – the Digital Cultures Research Centre (DCRC) – to revitalise this area of work within the university's media and design work at a time when the wider city was developing a digital focus through the partnership association Connecting Bristol. In line with the UWE's policy of partnering with key cultural organisations in the city described above, the faculty management was supportive of this centre and its newly-recruited director being located off-campus in the new studio. The DCRC is a 'soft' research centre that draws its membership from researchers interested in the study as well as creation of digital and interactive media from across UWE. In addition to securing external funding (including several projects from the AHRC-led Connected Communities programme), an internal system of supporting research leave was set-up to allow academics to become studio residents whilst working on their sabbatical projects. The Pervasive Media Studio also hosts PhD researchers from UWE and visiting students from international institutions. This means academics can contribute to and benefit from the culture of presenting work and sharing ideas with other residents that is a key part of the studio's collective working practices. In this way The Pervasive Media Studio and the DCRC have evolved together. A member of the University reflected on this approach of transposing an academic research centre into the non-conventional environment of a creative media studio:

> A studio is a creative environment in which, in this case, technology and new ways of delivering media play a lead part. If we think about a research centre, and in this case a research centre that believes in criticality, creativity, and application, then we can plug into the creative process of the studio – clearly there's an immediate overlap between our creative bit and their creative bit. So they're conterminous in a way; they're the same process. In terms of criticality, obviously what we offer is an analytic frame for reflection for the people who are involved in the creative process of the studio. . . . These activities in the studio [also] develop our critical resources. They help us to be creative in new ways. For me it's been a huge learning curve to work in this environment, to think about more agile ways of developing ideas, to think about new workshop methods, new ways of teaching.
>
> [*Interviewee, University of the West of England, 24/10/11*]

The creative industries component of The Pervasive Media Studio changed in 2009 when HP Labs scaled back their operation in the South West of England. This meant The Pervasive Media Studio no longer had a large corporate presence, but created opportunities for the studio to work with the new smaller enterprises formed by ex-employees of HP Labs. The studio also has a New Talent Residency scheme that provides graduates with an opportunity to develop a project or business idea in its environment. The open collaborative ethos of the studio provides an interface between academic and commercial actors. Interviewees in particular emphasised the studio's intermediary role in connecting the different working practices and rhythms of these two types of organisations.

> [T]hat's one of the functions I think we play in knowledge exchange; we as academics are really planning for five to ten years ahead, people in business are usually planning for the next quarter or the next six months or the next year. There are different temporalities, and one of the things that we can do is try to use our expertise to catch some of the things that they don't really have time to reflect on, or have the analytical purchase on, and play it back to them, and help them enrich their own process.
>
> *[Interviewee, University of the West of England, 24/10/11]*

> We I think resemble and learn from the working practices of the creative industries companies, who are agile, who are rapid, and who know that this territory is moving on. I think one of the benefits of working with academics is that they provide a kind of stability in the way we work.... There is a space in the middle where they can collaborate which is the work that might come out in two to three years. And then there's the horizon work, which the academy is in a much better place to look at, because it hasn't got the commercial constraints.... But the studio acts as a kind of gearing mechanism to try and help those timescales, agendas, cash flows, find each other and work together.
>
> *[Interviewee, Watershed/The Pervasive Media Studio,*
> *24/10/11 (2nd interviewee)]*

The terms used here reflect the distinction between the complementary roles of universities and firms in regional innovation systems that was proposed in Chapter 4: universities as non-market actors can provide the temporal 'slack' needed for adaptation to new technology or product pathways. The intermediary role of the studio captured in the gearing mechanism metaphor above also reflects the concept of a 'creative ecosystem of innovation' that Watershed more widely has developed to describe itself and the approach of brokering projects driven primarily by cultural rather than financial capital (see Leicester and Sharpe 2010).

At the time we finished our fieldwork research in Bristol (October 2011) The Pervasive Media Studio was on the verge of a major change, involving re-location to a bigger space back in the main Watershed building, and the widening of its partnership to also formally include the University of Bristol (involving members of this institution also moving into the new space).

The underlying relationship is going to be a five-year collaboration agreement between the three [organisations] at a corporate level, which we are calling a creative technologies collaboration. So it's for research, innovation and teaching in what we are broadly calling creative technologies; so that cross-over space between what you would normally call creative content and what you would normally call digital computing. This mixed up space that none of us quite understand.... So it is an active collaborative space, which adds value to what the universities can do in their own faculties, on their premises, on their own.

> [*Interviewee, Watershed/The Pervasive Media Studio,*
> *24/10/11 (1st interviewee)*]

As part of this newly configured partnership, both university collaborators will use the Studio for teaching. In its early stages this arrangement has facilitated joint projects between product design BA students from UWE and Computer Science MSc students from the University of Bristol. The Pervasive Media Studio will also host an even broader consortium of universities from throughout the South West of England (the two Bristol-based institutions and the universities of Bath and Exeter) and Wales (Cardiff University) as part of an AHRC-funded Knowledge Exchange Hub for the Creative Economy (REACT). This hub will use an established Watershed/Pervasive Media Studio commissioning methodology ('sandbox') to fund creative economy projects involving members of the partner universities, and in doing so seek to create new relationships and cross-disciplinary collaborations between academics from the humanities as well as creative arts and media.

Facilitating this type of broad interdisciplinary creative practice in an academic context is one of the key features of both The Pervasive Media Studio and Culture Lab examples discussed together in this section. These two centres do, however, occupy quite different positions in the cultural sector of their respective cities. These differences, in terms of their institutional parentage and geographical location, illustrate some of the wider themes of this chapter which we will now discuss in the concluding section.

Conclusion

This chapter has examined university relations with the cultural sector of cities through the particular lens of the various types of cultural venues or space through which this institutional or academic engagement takes place. We have distinguished between these spaces in terms of their on-campus and off-campus locations, and sought to show how this spatiality is itself an important component of university cultural strategies. In particular, we have highlighted examples from both cities of institutional resources being located off-campus (e.g. Northumbria University's Baltic 39, Culture Lab OnSite, UWE across various sites in central Bristol) for purposes including strengthening partnerships with creative arts organisations, increasing accessibility of the academic work to members of the public, and gaining access to extra space or new types of working environment.

These two types of space have different relationships to culture-based urban development.

Urban university campuses and surrounding areas are themselves often the location of cultural venues, which can be part of the institution's structures or operated by an independent organisation. These may be inherited assets from the university's past as a civic institution (for instance, the University of Bristol's Victoria Rooms and Wickham Theatre, or Newcastle University's Great North Museum), or they may be more recent facilities established primarily to support and enhance creative academic practice (such as Culture Lab or Northumbria University's Gallery North) that nevertheless have developed an external dimension beyond that of standard university departments or research centres. The public events or exhibitions that these types of venues host can bring an audience of people (and visiting groups such as local schoolchildren) otherwise unconnected to the university on to campus; although the often selective social makeup of this audience and disconnect from other parts of the university means that they add to the only ambivalent status of large central city based campuses as public spaces (c.f. Gumprecht 2007 on US college towns). The location of these venues on university campuses also means that they are unlikely to play the same role in culture-led regeneration, through for instance attracting tourism, property development or creative industry firms, that other more recognised 'cultural quarters' in the city assume (despite, for instance, Newcastle University's involvement in its city's bid to become European Capital of Culture).

In comparison, location of facilities off-campus can help universities tap into wider metropolitan creative energies and positive aspects of culture-based city development. This assumes a different form in the two cities discussed in this chapter. In Newcastle, this external environment has been reshaped by the public-funding-driven cultural regeneration strategy followed over the past fifteen years (jointly by Newcastle and Gateshead). Although Newcastle University made early teaching and research links with the two major arts organisations established at this time (the Baltic Centre for Contemporary Art and Sage Gateshead), more recently Northumbria University has taken this model of engagement in the city forward through its partnership with the Baltic and their shared facility in the centre of Newcastle that provides space for independent artist studios, a public gallery, and university teaching and practice. In Bristol, the external cultural environment is based more around the creative industries and established art organisations such as Watershed. Our more detailed example in this city, The Pervasive Media Studio, provides a distinctive type of off-campus setting and set of collaborative methods through which academics (initially from UWE but now also the University of Bristol and other collaborating institutions in the South West) can work in an environment that brings them into closer contact with creative industry practitioners in fields related to digital media and ubiquitous computing.

10 The embeddedness of universities in the city and the city in the university

Introduction

In the first part of this book we reviewed the links between universities and cities in terms of the impact of universities on the built form of the city, the urban economy and society. In the second part we have endeavoured to reveal how individual universities are embedded in particular cities – and how these cities are in turn embedded in the universities – by focusing on three urban themes, namely sustainable, healthy and creative cities. The four cities (and nine universities) that we have examined have been set in the context of a rapidly-changing policy environment for both higher education and city and regional development. In this concluding chapter we seek to connect the two halves of the book by examining: the role of the universities as civic institutions in enhancing capacity for innovation in the cities; the interconnectedness between the physical, economic and social dimensions of university embeddedness in the cities; the challenge of collaborative working, between disciplines and between institutions (different universities, public authorities and intermediate organisations); and finally the challenge of a turbulent public policy environment around higher education and urban development, in particular the ongoing period of austerity in public finances.

Universities and urban innovation

Chapters 4 and 5 highlighted the need to connect the economic and societal roles of universities in city development. In Chapter 4 we proposed the idea of the university as a source of 'slack' in a city or regional economy with the potential to enhance long term adaptability through generating new knowledge that can contribute to technological development in the private sector. In Chapter 5 we argued that a corresponding role in developing capacity in local civil society to shape future developments in the public interest, and in the process link the economic and societal domains, is just as important. In these respects the triple helix of universities, business and government becomes the quadruple helix which also embraces civil society. As Arnkil *et al.* note:

> The quadruple helix, with its emphasis on broad co-operation in innovation, represents a shift towards systemic, open and user centric innovation. An

era of linear, top-down, expert driven development is giving way to different forms and levels of co-production with consumers, customers and citizens.

(Arnkil *et al.* 2010)

An equally important concept is that of social innovation. According to the Board of European Policy Advisors, social innovations are:

> innovations that are social in both their ends and means. Specifically we define social innovations as new ideas (products, services and models) that simultaneously meet social needs ... and create new social relationships or collaborations. They are innovations that are not only good for society but enhance society's capacity to act. The *process of social interactions* between individuals undertaken to reach certain outcomes is participative, involves a number of actors and stakeholders who have a vested interest in solving a social problem, and empowers the beneficiaries.
>
> (BEPA 2011: 9–10; emphasis in original)

Such perspectives imply moving on from the model of the entrepreneurial university in which the principle driver is to act as a business by generating income principally from the private sector, to the civic university engaged across a wide range of disciplines with an equally wide range of stakeholders in a diverse external environment. To what extent have the universities in the cities that we have studied contributed towards building adaptive capacity, quadruple helix partnerships and social innovation in the inherently public interest domains of sustainability, health and culture?

In the area of sustainable development, the partnership between universities in the form of Manchester Knowledge Capital did play a key role in putting this topic on the local agenda and getting it embedded in the concerns of a new combined local authority structure through its standing Environment Commission. Corridor Manchester is a special purpose vehicle that combines university, public and private interests. In Newcastle, the Newcastle Science City partnership is building long term capacity for collaborative working around sustainability, with researchers in the Newcastle Institute for Research on Sustainability viewing the city as a 'living lab'. According to the Co-Director:

> The notion of treating our city and its region as a seedbed for sustainability initiatives is a potent one....The vision is of academics out in the community, working with local groups and businesses on practical initiatives to solve problems and promote sustainable development and growth .... This necessitates that we proceed in a very open manner to overcome barriers to thought, action and engagement; barriers between researchers and citizens, between the urban and the rural, between the social and natural sciences, between teaching, research and enterprise.
>
> (Personal communication, Philip Lowe to John Goddard, 4/4/2011)

In the field of health in Newcastle and Sheffield, the generation of new knowledge in human genetics and ageing, and around the determinants of ill health and the delivery of public health services, is highly embedded in urban institutions like NHS trusts and public health authorities in the cities. Genetic research is heavily dependent on local populations, and health service research works with the community in developing and evaluating new ways of delivering services that could be classified as social innovations. In the area of ageing research in Newcastle, the VOICENorth forum is playing a key role in the co-production of knowledge, and in the area of human genetics the University's Policy, Ethics and Life Sciences centre has helped through its Café Scientifique programme in raising public awareness of the ethical issues of stem cell research. And while the Newcastle science-based research may not quickly build a new economic base via high-tech spin-out companies, the development of assistive technologies for the elderly, new modes of retailing, new genetic testing tools and health service delivery improvements do offer the potential to build a stronger 'health economy', and at the same time break down health divides in the city.

Finally, in the cultural sphere, the generative and developmental roles of the universities in Newcastle and Bristol is even more intertwined in the fabric of urban institutions, and quintessentially bridges the economic and social domains. Unlike the other areas, the cultural and creative sectors are not dominated by monolithic organisations like the NHS and local authorities, and it has been even more necessary for the universities to be involved with intermediary organisations like Watershed in Bristol and New Writing North in Newcastle, and networks like the Bristol Cultural Development Partnership. Here the boundary between research, teaching and creative practice, and between the professional/commercial world and the general public, is even more blurred. ICT-based developments in pervasive media, being designed and tested not only in the lab but out in the city of Bristol in partnerships with companies and the community, will only accelerate this blurring. So, from whatever angle one looks at universities as civic institutions, it is clear that they are key actors in city-based creative economy ecosystems.

Critically, in all three fields the universities have worked with organisations specifically created to build bridges between the knowledge base, public authorities, business and the community – in effect to articulate the quadruple helix. And in several instances these networks have been facilitated by co-location of activities at a physical 'hub', often in a strategic location within the city, a subject to which we now turn.

The university footprint in the city – the physical, economic and societal dimensions

In Chapter 2 we highlighted the role of the university in 'place making' through its physical presence in the city. Our case studies go on to suggest that specific sites where academic and non-academic activities combine to deliver conjoint benefits can be equally important in embedding the university in the institutional fabric of the city, and on occasions facilitate the linking of the economic and social domains. For example, the Oxford Road corridor in Manchester is a site where the local authority, two universities and the health authority are working together as institutions to regenerate a part of the city in a sustainable way. The corridor is a site for academic research as a form of urban laboratory and, through the Low Carbon Economic Area, the monitoring of the environmental effects of changing traffic patterns. Likewise, the former Newcastle Brewery site (Science Central) being developed as part of Newcastle Science City is being used for experiments in exploring new forms of renewable energy, and as a potential opportunity for attracting mobile knowledge-based inward investment to the city centre. Both are adjacent to areas of social deprivation and, in the case of Manchester, the site of a new campus for one of the universities where it will be embedded in the local community.

In terms of the healthy city, off-campus dedicated sites are one of the means of achieving economic and social benefits of academic work in Newcastle. The Campus for Ageing and Vitality in the City's deprived West End combines leading-edge genetic science, work with patients with Parkinson's and Alzheimer's disease, research commercialisation (for example around assistive technologies), and links with the community and voluntary sector organisations based on the site. The International Centre for Life in Newcastle's city centre similarly houses scientific work undertaken through the University's Institute of Human Genetics, the NHS Fertility Testing Service (which is a source of human embryo stem cells), a 'manufacturing' facility to generate stem cells for clinical applications, a business incubator, conference facilities, and a visitor attraction focusing on the life sciences.

In terms of the creative city, on- and off-campus sites have been important loci for combining academic work and cultural practice, facilitating community engagement with the arts, and contributing to the creative economy. In Bristol, the Watershed building, which was part of a dockland physical regeneration scheme, has been a critical location for the development of pervasive media with the two universities, and acts as an interface with Bristol's vibrant digital media sector. The Baltic Centre for Contemporary Art in Gateshead and its extension in Newcastle (Baltic 39) are now central to the work of Northumbria University's Department of Arts, and the Sage music centre (also in Gateshead) was the initial home for Newcastle University's Folk and Traditional Music degree. In these sites, innovative creative practice in the academy interfaces with the general public in many ways, and contributes to the vitality of the city as a place to live and work (also Chapter 3).

On-campus dedicated sites (as distinct from academic departmental areas) have played a similar role as off-campus sites in the creative city. In Bristol, the University's Department of Music is based in a civic building with public performance space, and the Department of Drama has facilities in a theatre that shows productions by students alongside those of touring companies in its public programmes. Newcastle University's Culture Lab has provided a space for digital media experimentation and performance, and was previously home for the creative writing development agency New Writing North, which was linked to the University's School of English Language, Literature and Linguistics. This School has also made use of the University's Theatre run by the independent company Northern Stage for its work with young people. Last but not least, Newcastle University's Great North Museum is a major destination for young people learning about natural history, archaeology and the environment. Together, these sites could be viewed as a 'cultural quarter' on campus through which the city is physically embedded into the University.

These examples illustrate how difficult it is in practice to separate the physical, economic and social imprint of universities on their cities. The existence of university and non-university institutions, such as multi-disciplinary research institutes, visitor attractions and special purpose intermediary organisations like Newcastle's International Centre for Life, would, on the surface, appear to contribute to these synergies. We will now probe these conclusions by examining the actual collaboration process and mechanisms in action, both within the universities and between the universities and the city.

University/city partnership in action

In Chapter 4 we described the university as a 'loosely-coupled' organisation along three different lines: horizontally between different functional units (academic and service departments); vertically between different levels of the academic hierarchy (departments, faculties and central management); and in terms of links with the external environment, including the city (Rubin 1979). In our case studies we have focused on individual academic units and their responses to the challenges and opportunities of the external environment. Nevertheless, these units are all embedded in internal and external structures, where the university plays – and is expected to play – a role as a civic institution, mobilising its resources to meet quintessentially multi-disciplinary challenges, like urban sustainability, health and culture. Thus, achieving more sustainable urban development needs inputs from social scientists with interests in such topics as household behaviour, urban governance and economic regulation, as well as engineers focused on technical solutions such as energy use and distribution. Likewise, improving urban public health and the quality of life of an ageing population is not simply a matter for medical scientists. And enhancing the cultural vitality of cities in a digital age increasingly requires a blend of academic skills, which includes computer scientists as well as artists, musicians and creative writers.

As we have already noted with respect to sustainable development, the city can provide a 'living lab' in which academics can translate new ideas into practice. But achieving this is not without its challenges in terms of the ways in which different disciplines approach the laboratory. Is the city merely a source of subjects (as is usually the case in medical science), a site for detailed observation 'at a distance' of what is going on (classic social science) or for producing technical solutions to current problems (engineering)? Or can the city be a place for genuine co-production of multi-disciplinary knowledge involving a wide range of users and beneficiaries? As we noted in Chapter 4, in meeting these challenges there can be flexibility and openness on the part of individual academics, but the internal rigidity of the disciplinary-based university as an institution can create barriers to realising the potential of the university as a whole, not least because institutional change is slow. And because of this, an intermediary body operating between the university and the environment can play a role in accelerating the pace of change.

How have these coupling challenges been met in our case study cities and institutions? As revealed in our survey of individual academics and reported in Appendix B, researchers operating in the cross-disciplinary areas of sustainability, health and culture behave in a different way from the academic community as a whole. For example: in the area of sustainability, researchers from a range of disciplines are more likely to be involved in technological development, innovation and contributions to the economy through working with business and consultancy; a wide range of disciplines in addition to medical science are involved in the health field and are specifically seeking impact on socially-excluded or disadvantaged groups and on the delivery of health services; and in the area of arts and culture, public benefits are more highly rated than in other fields. But notwithstanding the stances of individual academics, handling these cross-disciplinary themes at an institutional level can be a challenge, particularly for research-intensive universities where the majority of academics are resourced via – and owe their allegiance to – disciplinary-based schools or departments, which are also usually the locus for undergraduate teaching. Such universities have characteristically sought to circumnavigate these challenges by the establishment of multi-disciplinary research groupings, which range from 'hard' research institutes employing their own staff, through 'soft' institutes sharing researchers with disciplinary departments and schools, to focused research centres accountable to specific schools.

We can see from our case studies that external university-level city partnerships can strengthen these internal structures, especially when these give academics access to new funding opportunities, space and key stakeholders outside of the university. We would highlight this interconnection between internal and external structures as one of the features that distinguishes the civic university from the entrepreneurial (where the focus is on income generation with less explicit external partnerships in civil society). Thus the International Centre for Life, established in Newcastle as an act of urban regeneration, enabled researchers from a wide range of disciplines in Newcastle University to come together in a 'hard' off-campus Institute of Human Genetics, and made it possible for the researchers to work alongside the NHS Genetic Testing Service. Likewise, the Campus for Ageing on the former site of the Newcastle General Hospital brings together researchers from a wide range of disciplines in a 'hard' Institute for Aging and Health. Stimulated by the need for a unified face to the Newcastle Science City partnership, Newcastle University established the 'soft' Newcastle Institute for Research on Sustainability (significantly without the word University in the title as an acknowledgement of the partnership with the city). The institute now leads on one of the University's three Societal Challenge themes (the others being Ageing and Social Renewal) with each being 'owned' by one of the University's three faculties. While the University of Sheffield's School of Health and Related Research (ScHARR) is an academic unit within the Faculty of Medicine, Dentistry and Health (like

Newcastle University's Institute of Health and Society), it is linked to a soft cross-faculty Centre for Health and Wellbeing in Public Policy, with the latter facilitating cross-disciplinary research with the social sciences – research which can have a specific urban focus. Within the University of Manchester, the highly-focused Corridor Manchester partnership has been supported by – and provided a focus for – research centres within the planning and architecture schools with externally funded programmes like EcoCities, even though the University has chosen not to establish a research institute in this area. Finally, in the field of urban culture and creativity, The Pervasive Media Studio in Bristol and Newcastle University's Culture Lab are venues where university-based artists and computer scientists have come together with those from outside the university to create new product for the digital age. Culture Lab is also home for a major externally-funded multi-disciplinary research programme on Social Inclusion in the Digital Economy.

By way of contrast, in the less research-intensive universities, the structures to facilitate engagement with the challenges of the city are often more clearly embedded in the basic organisational structure of the institution, as distinct from autonomous or semi-autonomous research entities. Thus Sheffield Hallam has a whole faculty of Health and Wellbeing which trains a range of health professionals, a Faculty level Centre for Health and Social Care Research, and an administrative Public Health Hub which acts as a portal to the external world. In the University of the West of England there is a whole Faculty of Arts, Creative Industries and Education, with the Department of Creative Industries running professional training programmes organised through its Bristol School of Animation. In both universities the organisational structures have made a close integration of teaching and research possible. This means that city-based professionals educated in the universities in fields related to health and the cultural industries have established the social relations through which knowledge exchange benefiting both the university and the city can take place.

How do these different types of university within the same city collaborate with each other and third parties in tackling urban challenges? Each of our cities contains two (three in the case of Greater Manchester) universities with different potential contributions to city development. In Greater Manchester, all of the universities worked together through Manchester Knowledge Capital, which provided a forum for new ideas and acted as a catalyst for collaborative projects around the sustainable city. Manchester University and Manchester Metropolitan University are both partners in Corridor Manchester. Newcastle Science City is a formally-constituted partnership between Newcastle University, Newcastle City Council and, up to its closure, the Regional Development Agency One NorthEast. (But the partnership did not include Northumbria University.) In Bristol, both universities are now partners in The Pervasive Media Studio located in the Watershed facility, thereby enhancing Watershed's role as a bridge between both universities and the digital culture scene in the city.

Alongside these formal institutional-level structures, academics from both Pre and Post 92 institutions work collectively in two of the urban challenge areas – health and culture – where the public sector has its own collaborative multi-level mechanisms that cannot be ignored. Thus in Sheffield, staff from the two universities work together with a number of NHS trusts from across the city region in a nationally-funded programme on Collaboration for Leadership in Applied Health Research and Care (CLAHRC), designed to improve the translation of medical and health research into clinical practice or products. Similarly in Newcastle, staff from Newcastle and Northumbria universities collaborate in one of the national Public Health Research Centres of Excellence. In both cities, individual academics have participated in the World Health Organisation's Healthy City initiative, and the institutions participate formally in local authority-based Local Strategic Partnership groupings dealing with health. In the cultural field, limited life initiatives like those organised around bids for designation as a Capital of Culture in both Bristol and Newcastle have engaged the universities. In summary, the diversity of models adopted by the universities to organise themselves internally to reach out to the city and the wider world is mirrored by the diversity of external structures through which cities engage with universities individually and collectively, and which range from the formal to the informal. It is a complex picture and many of the structures are fragile and susceptible to breaking down in a changing policy environment, both for universities and cities, a topic to which we now turn.

The challenge of a turbulent environment

Many of the collaborations between universities and cities that we have studied here have evolved over a decade or more and have taken different forms over this period. However, the 2008 financial crisis and the period of public austerity that has ensued – particularly under a new pro-market government intent on rolling back the boundaries of the state – has provided a real challenge to urban engagement by universities. Most significant have been the abolition of the Regional Development Agencies (RDAs) and the loss of the significant financial resources they brought to bear on urban regeneration and economic development, which universities have benefited from. (The demise of the RDAs has also removed one of the principle rationales for formal regional association of universities in each of the nine English regions which brought together universities with different missions – most of these have now been wound up.) RDAs have been replaced by private sector and local authority Local Enterprise Partnerships with limited financial and human resources that could enable them to work with universities. Despite the Government's purported commitment to localism, local authorities have come under severe financial pressure, as have bodies responsible for funding the performing arts, museums and galleries. In the latter area, the fiscal pressure has led to a concentration of resources on key venues, possibly at the expense of collaborative ventures with universities. Throughout the previous decade, the National Health Service has been subjected to frequent organisational change. Perhaps the most significant in relation to our concerns is the impending transfer of public health functions from the NHS to local government – a change that will inevitably disturb long-established relationships with university faculties of medicine and health. At the same time, the squeeze on NHS budgets will inevitably reduce expenditure on continuing professional training in universities for disciplines allied to medicine, which will affect universities like Sheffield Hallam and Northumbria offering these programmes and the knowledge exchange mechanisms that have flowed from such programmes.

The universities themselves have been subject to a major upheaval as a result of the Government's creation of a student marketplace though variable fees underwritten by the state and the withdrawal of direct government support for teaching in non-science subjects. Universities are now expected to compete for the best qualified students or lower their fees. At the same time, access agreements with the Government will require universities to recruit specified numbers of students from more disadvantaged backgrounds, regardless of location. So competition between universities nationally and locally, focused on the quality of its student experience and employment outcomes, will inevitably increase. To some extent, teaching and learning programmes that increase exposure to urban challenges may enhance the student experience and positively contribute to city development.

Budgets for university research have been protected, but there is a greater expectation that research should be designed to have a demonstrable impact on society, broadly defined. This may encourage more involvement of academics with the city on their doorstep and where such impacts may be more transparent. But given the fragility of the organisations academics might want to partner with to deliver these impacts and the absence of match funding, this may be difficult to achieve.

Universities and cities in an age of austerity

Although the empirical focus of our book has been England, austerity in public finances is an issue throughout the developed world and, both publicly-funded universities *and* cities are having to review their business and organisational models. Does this foreshadow a coming together of universities and cities on the basis on shared interests or a growing separation? In the case of higher education, some European countries are moving towards the introduction of significant student fees for those studying at public universities, 'modernising' their universities by the introduction of more managerial structures and, last but not least, concentrating public resources for research in a few elite institutions able to compete on the global stage for academic talent. In most countries these changes are being made with scant regard to the urban and regional consequences, because higher education and territorial policy remain separate domains. And yet we have demonstrated that in a number of ways universities are key assets for cities – as anchor institutions and important actors in urban innovation broadly defined. Like city governments, universities are key civic institutions engaged in a wide range of urban issues – business support, new enterprise formation, attracting inward investment, human capital development, health improvement, physical regeneration and place making, student housing and cultural production and consumption.

But unlike city authorities, universities do not operate within bounded territories and have the capacity to link the global and the local. In short, universities contribute to city development in the round. And within an individual city, different higher education institutions can play complementary roles.

But because of the separation of urban policy and higher education, and a general obsession with the higher education business interface, the full potential of universities as civic institutions has hitherto not been realised. Indeed, as we have noted for England, the outcome of changes in higher education policy, such as possible institutional failures, mergers and reductions in the number of non-local students, could have unintended consequences for individual cities. Likewise, the focus on competition for students could lead to less civic engagement and inter-university collaboration within cities. While cities may need a range of higher education institutions to achieve sustainable economic, social and cultural development, in many countries city authorities currently have no say in shaping the higher education sector, and indeed in the light of fiscal austerity may, like universities, be forced to look inwards and focus on the delivery of basic public services. In summary, civic engagement by universities is not only influenced by policy drivers from within higher education (the knowledge supply side) but by what is happening on the demand side locally and globally, and in the public as well as the private spheres. Given general austerity, there are very real dangers that bridges that have been built between universities and cities might collapse because the supporting pillars on both sides are knocked away.

However, this outcome is not inevitable if the mutual interests of the city and the university are fully appreciated on both sides and the economies that could arise from shared action identified. From the universities side, there is a great incentive to demonstrate their role in creating public benefits – not only what they are good at but what they are good for – and the city is one obvious arena within which to do this. This is particularly true in relation to such societal challenges as climate and demographic change and social inclusion. But this will require the university to make transparent to a broad audience their multi-faceted contributions to the city of the kind we have revealed in our case studies – to demonstrate that they are not only *in* the city but *of* the city. This is a challenge for the university insofar as much civic engagement takes place below the radar screen of institutional managers and is difficult to capture in conventional metrics.

For their part, city authorities need to explore with their universities what strategic functions the universities can perform individually and collectively with and for the city in terms of addressing the societal challenges it faces, whilst at the same time maintaining the university's integrity as an academic institution. In the process, it may be possible to identify fiscal savings for all concerned and developmental gains for the city that could arise from collaborative working. Across the world, OECD has been facilitating the building of such collaborations by a process of self evaluations and international peer reviews of university, city and regional partnerships. We hope that the insights from our book will underpin this ongoing process and contribute to the building of a global network of civic universities.

Appendix A: Interviews

The main method used for the research in this book was semi-structured qualitative interviews (see Chapter 6). In total 48 interviews were carried out across the four cities between January 2010 and November 2011. The interviews lasted between an hour and an hour and a half. Some interviews were with two interviewees (indicated over page).

In addition, where relevant, we have also drawn on interview material from two other projects. The first, a scoping project for a potential leadership development programme between universities and cities (in partnership with the Leadership Foundation for Higher Education and funded by the HEFCE Leadership, Management and Governance Fund), involved interviews with senior management in universities, city councils and other organisations in Bristol, Newcastle and Sheffield during 2009 (see Goddard *et al.* 2010). The second involved interviews with representatives from technology and innovation centres, the regional development agency, and Newcastle University in the North East of England during 2010 (see Goddard *et al.* 2012).

These interviews are listed over page by city and, for Newcastle, by the thematic area to which the interview corresponded. Because Newcastle was used as a case study across all three areas, several of the interviews in this city and the wider North East region were cross-thematic and have been drawn on for more than one chapter (as indicated). The right hand column lists the additional interviews from other projects that were used.

Newcastle interviews
Cross thematic area
1 One North East (RDA) – 29/01/10
2 Newcastle Science City Ltd – 08/02/10
3 Durham University – 17/02/10
4 Newcastle City Council – 18/02/10
5 Newcastle University – 05/03/10
6 Northumbria University – 30/03/10

Sustainability
1 Newcastle University – 11/04/10
2 Northumbria University – 01/06/10
3 Newcastle City Council – 07/07/11

Health
1 Newcastle University (2 interviewees) – 29/01/10
2 International Centre for Life (2 interviewees) – 17/02/10
3 Newcastle University – 03/03/10
4 Northumbria University – 09/06/10
5 Newcastle University – 19/07/11

Culture
1 Newcastle University – 08/02/10 and 17/02/10
2 Newcastle University – 19/07/10
3 Northumbria University – 20/07/10
4 New Writing North – 23/07/10
5 Newcastle University – 14/07/11
6 Northumbria University – 22/11/11
7 Northumbria University (2 interviewees) – 23/11/11

Newcastle interviews other projects
First project
1 Newcastle University (2 interviewees) – 19/05/09
2 Northumbria University – 15/06/09
3 Newcastle Science City Ltd – 25/06/09
4 Newcastle upon Tyne Hospitals NHS Foundation Trust– 26/06/09
5 Newcastle City Council – 06/07/09

Second project
1 Newcastle University – 08/07/10
2 One North East – 29/07/10
3 National Renewable Energy Centre (Narec) – 27/07/10

Manchester interviews
1 The University of Manchester – 12/05/10
2 ARUP consultants – 12/05/10
3 Manchester Commission for the New Economy – 26/05/10
4 The University of Salford – 26/05/10
5 Manchester City Council – 26/05/10
6 Manchester Metropolitan University – 14/06/10
7 North West Development Agency (RDA) – 14/06/10
8 Manchester: Knowledge Capital – 07/07/10
9 The University of Manchester – 18/08/10
10 Manchester Metropolitan University (2 interviewees) – 18/08/10
11 The University of Salford– 28/02/11
12 Corridor Manchester – 28/02/11
13 The University of Salford – 01/04/11

Sheffield interviews
1 Sheffield Hallam University (2 interviewees) – 18/05/10
2 Sheffield Hallam University – 21/07/10a
3 Sheffield Hallam University – 21/07/10b
4 NHS Sheffield – 02/06/11
5 The University of Sheffield – 02/06/11
6 The University of Sheffield – 28/07/11a
7 Sheffield City Council – 28/07/11
8 The University of Sheffield – 28/07/11b

Sheffield interviews other projects
First project
1 Sheffield Hallam University – 01/05/09
2 Sheffield City Council – 15/05/09
3 The University of Sheffield (2 intervie-wees) – 21/05/09
4 Sheffield NHS Foundation Trust – 29/06/09

Bristol interviews
1 University of the West of England – 17/05/11
2 National Co-ordinating Centre for Public Engagement – 17/05/11
3 The University of Bristol – 17/05/11a
4 The University of Bristol – 17/05/11b
5 Watershed/Pervasive Media Studio (2 interviewees) – 24/10/11
6 University of the West of England – 24/10/11

Bristol interviews from other projects
First Project
1 The University of Bristol – 27/03/09
2 University of the West of England – 27/03/09
3 Bristol West/Bristol Cultural Development Partnership (2 interviewees) – 08/05/09

Appendix B: Findings from a survey of individual academics' research impacts

1 Introduction

This appendix summarises results from an online questionnaire survey that explored the ways in which academics across different institutions and disciplines understand their research to have an 'impact' in the broadest possible sense. The aim of this piece of research was to contribute to a better understanding of the range of both academic and non-academic impacts that result from different forms of research and their possible relationships to activities such as teaching, consultancy, professional practice, commercialisation and public engagement. The position of this survey in this book is explained in the first section of Chapter 6. Chapter 6 also discusses the introduction of societal impact as criteria for research assessment in the UK higher education system, which formed a broader context for this survey.

The purpose of the survey (stated in the introduction to the questionnaire) was not to measure the impact of participants' research, but to determine: in which areas this impact lies; the factors that affect this; and how these vary across different disciplinary areas, academic positions and institutions. Most of the results cited in this appendix refer to the number of individual participants (expressed as a percentage) who indicated that they thought their research has a certain impact, without considering how the size of that impact varies between academics in different positions and universities. The survey was predicated on the assumption (also stated in the introduction) that all forms of academic research potentially have some form of wider impact.

In summer of 2010, invitations to participate in the survey were sent to a random sample (one third) of all academic staff (including research staff) from six universities in three of the same four English cities featured in the empirical work in this book – Bristol, Newcastle and Sheffield (but not Manchester) during the summer of 2010. In total, 711 responses were received from a sample of 2,372. Table B.1 breaks these 711 participants down according to the only two question fields in the survey that required a response: their university and with which of twelve disciplinary areas they most closely identified. The differences in

Table B.1 Number of participants by university and disciplinary areas

University	Participants	Disciplinary areas	Participants
Bristol University	168	Medicine and Health Sciences	131
Newcastle University	190	Biological Sciences	76
The University of Sheffield	157	Physical Sciences	65
		Mathematics and Statistics	36
		Computer Science	20
		Engineering	57
Pre 1992 total	*515*	*NAFS total*	*385*
University of the West of England	65	Business, Management, Economics	42
Northumbria University	75	Architecture, Planning, Built Environment	40
Sheffield Hallam University	56	Social Sciences	116
		Law	21
		Humanities and Languages	80
		Arts and Design	27
Post 1992 total	*196*	*HSS total*	*326*
Total	*711*	*Total*	*711*

numbers of participants between the Pre 1992 and Post 1992 universities largely reflect the different population sizes of eligible academic staff that we could identify from the institution's website, rather than large disparities in response rates. For simplicity, in the summary that follows, we frequently employ a distinction between the top six disciplinary areas in Table B.1 – a group that we will refer to collectively as the 'natural, applied and formal sciences' (NAFS) – and the bottom six – that we will refer to as the 'human or social subject' areas (HSS).

Table B.2 below also shows the numbers of participants by the type of academic position they identified themselves as holding, and how this varies between participants from the NAFS and HSS disciplines, and Pre 1992 and Post 1992 universities. The three groups shown here – Professors and Readers, Lecturers, and Research Fellows and Associates – are collated from eight options given in the question. This was not a compulsory question in the survey, but received 707 responses out of 711 participants in total.

The questionnaire had three sections:

1   *Research Profile* – consisted of background questions about the participant and their research activities, including their institution, disciplinary area and position.
2   *Research Impact* – consisted of questions about the areas of their research impacts, the groups or organisations who are beneficiaries of the research,

Table B.2 Number of participants by academic position: overall, NAFS and HSS disciplinary area groupings, and Pre and Post 1992 universities

| | Professors and Readers | | Lecturers | | Research Fellows and Associates | | Total |
	Number	%	Number	%	Number	%	Number
Overall	245	34.6	313	44.3	149	21.1	707
NAFS	141	36.6	136	35.3	108	28.1	385
HSS	104	32.3	177	55.0	41	12.7	322
Pre 1992	193	37.7	199	38.9	120	23.4	512
Post 1992	52	26.7	114	58.5	29	14.9	195

and the 'mechanisms' and 'intermediaries' they use to deliver these research impacts.

3   *Research Drivers and Barriers* – consisted of questions about the personal, institutional and wider environmental factors that encouraged or supported their research and its intended impact, and the factors that they had experienced as barriers to their research and its intended impact.

This appendix will outline the main findings and preliminary statistical analysis for the questions from section 2 only, because this represents material about forms of engagement through academic research that is of relevance to the rest of the book. Other results from this survey, including those for the questions in section 3, can be found in Vallance *et al.* (2011).

Section 2 of the questionnaire had three main questions, which enquired about, respectively: the broad areas in which participants thought their research was having an impact; the groups or organisations that are beneficiaries of the research; and the mechanisms they use to deliver these research impacts. For these three questions we introduced a qualitative distinction between 'primary' and 'secondary' research impacts or beneficiaries to distinguish between the different more direct and less direct ways in which academic research can have a societal impact. This distinction was presented in the questionnaire using the following definitions:

> By a primary impact or beneficiary we mean the main areas or groups for which your research is designed to directly and intentionally result in benefits. By a secondary impact or beneficiary we mean the other areas or groups that your research may indirectly benefit, even if this impact is not one of the main aims of the research.

In the three question areas, participants were asked to indicate, for various given categories, whether they thought they were having a primary impact, secondary impact or no impact, or whether the option was not applicable to them. Between

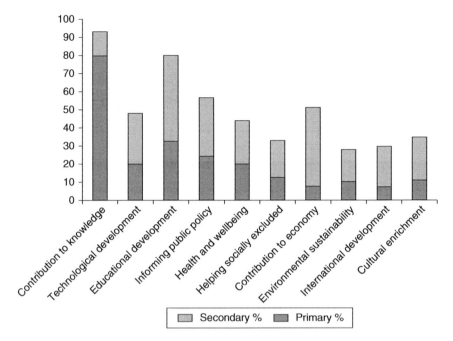

Figure B.1 'In which of the following areas do you think your research is having either a primary or secondary impact?': Overall (n = 711).

ten and fourteen potential areas, beneficiaries or mechanisms were selected as categories for each of these three questions. These were chosen through the survey design process to give as broad and inclusive range of both 'academic' based categories and 'non-academic' based categories of impact as possible.

These categories are shown along the x-axis of figures B.1 to B.3. Slightly shortened labels are used for the categories in these figures, but elsewhere in this appendix, the full wording is used as it appeared in the questionnaire. These graphs show overall response levels (percentages of all participants in the survey) for the primary impact and secondary impact options in these three questions. These are presented as a stacked bar so that the level of total positive response (primary + secondary impact) is also displayed.

This summary is divided into five further brief sections. Section 2 discusses the main patterns in the results for all participants shown in figures B.1 to B.3 and analyses how they vary by disciplinary area. Section 3 outlines and discusses differences in results by participants from Pre and Post 1992 universities. Sections 4 through 6 use results from the survey to shed light on research impacts connected to the three areas that were covered in the empirical chapters in Part II, namely sustainable development, public health and wellbeing, and links with the cultural sector.

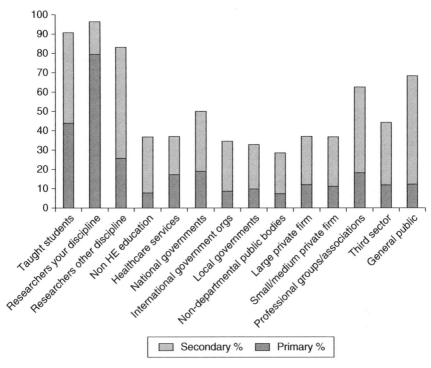

Figure B.2 'Which of the following types of group or organisation do you think are either primary or secondary beneficiaries of your research?': Overall (n = 711).

2   Academic and non-academic impacts

Figures B.1 to B.3 show that, at this level of all participants, the categories receiving clearly the biggest response for primary impact and total positive response (primary + secondary impact) relate to 'academic' rather than 'non-academic' impacts for all three questions – 'contribution to scientific/academic knowledge or method' (area of research impact), 'academics or postgraduate researchers in your discipline' (beneficiaries of research impact), and 'dissemination through academic publications or conferences' (mechanism of research impact). Respectively, 93.4, 96.2, and 97.9 per cent of all participants responded that these categories were either a primary or a secondary impact. Moreover, most participants indicated that their impact in these categories was a primary impact (79.9, 79.7 and 90.7 per cent respectively), which means that it is a direct and intended product of their research activity.

These overall results could in part be explained by these academic impacts being more generally relevant across all disciplinary groups than the other

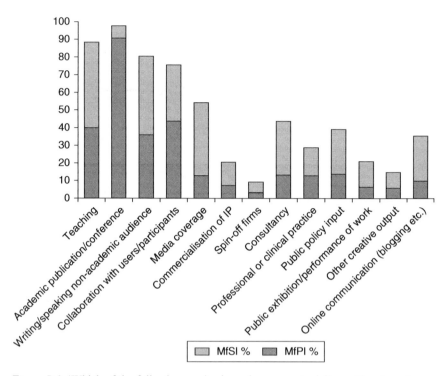

Figure B.3 'Which of the following mechanisms do you use to deliver either the primary or secondary impacts of your research?': Overall (n = 711).

categories that often will only be more widely applicable within certain specialist fields. It is, therefore, important to examine how these results vary at the level of individual disciplinary areas. In this case, however, the same broad pattern is also seen for almost all academic fields. Table B.3 shows the ranking of disciplinary areas by total positive response (primary + secondary impact) for the 'contribution to scientific/academic knowledge or method' category in the first question. This shows that, for all but one of the disciplinary areas, over 80 per cent of participants responded that this was an area of either primary or secondary impact, and for three of them the total positive response was 100 per cent. A very similar pattern (with slight variations in the ranking of the disciplinary areas) exists here for the 'academics or postgraduate researchers in your discipline' and 'dissemination through academic publications or conferences' categories in the other two questions.

The other important measure in these ranking tables is the level of primary impact, which indicates the extent to which any impact comes directly and intentionally from the participant's research. The *Primary%/Total%* column shows the proportion of the total positive impact that is a primary impact (between 0

Table B.3 Disciplinary area ranking for 'Contribution to scientific/academic knowledge or method' (as an area of research impact)

Rank	Discipline area (n)	Primary %	Secondary %	Total %	Primary%/ Total%
1	Physical Sciences (65)	96.9	3.1	100.0	0.97
2	Biological Sciences (76)	90.8	9.2	100.0	0.91
3	Medicine and Health Sciences (131)	90.1	9.9	100.0	0.90
4	Social Sciences (116)	70.7	25.9	96.6	0.73
5	Engineering (57)	75.4	19.3	94.7	0.80
6	Architecture, Planning, Built Environment (40)	70.0	22.5	92.5	0.76
7	Mathematics and Statistics (36)	86.1	5.6	91.7	0.94
8	Computer Science (20)	85.0	5.0	90.0	0.94
9	Business, Management, Economics (42)	66.7	21.4	88.1	0.76
10	Humanities and Languages (80)	78.8	3.8	82.6	0.95
11	Law (21)	66.7	14.3	81.0	0.82
12	Arts and Design (27)	44.4	22.2	66.6	0.67

and 1). So in Table B.3, this is high (e.g. > 0.75) for most of the disciplinary areas and very high (e.g. ≥ 0.9) for half of them. Again, there is a similar pattern for the other main 'academic' beneficiary or mechanism categories in the second and third questions of this section. This strongly suggests that most of the survey participants' research activity is orientated towards, in the first place, contributing to (mainly disciplinary) knowledge and generating academic outputs (e.g. publications, etc.).

The other main form of broadly 'academic' research impacts were in categories that indicated a relationship between research and teaching – 'undergraduate or postgraduate taught students' as beneficiaries of research (Figure B.2), and 'teaching' as a mechanism for delivering research impact (Figure B.3). These are both the categories with the second largest positive response at the level of the overall participation for their questions – respectively 91.1 and 88.8 per cent (primary + secondary impact). Table B.4 shows how the results for the 'teaching' as a mechanism for delivering research impact category varies between participants from disciplinary areas on the NAFS and HSS sides of our classification (see Table B.1). The most notable difference here is that the mechanism for primary impact response is much higher for the HSS disciplines (53.1 per cent) than it is for the NAFS disciplines (29.1 per cent). This indicates that teaching is more integral to the delivery of the main intended benefits of research in HSS disciplinary areas (e.g. Humanities and Languages, Law, or Business, Management and Economics) than it is in the main scientific disciplines.

Table B.4 also shows the results for those that are classified as Lecturers, and not Professors/Readers or Research Associates/Fellows (see Table B.2) who may not be directly involved with teaching. Unsurprisingly, the response for both primary and total impact is higher for the lecturers sub-group than it is for the overall participation, indicating that this relationship between research and teaching

Table B.4 Results for 'Teaching' (as a mechanism of delivering research impact): Overall and Lecturers only

	MfPI[a] %	MfSI[a] %	Total %	MfPI%/Total%
Overall (n = 711)	40.1	48.7	88.8	0.45
NAFS (n = 385)	29.1	57.7	86.8	0.34
HSS (n = 326)	53.1	38.0	91.1	0.58
Lecturers only (n = 313)	46.0	46.0	92.0	0.50
NAFS (n = 136)	30.9	58.8	89.7	0.34
HSS (n = 177)	57.6	36.2	93.8	0.61

Note
a Key: MfPI = mechanism for primary impact, MfSI = mechanism for secondary impact.

is further strengthened when only participants who are likely to teach are considered. This also shows that the divide between the HSS and NAFS disciplines remains present for this sub-group, demonstrating that this is not caused by the higher proportion of lecturers amongst respondents from the HSS side (see Table B.2).

Unsurprisingly, the 'non-academic' categories of research impact included in these questions have lower response levels amongst all participants (figures B.1, B.2, B.3). These also vary much more between disciplinary areas, reflecting different areas of specialisation and engagement across different academic fields. This is illustrated by tables B.5 and B.6, which gives the ranking of the top eight disciplines for the 'technological development or innovation' and 'helping socially excluded or disadvantages groups' categories in question 1. These show that only in selected cases (for instance with computer science for 'technological development or innovation') do individual disciplinary areas reach the levels of total positive (primary + secondary) impact (e.g. > 90 per cent) typical of the main categories of academic impact discussed above (see Table B.3). These two tables also demonstrate the division between disciplinary areas on the HSS and NAFS sides of our classification (see Table B.1) observable in some categories: 'technological development or innovation' has the six NAFS areas in the top six places, while conversely the top eight for 'helping socially excluded or disadvantaged groups' is made up predominately (but not exclusively) of disciplines from the HSS side.

The 'non-academic' categories of research impact differ from the main 'academic' categories even more markedly in terms of the proportion of their total positive response, that is for primary impact. In most cases, even at the level of individual disciplinary areas, the *Primary%/Total%* measure is less than 0.5 for non-academic categories of research impact (compare to Table B.3). This indicates that, for most participants, impact relating to these categories is secondary or indirect to the main purpose of their research activity. Interestingly, this pattern is particularly strong for the 'contribution to the economy' category: only 7.6 per cent of all participants responded that their research had a primary impact

Table B.5 Disciplinary area ranking (top 8) for 'Technological development or innovation' (as an area of research impact)

Rank	Discipline area (n)	Primary %	Secondary %	Total %	Primary%/ Total%
1	Computer Science (20)	50.0	45.0	95.0	0.53
2	Engineering (57)	56.1	29.8	85.9	0.65
3	Physical Sciences (65)	33.8	50.8	84.6	0.40
4	Biological Sciences (76)	23.7	47.4	71.1	0.33
5	Mathematics and Statistics (36)	30.6	33.3	63.9	0.48
6	Medical and Health Sciences (131)	22.1	35.9	58.0	0.38
7	Arts and Design (27)	14.8	29.6	44.4	0.33
8	Architecture, Planning, Built Environment (40)	17.5	20.0	37.5	0.47

Table B.6 Disciplinary area ranking (top 8) for 'Helping socially excluded or disadvantaged groups' (as an area of research impact)

Rank	Discipline area (n)	Primary %	Secondary %	Total %	Primary%/ Total%
1	Social Sciences (116)	30.2	39.7	69.9	0.43
2	Architecture, Planning, Built Environment (40)	15.0	30.0	45.0	0.33
3 =	Business, Management, Economics (42)	21.4	21.4	42.8	0.50
3 =	Law (21)	19.0	23.8	42.8	0.44
5	Medical and Health Sciences (131)	15.3	27.5	42.8	0.36
6	Computer Science (20)	15.0	20.0	35.0	0.43
7	Arts and Design (27)	14.8	11.1	25.9	0.57
8	Humanities and Languages (80)	7.5	17.5	25.0	0.30

in this area (compared to 44.2 per cent a secondary impact, Figure B.1). Table B.7 gives the disciplinary ranking for this category.

Here, the *Primary%/Total%* measure remains low (< 0.3) for all the disciplinary areas including engineering and computer science. This broad pattern is repeated for economic-related categories in the other two questions; for instance 'large' and 'small or medium firms in the private sector' as the beneficiaries of research, and 'consultancy', 'commercialisation of intellectual property' and 'spin-off firms' for the mechanisms. This means that, while many academics feel that their research makes some contribution to the economy, little of this is direct.

3   Pre 1992 and Post 1992 universities

The survey included three Pre 1992 and three Post 1992 universities to allow investigation of whether there was evidence that perceived differences between these two types of institutions (see Chapter 6) had an observable effect on the

Table B.7 Disciplinary area ranking for 'Contribution to the economy' (as an area of research impact)

Rank	Discipline area (n)	Primary %	Secondary %	Total %	Primary%/ Total%
1	Engineering (57)	24.6	61.4	86.0	0.29
2	Computer Science (20)	15.0	55.0	70.0	0.21
3	Physical Sciences (65)	10.8	56.9	67.7	0.16
4	Business, Management, Economics (42)	14.3	52.4	66.7	0.21
5	Biological Sciences (76)	6.6	55.3	61.9	0.11
6	Architecture, Planning, Built Environment (40)	5.0	50.0	55.0	0.09
7	Mathematics and Statistics (36)	2.8	50.0	52.8	0.05
8	Arts and Design (27)	14.8	37.0	51.8	0.29
9	Medicine and Health Sciences (131)	3.8	40.5	44.3	0.09
10	Social Sciences (116)	4.3	31.9	36.2	0.12
11	Humanities and Languages (80)	1.3	30.0	31.3	0.04
12	Law (21)	4.8	23.8	28.6	0.20

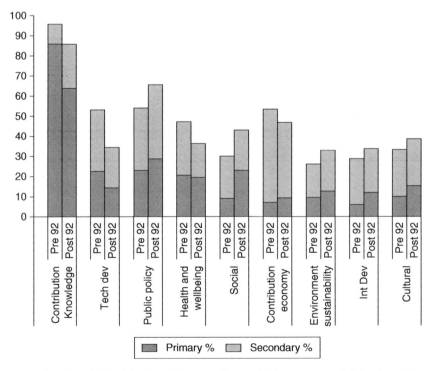

Figure B.4 'In which of the following areas do you think your research is having either a primary or secondary impact?': Overall Pre and Post 1992 universities (n = 515/196).

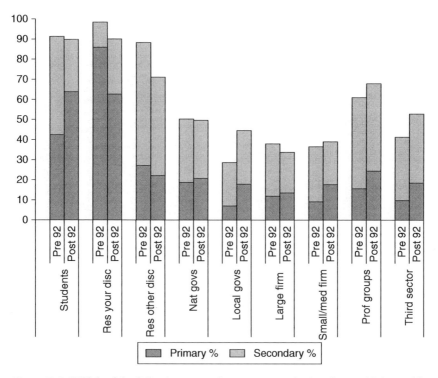

Figure B.5 'Which of the following types of group or organisation do you think are either primary or secondary beneficiaries of your research?': Overall Pre and Post 1992 universities (n = 515/196).

research practice of individual academics. Figures B.4 to B.6 compare the differences in response for all participants from Pre 1992 and Post 1992 universities for the three questions in section 2 of the questionnaire (with selected categories shown and shortened labels on the x-axis).

The graphs show several clear differences (generally more in levels of primary impact than total impact) on some points that we may expect for these two types of institution. For instance, the Pre 1992 universities have higher (percentage) levels for the main areas of 'academic' impact discussed above, while Post 1992 universities have clearly higher primary impact response levels for various categories with which they may be more readily associated, for example: 'helping socially excluded' (Figure B.4); 'local governments' and 'small and medium private firms' (Figure B.5); and 'teaching' and 'consultancy' (Figure B.6). However, this comparison does not take into account the differences in composition of the Pre and Post 1992 participants in terms of disciplinary areas. Table B.8 shows this breakdown along the lines of the split between the six NAFS disciplines and the six HSS disciplines. This shows that the share varies significantly: 64.3 per cent of Pre 1992 university participants came from the NAFS side and 35.7 per cent from

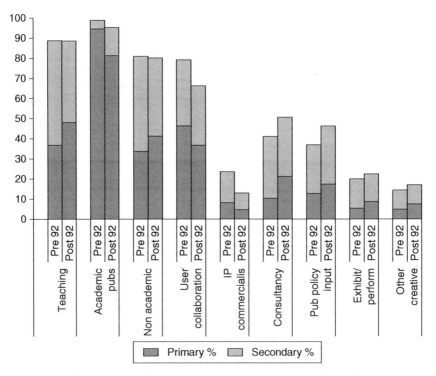

Figure B.6 'Which of the following mechanisms do you use to deliver either the primary or secondary impacts of your research?': Overall Pre and Post 1992 universities (n = 515/196).

the HSS side, compared to 27.6 per cent NAFS and 72.4 per cent HSS for the Post 1992 participation. This, we would suggest, is above all a reflection of the comparative rarity of large-scale medical, science and engineering research communities in Post 1992 universities.

This raises the possibility that the overall differences observed in figures B.4 to B.6 could just be caused by these differences in the composition of populations, rather than attributable to any institutional differences between Pre and Post 1992 universities. For instance, the higher response by participants from Pre 1992 universities for the 'technological development and innovation' or 'healthcare or public health and wellbeing' categories in the areas of research impact question (Figure B.4) could largely be due to the higher proportion of Pre 1992 participants from disciplinary areas such as Engineering or Medicine and Health Sciences.

To examine the effect that these variations in sample composition have, we have also compared the results for Pre and Post 1992 university participants for the NAFS and HSS groupings to see if similar differences in response recur for these smaller units. Tables B.9 to B.11 show, for selected categories in each of the

Table B.8 Number of participants by disciplinary area from Pre and Post 1992 universities

Disciplinary area	Pre 1992		Post 1992	
	Number	%	Number	%
Medicine and Health Sciences	112	21.7	19	9.7
Biological Sciences	68	13.2	8	4.1
Physical Sciences	58	11.3	7	3.6
Mathematics and Statistics	30	5.8	6	3.1
Computer Science	13	2.5	7	3.6
Engineering	50	9.7	7	3.6
NAFS	*331*	*64.3*	*54*	*27.6*
Business, Management, Economics	15	2.9	27	13.8
Architecture, Planning, Built Environment	17	3.3	23	11.7
Social Sciences	79	15.3	37	18.9
Law	6	1.2	15	7.7
Humanities and Languages	60	11.7	20	10.2
Arts and Design	7	1.4	20	10.2
HSS	*184*	*35.7*	*142*	*72.4*
Total	*515*		*196*	

Table B.9 Differences in primary impact between Pre and Post 1992 universities for selected areas of research impact: Overall participation, NAFS and HSS

	Pre 1992	Post 1992	Difference
	Primary %	Primary %	%
Contribution to scientific/academic knowledge or method			
Overall (n = 515/196)	86.0	63.8	+ 22.2
NAFS (n = 331/54)	90.3	77.8	+ 12.5
HSS (n = 184/142)	78.3	58.5	+ 19.8
Technological development or innovation			
Overall (n = 515/196)	22.7	14.3	+ 8.4
NAFS (n = 331/54)	31.7	31.5	+ 0.2
HSS (n = 184/142)	6.5	7.7	− 1.2
Healthcare or public health and wellbeing			
Overall (n = 515/196)	20.6	19.4	+ 1.2
NAFS (n = 331/54)	25.7	37.0	− 11.3
HSS (n = 184/142)	11.4	12.7	− 1.3
Helping socially excluded or disadvantaged groups			
Overall (n = 515/196)	9.1	23.0	− 13.9
NAFS (n = 331/54)	5.7	16.7	− 11.0
HSS (n = 184/142)	15.2	25.4	− 10.2

Table B.10 Differences in primary impact between Pre and Post 1992 universities for selected beneficiaries of research impact: Overall participation, NAFS and HSS

	Pre 1992	Post 1992	Difference
	Primary %	Primary %	%
Academics or postgraduate researchers in your discipline			
Overall (n = 515/196)	86.2	62.8	+ 23.4
NAFS (n = 331/54)	85.8	68.5	+ 17.3
HSS (n = 184/142)	87.0	60.6	+ 26.4
Local governments			
Overall (n = 515/196)	7.6	17.9	− 10.3
NAFS (n = 331/54)	3.9	16.7	− 12.8
HSS (n = 184/142)	14.1	18.3	− 4.2
Small or medium firms in the private sector (under 250 employees)			
Overall (n = 515/196)	9.1	17.9	− 8.8
NAFS (n = 331/54)	11.2	20.4	− 9.2
HSS (n = 184/142)	5.4	16.9	− 11.5
Third sector			
Overall (n = 515/196)	9.7	18.4	− 8.7
NAFS (n = 331/54)	6.9	7.4	− 0.5
HSS (n = 184/142)	14.7	22.5	− 7.8

three questions, the difference in primary (and not total) impact response between Pre and Post 1992 universities for the overall, NAFS and HSS participation. A positive figure in the 'Primary % Difference' column shows where the Pre 1992 positive impact response is higher than the Post 1992 response and by how much, and a negative figure where the Post 1992 response is higher than the Pre 1992.

These tables show that for some categories clear differences between participants from Pre and Post 1992 universities in the overall response also exist for participants from both the NAFS and HSS sides. This corroborates that in these areas the varying institutional orientation and culture of these two types of university does seem to have a demonstrable effect on individual research practice. Categories for which the Post 1992 university response is clearly higher for different disciplinary groupings (by those indicating that their research has a primary impact) are: 'helping socially excluded or disadvantaged groups' (areas of research impact); 'small or medium firms in the private sector' (beneficiaries of research impact); and 'consultancy' (mechanisms of research impact). Categories for which the Post 1992 response is higher, but by a less conclusive amount, or for only one of either the NAFS or HSS disciplinary groups, are: 'local governments' and 'third sector' (beneficiaries of research impact); and 'dissemination through writing or speaking for non-academic audiences' and 'teaching' (mechanisms of research impact).

Table B.11 Differences in primary impact between Pre and Post 1992 universities for selected mechanisms of research impact: Overall participation, NAFS and HSS

	Pre 1992	Post 1992	Difference
	Primary %	Primary %	%
Dissemination through academic publications/conferences			
Overall (n = 515/196)	94.4	81.1	+ 13.3
NAFS (n = 331/54)	96.7	87.0	+ 9.7
HSS (n = 184/142)	90.2	78.9	+ 11.3
Teaching			
Overall (n = 515/196)	37.1	48.0	−10.9
NAFS (n = 331/54)	28.7	31.5	−2.8
HSS (n = 184/142)	52.2	54.2	−2.0
Dissemination through writing/speaking for non-academic audiences			
Overall (n = 515/196)	33.8	41.3	−7.5
NAFS (n = 331/54)	29.0	35.2	−6.2
HSS (n = 184/142)	42.4	43.7	−1.3
Collaboration with research participants or users			
Overall (n = 515/196)	46.4	36.7	+ 9.7
NAFS (n = 331/54)	53.2	44.4	+ 8.8
HSS (n = 184/142)	34.2	33.8	+ 0.4
Consultancy			
Overall (n = 515/196)	10.5	21.4	−10.9
NAFS (n = 331/54)	12.1	20.4	−8.3
HSS (n = 184/142)	7.6	21.8	−14.2

The only categories for which the Pre 1992 response is consistently much higher for all the groupings looked at are the main 'academic' forms of research impact for each question mentioned above (respectively, 'contribution to scientific/ academic knowledge or method', 'academics or postgraduate researchers in your discipline' and 'dissemination through academic publications or conferences'). 'Collaboration with research participants or users' (mechanisms of research impact) also has a clearly higher response from Pre 1992 participants from the NAFS side, but only marginally from the HSS side.

4   Sustainability

Each of the three areas covered in the preceding empirical chapters broadly corresponds to one or more categories covered in the questions in section 2 of the survey discussed above. In the remaining three sections of this appendix we will take these themes, starting with sustainability (Chapter 7), and analyse the categories in more detail to elucidate patterns of academic engagement through

Table B.12 Disciplinary area ranking (top 8) for 'Sustainable development or environmental protection' (as an area of research impact)

Rank	Discipline area (n)	Primary %	Secondary %	Total %	Primary%/ Total%
1	Architecture, Planning, Built Environment (40)	30.0	40.0	70.0	0.43
2	Engineering (57)	26.3	38.6	64.9	0.41
3	Physical Sciences (65)	9.2	24.6	33.8	0.27
4	Business, Management, Economics (42)	14.3	19.0	33.3	0.43
5	Biological Sciences (76)	15.8	15.8	31.6	0.50
6	Social Sciences (116)	12.9	18.1	31.0	0.42
7	Arts and Design (27)	3.7	25.9	29.6	0.13
8	Mathematics and Statistics (36)	11.1	13.9	25.0	0.44

research. For this we use disciplinary rankings to show how engagement varies across different fields, and we use cross-tabulations with other categories to show where there are possible relationships with other forms of research impact area, beneficiaries or mechanisms.

Table B.12 shows the disciplinary area ranking for the 'sustainable development or environmental protection' category from the first areas of research impact question. The notable feature of this table – more so than the disciplinary ranking for other areas of research impact – is the evenness of the split in ranking between areas from the NAFS and HSS side in our classification outlined in Table B.1; starting with the two highest ranking disciplines of Architecture, Planning, Built Environment and Engineering. This equal distribution gives a clear reflection of the diverse technical and sociological nature of the scientific problems associated with this field.

Table B.13 shows this 'sustainable development or environmental protection' category cross-tabulated against selected categories from each of the questions in this section of the survey. This analysis shows whether participants who responded that their research had a primary impact in sustainability were more or less likely to also have a primary or secondary impact relating to other fields (the 'other' non-primary group combines those who responded secondary impact, no impact, not applicable or skipped this sustainability category). To ensure these two groups are broadly comparable in terms of disciplinary composition, we have just taken participants from the top six ranking disciplinary areas for the 'sustainable development or environmental protection' category shown in Table B.12 (Architecture, Planning, Built Environment; Engineering; Physical Sciences; Business, Management, Economics; Biological Sciences; Social Sciences).

This table shows that participants who identified their research as having a primary impact in 'sustainable development or environmental protection' were much more likely to indicate they also had a primary impact in the related areas of 'technological development or innovation' and 'contribution to the economy'. This pattern is also seen in economic-based categories of research beneficiaries

Table B.13 Cross-tabulations of 'Sustainable development or environmental protection' (top 6 disciplinary areas) against other areas, beneficiaries and mechanisms of research impact

Areas	Contribution to knowledge			Technological development			Informing public policy			Helping socially excluded			Contribution to the economy			International development		
Sustainable development	P%	S%	N%	P%	S%	N%	P%	S%	N%	P%	S%	N%	P%	S%	N%	P%	S%	N%
Primary (66)	**78.8**	15.2	6.0	**45.5**	21.2	33.3	**47.0**	36.4	16.6	**25.8**	16.7	57.5	**30.3**	43.9	25.8	**28.8**	28.8	42.4
Other (330)	**79.1**	17.6	3.3	**17.6**	30.9	51.5	**25.8**	32.1	42.1	**11.5**	21.2	67.3	**5.8**	49.7	44.5	**4.5**	26.1	69.4

Beneficiaries	Researchers your discipline			Researchers other disciplines			National governments			Local governments			Large firms			Small/medium firms		
Sustainable development	P%	S%	N%	P%	S%	N%	P%	S%	N%	P%	S%	N%	P%	S%	N%	P%	S%	N%
Primary (66)	**74.2**	18.2	7.6	**21.2**	62.1	16.7	**53.0**	25.8	21.2	**33.3**	34.8	31.9	**34.8**	22.7	42.5	**36.4**	18.2	45.4
Other (330)	**82.4**	16.7	0.9	**25.5**	62.1	12.4	**17.3**	36.7	46.0	**11.8**	22.1	66.1	**13.3**	29.4	57.3	**10.3**	32.4	57.3

Mechanisms	Teaching			Academic publication/ conference			Writing/speaking for non-academic audience			Collaboration with research users/ participants			Commercialisation of intellectual property			Consultancy		
Sustainable development	P%	S%	N%	P%	S%	N%	P%	S%	N%	P%	S%	N%	P%	S%	N%	P%	S%	N%
Primary (66)	**48.5**	39.4	12.1	**90.9**	9.1	0.0	**56.1**	34.8	9.1	**63.6**	27.3	9.1	**15.2**	18.2	66.6	**40.9**	28.8	30.3
Other (330)	**36.7**	52.1	11.2	**90.9**	8.2	0.9	**36.4**	44.2	19.4	**42.1**	35.8	22.1	**7.0**	13.6	79.4	**11.5**	32.7	55.8

and mechanism, such as 'large' and 'small firms', and in particular 'consultancy' (but much less so for 'commercialisation of intellectual property'). This analysis also suggests a relationship between sustainability and 'informing public policy' as an area of research impact and government at different scales (national, local, international) as beneficiaries. By comparison, the academic categories (e.g. 'contribution to scientific/academic knowledge or method', 'academic or postgraduate researchers in your discipline') showed little difference between the primary and non-primary group. Interestingly, 'academic or postgraduate researchers in other disciplines' was slightly less for the primary group, suggesting that cross-disciplinary work is not widely practiced in this field, despite the interdisciplinary nature of the problems it involves.

5   Health

The Medical and Health Sciences was the largest of twelve disciplinary areas in terms of numbers of participants in the survey (131 out of 711 in total, Table B.1). It was, unsurprisingly, the disciplinary area with clearly the highest proportion of participants responding that their research had either a primary or secondary impact for categories with a direct connection to health: 'healthcare or public health and wellbeing' (area of research impact); 'healthcare services' (beneficiaries of research impact); 'professional or clinical practice' (mechanism of research impact). However, it also ranked highly for other categories of both scientific and societal impact. Table B.3 above shows that all participants from this field responded that they had either a primary or secondary impact relating to 'contribution to scientific/academic knowledge or method'. Table B.6 above also shows that this was the highest ranking disciplinary area on the NAFS side of our distinction for the category 'helping socially excluded or disadvantaged groups', which was a result repeated across other societal-based categories of research impact not shown here.

However, impact within the field of health (Chapter 8) is not just restricted to the Medical and Health Sciences. Table B.14 gives the disciplinary ranking for the category of 'healthcare or public health and wellbeing' as an area of research impact. Below the Medical and Health Sciences there are HSS-side disciplines (such as Social Sciences and Business, Management, Economics) as well as other NAFS-side disciplines (principally Biological Sciences). It should be noted, however, that the level of primary impact in this category is much lower for all these disciplines than it is for Medical and Health Sciences (59.5 per cent).

Again, we have cross-tabulated this 'healthcare or public health and wellbeing' category against other forms of research impact for the top six ranking disciplinary areas shown in Table B.14 (Medical and Health Sciences; Biological Sciences; Physical Sciences; Social Sciences; Business, Management, Economics; Computer Science). The results, shown in Table B.15, indicate the strongest relationship is with healthcare services as a beneficiary of research impact: an extremely high 72.8 per cent of those who responded that they had a primary impact for 'healthcare or public health and wellbeing' also responded

Table B.14 Disciplinary area ranking (top 8) for 'Healthcare or public health and wellbeing' (as an area of research impact)

Rank	Discipline area (n)	Primary %	Secondary %	Total %	Primary%/ Total%
1	Medical and Health Sciences (131)	59.5	32.1	91.6	0.65
2	Biological Sciences (76)	11.8	50.0	61.8	0.19
3	Physical Sciences (65)	6.2	32.3	38.5	0.16
4	Social Sciences (116)	18.1	19.8	37.9	0.48
5	Business, Management, Economics (42)	19.0	16.7	35.7	0.53
6	Computer Science (20)	25.0	10.0	35.0	0.71
7 =	Engineering (57)	10.5	22.8	33.3	0.32
7 =	Mathematics and Statistics (36)	8.3	25.0	33.3	0.25

that 'healthcare services' were a primary beneficiary of their research, against only 5.2 per cent in the non-primary group. By comparison, the corresponding results for the proportion of this primary group for whom other types of organisations active in this field of public health – 'local governments' and 'third sector' – are also primary beneficiaries of their research are much lower (17.6 and 19.2 per cent respectively). The other interesting pattern here is that the primary group for 'healthcare or public health and wellbeing' were not more likely than the non-primary group to respond that their research also had a primary impact for 'contribution to the economy' and related categories (e.g. 'small/medium firms in the private sector', 'commercialisation of intellectual property'). This reinforces questions raised in Chapter 8 about the widespread scale of economic development benefits that may be leveraged from medical science expertise in universities.

6 Culture

For links with the cultural sector we have chosen to highlight two categories from the mechanisms of research impact question, namely 'public exhibition or performance of work' and 'other creative output'. Taken together, these complementary categories give the closest approximation to the concerns of Chapter 9 out of any of the options included in the survey design. For analysis, we have combined these categories in the disciplinary ranking shown in Table B.16. Participants who indicated that they used either (or both) of these mechanisms for their primary research impacts are counted as primary respondents and, of those remaining, those who indicated that they used either mechanism (or both) for their secondary research impacts are counted as secondary respondents.

This table shows that, perhaps unsurprisingly, the disciplinary area with the highest response for these combined categories is Arts and Design, followed by Humanities and Languages. However, other disciplines such as Computer Science and Architecture, Planning, Built Environment also have a fair proportion of

Table B.15 Cross-tabulations of 'Healthcare or public health and wellbeing' (top 6 disciplinary areas) against other areas, beneficiaries and mechanisms of research impact

Areas	Contribution to knowledge			Technological development			Informing public policy			Helping socially excluded			Contribution to the economy			International development		
Healthcare/ public health	P%	S%	N%	P%	S%	N%	P%	S%	N%	P%	S%	N%	P%	S%	N%	P%	S%	N%
Primary (125)	**88.0**	11.2	0.8	**25.6**	26.4	48.0	**45.6**	36.8	17.6	**26.4**	30.4	43.2	**6.4**	45.6	48.0	**9.6**	18.4	72.0
Other (325)	**82.2**	14.8	3.0	**17.2**	35.1	47.7	**22.2**	34.8	43.0	**11.1**	20.9	68.0	**7.1**	44.6	48.3	**7.4**	24.3	68.3

Beneficiaries	Researchers your discipline			Healthcare services			National governments			Local governments			Small/medium firms			Third sector		
Healthcare/ public health	P%	S%	N%	P%	S%	N%	P%	S%	N%	P%	S%	N%	P%	S%	N%	P%	S%	N%
Primary (125)	**73.6**	23.2	3.2	**72.8**	21.6	5.6	**32.8**	34.4	32.8	**17.6**	27.2	55.2	**5.6**	24.0	70.4	**19.2**	47.2	33.6
Other (325)	**82.2**	16.0	1.8	**5.2**	25.5	69.3	**18.2**	34.8	47.0	**9.5**	21.5	69.0	**12.0**	28.3	59.7	**11.4**	32.3	56.3

Mechanisms	Academic publication/ conference			Teaching			Writing/speaking for non-academic audience			Collaboration with research users/ participants			Commercialisation of intellectual property			Professional or clinical practice		
Healthcare/ public health	P%	S%	N%	P%	S%	N%	P%	S%	N%	P%	S%	N%	P%	S%	N%	P%	S%	N%
Primary (125)	**97.6**	2.4	0.0	32.8	56.0	11.2	**47.2**	40.8	12.0	**46.4**	37.6	16.0	**7.2**	10.4	82.4	**37.6**	29.6	32.8
Other (325)	**91.7**	6.8	1.5	40.0	49.8	10.2	**35.7**	44.0	20.3	**45.5**	31.7	22.8	**7.4**	15.4	77.2	**7.7**	13.5	78.8

Table B.16 Disciplinary area ranking (top 8) for 'Public exhibition or performance of work' and 'Other creative output' combined (as mechanisms of research impact)

Rank	Discipline area (n)	Primary %	Secondary %	Total %	Primary%/ Total%
1	Arts and Design (27)	59.3	22.2	81.5	0.73
2	Humanities and Languages (80)	15.0	27.5	42.5	0.35
3	Computer Science (20)	20.0	20.0	40.0	0.50
4	Architecture, Planning, Built Environment (40)	10.0	22.5	32.5	0.31
5	Biological Sciences (76)	3.9	25.0	28.9	0.14
6	Engineering (57)	5.3	17.5	22.8	0.23
7	Social Sciences (116)	6.0	14.7	20.7	0.29
8	Physical Science (65)	3.1	16.9	20.0	0.15

practitioners who use 'public exhibitions or performances' or 'other creative outputs' as mechanisms of delivering their research. We have taken these four disciplines to cross-tabulate these two combined categories against other mechanisms, areas and beneficiaries of research impact (Table B.17). Again, the primary group is made up of participants who responded that they used either of these mechanisms to deliver their primary research impacts. This table indicates that respondents who used these two mechanisms of research impact are more likely to have research impacts relating to 'cultural development or enrichment' (area), 'the general public' (beneficiary), and 'online communication' (mechanism). The table also suggests that use of these two mechanisms may have a negative relationship to the 'academic' form of impact 'contribution to scientific/academic knowledge or method' (area) and also possibly 'dissemination through academic publications or conferences' (mechanism). However, interestingly, this is not the case with the beneficiary categories of 'academic or postgraduate researchers in your discipline' or 'other disciplines'.

Table B.17 Cross-tabulations of combined 'Public exhibition or performance of work' and 'Other creative outputs' (top 4 disciplinary areas) against other areas, beneficiaries and mechanisms of research impact

Areas	Contribution to knowledge			Technological development			Informing public policy			Helping socially excluded			Contribution to the economy			Cultural development or enrichment		
Creative outputs	P%	S%	N%	P%	S%	N%	P%	S%	N%	P%	S%	N%	P%	S%	N%	P%	S%	N%
Primary (36)	**58.3**	16.7	25.0	**13.9**	25.0	61.1	**5.6**	44.4	50.0	**16.7**	22.2	61.1	**11.1**	38.9	50.0	**69.4**	19.4	11.2
Other (131)	**75.6**	9.9	14.5	**13.0**	16.0	71.0	**19.8**	26.0	54.2	**9.9**	19.1	71.0	**4.6**	38.9	56.5	**24.4**	35.9	39.7

Beneficiaries	Taught students			Researchers your discipline			Researchers other discipline			Large firms			Small/medium firms			General public		
Creative outputs	P%	S%	N%	P%	S%	N%	P%	S%	N%	P%	S%	N%	P%	S%	N%	P%	S%	N%
Primary (36)	**61.1**	33.3	5.6	**91.7**	2.8	5.5	**36.1**	52.8	11.1	**2.8**	19.4	77.8	**13.9**	25.0	61.1	**41.7**	55.6	2.7
Other (131)	**57.3**	37.4	5.3	**76.3**	17.6	6.1	**26.0**	55.7	18.3	**6.1**	14.5	79.4	**10.7**	13.7	75.6	**9.2**	61.1	29.7

Mechanisms	Teaching			Academic publication/ conference			Writing/speaking for non-academic audience			Collaboration with research users participants			Commercialisation of intellectual property			Online communication		
Creative outputs	P%	S%	N%	P%	S%	N%	P%	S%	N%	P%	S%	N%	P%	S%	N%	P%	S%	N%
Primary (36)	**47.2**	50.0	2.8	**75.0**	16.7	8.3	**50.0**	47.2	2.8	**47.2**	22.2	30.6	**11.1**	11.1	77.8	**36.1**	36.1	27.8
Other (131)	**52.7**	38.9	8.4	**88.5**	6.9	4.6	**29.0**	51.9	19.1	**35.9**	29.8	34.3	**3.8**	10.7	85.5	**7.6**	32.8	59.6

Notes

1 Introduction

1 Special issues on this subject include *GeoJournal* Volume 41, Number 4 (1997) edited by Herman van der Wusten; *Planning, Practice & Research* Volume 21, Number 1 (2006); and *Built Environment* Volume 37, Number 3 (2011) edited by Beth Perry and Tim May. In February 2012 the Association of American Geographers annual conference held in New York also included three paper sessions on this subject convened by Andrew Karvonen, James Evans and Bas van Heur.

3 The university in the city II: economic impacts

1 This section is limited to discussing national patterns of student migration, because although there is a significant literature growing on international student mobility, this is based predominantly on qualitative research addressing the role of education in issues such as reproducing social inequality and disadvantage (see Waters 2012).

4 Universities, innovation and economic development

1 See Feldman and Audretsch 1999 for a similar argument about 'complementary industries sharing a common science base'.

5 City social and economic development

1 An earlier and more detailed version of this chapter has previously been published as Goddard *et al.* (2011). This is part of a journal special issue entitled 'Building Knowledge Cities: The Role of Universities' edited by Beth Perry and Tim May. We are grateful for the input of the editors and two anonymous referees into the earlier version of this paper. We also acknowledge the work of those involved in the OECD reviews which we draw on in this chapter.

2 See OECD website (www.oecd.org/edu/imhe/regionaldevelopment, accessed 24 July 2012).

3 The Jyväskylä review uses the term Polytechnic instead. However, in the time since the review, these institutions have been renamed in the Finnish system as (what broadly translates into) UASs. In the rest of this chapter, we will use the term UAS when referring to this type of institution in general across all three national systems, but still refer to the specific institution of Jyväskylä Polytechnic as in the review.

4 Van den Berg *et al.* (2003) includes another case study of a Rotterdam social policy programme led by the municipality, in which the city's HEIs are not mentioned as participants at all.

6 Higher education and cities in the UK

1 London was not considered for the research because it represents a fundamentally different case to these other cities, both in terms of its economic function as a 'global
city', and in terms of the size and diversity of its higher education sector.
2 This may also have a historical basis: between 1982 and 1988, the polytechnics had
been under local authority control (Pratt 1997: 3).
3 Figures from Universities UK (http://www.universitiesuk.ac.uk/UKHESector/Pages/
OverviewSector.aspx#Q1, accessed 12th July 2012).
4 Following the 2010 election, the new coalition government introduced a bill to
increase tuition fees to a maximum of £9,000 per annum from the academic year
2012/2013 and drastically cut public spending for the higher education teaching grant.
5 Quote from RCUK website (http://www.rcuk.ac.uk/research/xrcprogrammes/Pages/
home.aspx, accessed 7th July 2012).
6 The large-scale projects that UDCs supported included the development of university
campuses in areas including Sunderland and Teesside in the North East of England.
7 Source: English HEI HEFCE recurrent grant funding 2010/2011 (Total Research
Funding) (http://www.hefce.ac.uk/pubs/hefce/2010/10_08/, accessed 16 July 2012).
Figures compiled by the authors.
8 This also led to the formation of formal Higher Education Regional Associations
between universities throughout England at this time.
9 See University of Salford website (http://www.salford.ac.uk/university/heritage,
accessed 16th July 2012).
10 Quote from the University of Manchester website (http://www.manchester.ac.uk/
aboutus/facts/, accessed 16th July 2012).

7 Universities, sustainability and urban development

1 See the HEFCE website (http://www.hefce.ac.uk/whatwedo/lgm/sd/carbon/, accessed
6th July 2012).
2 At this stage of its inception, Corridor Manchester was known as Manchester City
South Partnership. See the original strategic development framework (Manchester City
South Partnership 2008).
3 Low Carbon Economic Areas are an initiative set up by the previous Labour government to promote certain parts of the country as leading areas for the development of one
aspect of carbon-efficient technology and industry. For instance, the North East region
as a whole is designated the LCEA for Electric Cars, based mainly on the location of a
Nissan plant in Sunderland specialising in this field.
4 Information on these projects can be found on the University of Manchester EcoCities
website   (http://www.sed.manchester.ac.uk/architecture/research/ecocities/projects/,
accessed 25 June 2012).

8 Universities and health

1 Quote from The University of Sheffield CWiPP website (www.sheffield.ac.uk/cwipp,
accessed 25 June 2012).
2 See the South Yorkshire CLAHRC website (www.clahrc-sy.nihr.ac.uk/themes.html,
accessed 25 June 2012).

3 Durham University's medical school was part of the Newcastle-located King's College that in 1963 became the basis for the new independent University of Newcastle upon Tyne.
4 Quote from Newcastle University Institute for Human Genetics website (http://www. ncl.ac.uk/igm/services/ngs/, accessed 25 June 2012).
5 Quote from Cels group website (http://www.celsgroup.com/about.html, accessed 25 June 2012).
6 See Newcastle University website (http://www.ncl.ac.uk/research/impact/spinout/, accessed 25 June 2012).
7 Quote from the Institute of Ageing and Health website (http://www.ncl.ac.uk/iah/ ageing/volunteer/, accessed 25 June).

9 Universities and the cultural sector of cities

1 The Capital of Culture is an EU initiative (rotating between member states) for one or more cities every year to organise a programme of events that promotes local cultural development, which during its 25-year history has become increasingly coveted for the perceived economic benefits that it can bring to host cities (Richards and Wilson 2004; Griffiths 2006).
2 Quote from New Writing North website (http://www.newwritingnorth.com/about.html, accessed 18 July 2012).
3 A key part of the North East of England's arts funding environment through this period was the Northern Rock Foundation, a charity established to distribute a share of the profits of the Northern Rock bank in the region following its demutualisation as a local building society in 1997. In 2007, as a precursor to the wider financial crisis of the following year, Northern Rock became the first UK bank to come close to collapse, and in early 2008 was nationalised by the UK government (see Marshall *et al.* 2012). Although the Northern Rock Foundation has survived through these and subsequent changes, it now operates on a smaller scale with a currently more uncertain future (see Northern Rock Website: http://www.nr-foundation.org.uk/about/, accessed 20th July 2012).
4 This contrasts with the other gallery space on the campus (the University Gallery) which is centrally-run by the institution along more commercial lines and has little connection to the curriculum of the Department of Arts.
5 The value of the BBC to the city is illustrated by the formation of the BBC Bristol Anchor, a partnership with various local actors (including the two universities) to reaffirm the embeddedness of the corporation in the city and region through strengthening its economic and community links (partly in response to the re-location of some major national BBC facilities to Salford mentioned in Chapter 7).
6 See the University of Bristol website (http://www.bris.ac.uk/parip/index.htm, accessed 23 July 2012).
7 The Bristol Old Vic Theatre School, affiliated with the historical theatre and company in the city, is also an associate school of UWE based around a degree validation arrangement.
8 Quote from RCUK website (http://www.rcuk.ac.uk/research/xrcprogrammes/Digital/ Pages/home.aspx, accessed 20th July 2012).
9 Quote from Newcastle University website (http://www.ncl.ac.uk/culturelab/, accessed 22nd July 2012).
10 See the Ambient Kitchen project on the Culture Lab website (http://culturelab.ncl.ac. uk/research/digital-interaction/ambient-kitchen-cels, accessed 22 July 2012).
11 See article 'DShed: Past, Present & Future' on the Watershed website (http://www. watershed.co.uk/dshed/articles/dshed-past-present-future, accessed 22nd July 2012).
12 See the DShed platform hosted on the Watershed website (http://www.watershed.co. uk/dshed/articles/dshed-past-present-future, accessed 22 July 2012).

References

1NG (2010) *1Plan: an Economic and Spatial Strategy for NewcastleGateshead*. Gateshead: 1NG.

Abel, J. R. and Deitz, R. (2012) 'Do colleges and universities increase their region's human capital'. *Journal of Economic Geography*, *12*: 667–91.

Abreu, M. and Grinevich, V. (2011) 'Academic entrepreneurship in the creative arts', paper presented at *Regional Studies Association annual conference*, Newcastle upon Tyne, April 2011.

Abreu, M., Grinevich, V., Hughes, A. and Kitson, M. (2009) *Knowledge Exchange between Academics and the Business, Public and Third Sectors*. Cambridge: UK Innovation Research Centre.

Adams, C. (2003) 'The meds and eds in urban economic development'. *Journal of Urban Affairs*, *25*: 571–88.

AGMA (2009) *Prosperity for All: The Greater Manchester Strategy*. Wigan: AGMA. Available at http://neweconomymanchester.com/stories/842-greater_manchester_strategy (accessed 25 June 2012).

AGMA (2010) *Greater Manchester's Low Carbon Economic Area for the Built Environment (LCEA): Joint Delivery Plan – Final Version*. Wigan: AGMA.

Allen, P. (2006) 'New localism in the English National Health Service: What is it for?'. *Health Policy*, *79*: 244–52.

Allen, J. and Buswell, R. (2005) *Rutherford's Ladder: The Making of Northumbria University, 1871–1996*. Newcastle upon Tyne: Northumbria University Press.

Allinson, J. (2006) 'Over-educated, over-exuberant and over here? The impact of students on cities'. *Planning, Practice & Research*, *21*: 79–94.

Alm, J. and Winters, J. V. (2009) 'Distance and intrastate college state migration'. *Economics of Education Review*, *28*: 728–38.

Amin, A. and Cohendet, P. (2004) *Architectures of Knowledge: Firms, Capabilities, and Communities*. Oxford: Oxford University Press.

Amin, A. and Graham, S. (1997) 'The ordinary city'. *Transactions of the Institute of British Geographers*, *22*: 411–29.

Amin, A. and Thrift, N. (1995) 'Globalization, institutional "thickness" and the local economy', in Healey, P., Cameron, S., Davoudi, S., Graham, S. and Madanipour, A. (eds) *Managing Cities: The New Urban Context*. London: Wiley.

Amin, A. and Thrift, N. (2002) *Cities: Reimagining the Urban*. Cambridge: Polity Press.

Arbo, P. and Benneworth, P. (2006) *Understanding the Regional Contribution of Higher Education Institutions: A Literature Review*. Paris: OECD/IMHE.

Armstrong, H. W., Darrall, J. and Grove-White, R. (1997) 'Maximising the local economic, environmental and social benefits of a university: Lancaster University'. *GeoJournal, 41*: 339–50.

Arnkil, R., Järvensivu, A., Koski, P. and Piirainen, T. (2010) 'Exploring Quadruple Helix: Outlining User-Oriented Innovation Models. Final report on Quadruple Helix Research for the CLIQ project', *Työraportteja 85/2010 Working Papers*.

Arthur, D Little (2001) *Realising the Potential of the North East's Research Base: Report to One NorthEast*. Harrogate: Arthur D Little Limited.

ARUP and Manchester: Knowledge Capital (2010) *Sustainable Energy Action Plan: A Report to Inform and Help Shape Energy Priorities in Greater Manchester*. Wigan: AGMA. Online. Available at http://manchesterismyplanet.com/strategyandresearch/agma/seap-for-greater-manchester (accessed 24 July 2012).

Asheim, B. T. (1996), 'Industrial districts as 'learning regions': a condition for prosperity'. *European Planning Studies 4*: 379–400.

Asheim, B. T. and Cooke, P. (1999), 'Local learning and interactive innovation networks in a global economy', in Malecki, E. J. and Oinas, P. (eds), *Making Connections: Technological Learning and Regional Economic Change*. Aldershot: Ashgate.

Athey, G., Glossop, C., Harrison, B., Nathan, M. and Webber, C. (2007) *Innovation and the City: How Innovation has Developed in Five City-Regions*. London: NESTA.

Atkinson, R. and Easthope, H. (2008) 'The creative class *in utero*? The Australian city, the creative economy and the role of higher education'. *Built Environment, 34*: 307–18.

Austrian, Z. and Norton, J. S. (2005) 'An overview of university real estate investment practices', in Perry, D. C. and Wiewel, W. (eds) *The University as Urban Developer: Case Studies and Analysis*. Armonk: M. E. Sharpe.

Bailey, C., Miles, S. and Stark, P. (2004) 'Culture-led urban regeneration and the revitalisation of identities in Newcastle, Gateshead and the North East of England'. *International Journal of Cultural Policy, 10*: 47–65.

Bailey, N. (2003) 'Local strategic partnerships in England: the continuing search for collaborative advantage, leadership and strategy in urban governance'. *Planning Theory & Practice, 4*: 443–57.

Ball, L., Pollard, E. and Stanley, N. (2010) *Creative Graduates Creative Futures*. London: Institute of Employment Studies.

Barlow, M. (1998) 'Developing and sustaining an urban mission: Concordia University in Montreal', in van der Wusten, H. (ed.) *The Urban University and its Identity: Roots, Locations, Roles*. Dordrecht: Kluwer Academic Publishers.

Barnes, S. V. (1996) 'England's civic universities and the triumph of the Oxbridge ideal'. *History of Education Quarterly, 36*: 271–305.

Barnett, R. (2007) 'Recovering the civic university', in McIlrath, L. and Mac Labhrainn, I. (eds) *Higher Education and Civic Engagement: International Perspectives*. Aldershot: Ashgate.

Bartik, T. J. and Erickcek, G. (2007) 'Higher education, the health care industry, and metropolitan regional economic development: what can "eds & meds" do for the economic fortunes of a metro area's residents?', *Upjohn Institute Working Paper, No. 08-140*. Kalamazoo, MI: W.E. Upjohn Institute for Employment Research.

Bassett, K., Griffiths, R. and Smith, I. (2002) 'Cultural industries, cultural clusters and the city: the example of natural history film-making in Bristol'. *Geoforum, 33*: 165–77.

Beck, R., Elliott, D., Meisel, J. and Wagner, M. (1995) 'Economic impact studies of regional public colleges and universities'. *Growth and Change, 26*: 245–60.

Belfield, C and Morris, Z. (1999) 'Regional migration to and from higher education institutions: scale, determinants and outcomes'. *Higher Education Quarterly*, *53*: 240–63.

Bender, T. (1988a) 'Introduction', in Bender, T. (ed.) *The University and the City: From Medieval Origins to the Present*. Oxford: Oxford University Press.

Bender, T. (1988b) 'Afterword', in Bender, T. (ed.) *The University and the City: From Medieval Origins to the Present*. Oxford: Oxford University Press.

Bender, T. (1998) 'Scholarship, local life, and the necessity of worldliness', in van der Wusten, H. (ed.) *The Urban University and its Identity: Roots, Locations, Roles*. Dordrecht: Kluwer Academic Publishers.

Benneworth, P. and Charles, D. (2005) 'University spin-off policies and economic development in less successful regions: learning from two decades of policy practice'. *European Planning Studies*, *13*: 537–57.

Benneworth, P. and Hospers, G. (2007a) 'Urban competitiveness in the knowledge economy: Universities as new planning animateurs'. *Progress in Planning*, *67*: 105–97.

Benneworth, P. and Hospers, G. (2007b) 'The new economic geography of old industrial regions: universities as global-local pipelines'. *Environment and Planning C: Government and Policy*, *25*: 779–802.

Benneworth, P., Conroy, L. and Roberts, P. (2002) 'Strategic connectivity, sustainable development and the new English Regional Governance'. *Journal of Environmental Planning and Management*, *45*: 199–217.

Benneworth, P., Coenen, L., Moodysson, J. and Asheim, B. (2009) 'Exploring the multiple roles of Lund University in strengthening Scania's Regional Innovation System: towards institutional learning?'. *European Planning Studies*, *17*: 1645–64.

Benneworth, P., Charles, D. and Madanipour, A. (2010) 'Building localized interactions between universities and cities through university spatial development'. *European Planning Studies*, *18*: 1611–29.

BEPA (2010) *Empowering People, Driving Change: Social Innovation in the European Union*. Brussels: European Commission.

Bianchini, F. (1993) 'Remaking European cities: the role of cultural policies', in Bianchini, F. And Parkinson, M. (eds), *Cultural Policy and Urban Regeneration: The West European Experience*. Manchester: Manchester University Press.

Birch, K. (2008) 'Alliance-driven governance: applying a global commodity chains approach to the U.K. biotechnology industry'. *Economic Geography*, *84*: 83–103.

Blackwell, M., Cobb, S. and Weinberg, D. (2002) 'The economic impact of educational institutions: issues and methodology'. *Economic Development Quarterly*, *16*: 88–95.

Blanden, J. and Machin, S. (2004) 'Educational inequality and the expansion of UK higher education'. *Scottish Journal of Political Economy*, *51*: 230–49.

Bleaney, M. F., Binks, M. R., Greenway, D., Reed, G. V. and Whynes, D. K. (1992) 'What does a University add to its local economy?'. *Applied Economics*, *24*: 305–11.

Boal, F. W. and Logan, K. (1998) 'A shared space in a divided society: the Queen's University of Belfast', in van der Wusten, H. (ed.) *The Urban University and its Identity: Roots, Locations, Roles*. Dordrecht: Kluwer Academic Publishers.

Boschma, R. A. and Lambooy, J. G. (1999) 'Evolutionary economics and economic geography'. *Journal of Evolutionary Economics*, *9*: 411–29.

Boucher, G., Conway, C. and Van Der Meer, E. (2003) 'Tiers of engagement by universities in their region's development'. *Regional Studies*, *37*: 887–97.

Boyer, E. L. (1996) 'The scholarship of engagement'. *Bulletin of the American Academy of Arts and Sciences*, *49*: 18–33.

Braczyk, H.-J., Cooke, P. N. and Heidenreich, M. (eds) (1998) *Regional Innovation Systems: the Role of Governances in a Globalized World*. London: Routledge.

Brandt, A. M. and Gardner, M. (2000) 'Antagonism and accommodation: interpreting the relationship between public health and medicine in the United States during the 20th Century'. *American Journal of Public Health, 90*: 707–15.

Bromley, R. (2006) 'On and off campus: colleges and universities as local stakeholders'. *Planning, Practice & Research, 21*: 1–24.

Bromley, R. and Kent, R. B. (2006) 'Integrating beyond the campus: Ohio's urban public universities and neighbourhood revitalisation'. *Planning, Practice & Research, 21*: 45–78.

Brown, A., O'Conner, J. and Cohen, S. (2000) 'Local music policies within a global music industry: cultural quarters in Manchester and Sheffield'. *Geoforum, 31*: 437–51.

Brownill, S. (1999) 'Turning the East End into the West End: the lessons and legacies of the London Docklands Development Corporation', in Imrie, R., Thomas, H. (eds), *British Urban Policy: An Evaluation of the Urban Development Corporations*. London: Sage Publications.

Bulkeley, H. (2010) 'Cities and the governing of climate change'. *Annual Review of Environment and Resources, 35*: 229–53.

Bulkeley, H. and Betsill, M. M. (2005) 'Rethinking sustainable cities: multilevel governance and the 'urban' politics of climate change'. *Environmental Politics, 14*: 42–63.

Bulkeley, H., Broto, V. C., Hodson, M. and Marvin, S. (2010) 'Introduction', in Bulkeley, H., Castán Bronto, V., Hodson, M. and Marvin, S. (eds) *Cities and Low Carbon Transitions*. London: Routledge.

Bunnell, T. G. and Coe, N. M. (2001) 'Spaces and scales of innovation'. *Progress in Human Geography, 25*: 569–89.

Bunnell, G. and Lawson, C. T. (2006) 'A public university as city planner and developer: experience in the "capital of good planning"'. *Planning, Practice & Research, 21*: 25–43.

Calhoun, C. (2006) 'The university and the public good'. *Thesis Eleven, 84*: 7–43.

Castells, M. and Hall, P. (1994) *Technopoles of the World: The Making of 21st Century Industrial Complexes*. London: Routledge.

Champion, T. and Townsend, A. (2011) 'The fluctuating record of economic regeneration in England's second-order city-regions, 1984–2007'. *Urban Studies, 48*: 1539–62.

Chapain, C. and Comunian, R. (2010) 'Enabling and inhibiting the creative economy: the role of the local and regional dimensions in England'. *Regional Studies, 44*: 717–34.

Chapain, C. and Lee, P. (2009) 'Can we plan the creative knowledge city? Perspectives from western and eastern Europe'. *Built Environment, 35*: 157–64.

Chapain, C., Cooke, P., De Propris, L., MacNeill, S. and Mateos-Garcia, J. (2010) *Creative Clusters and Innovation: Putting Creativity on the Map*. London: NESTA.

Charles, D. (2003) 'Universities and territorial development: reshaping the regional role of UK universities'. *Local Economy, 18*: 7–20.

Charles, D. (2006) 'Universities as key knowledge infrastructures in regional innovation systems'. *Innovation, 19*: 117–30.

Charles, D. (2011) 'The role of universities in building knowledge cities in Australia'. *Built Environment, 37*: 281–98.

Charles, D. and Benneworth, P. (2001) 'Are we realizing our potential? Joining up science and technology policy in the English regions'. *Regional Studies, 35*: 73–9.

Chatterton, P. (1999) 'University students and city centres – the formation of exclusive geographies: The case of Bristol, UK'. *Geoforum, 30*: 117–33.

Chatterton, P. (2000) 'The cultural role of universities in the community: revisiting the university-community debate'. *Environment and Planning A, 32*: 165–81.

Chatterton, P. (2010) 'The student city: an ongoing story of neoliberalism, gentrification, and commodification'. *Environment and Planning A, 42*: 509–14.

Chatterton, P. and Goddard, J. (2000) 'The response of higher education institutions to regional needs'. *European Journal of Education 35*: 475–96.

Chatterton, P. and Style, S. (2001) 'Putting sustainable development into practice? The role of local policy partnership networks'. *Local Environment, 6*: 439–52.

Christie, H. (2007) 'Higher education and spatial (im)mobility: nontraditional students and living at home'. *Environment and Planning A, 39*: 2445–63.

Christopherson, S. (2009) 'Manufacturing: up from the ashes'. *Democracy, 14*: 25–30.

Christopherson, S. (2011) 'Green dreams in a cold light', in Pike, A., Rodríguez-Pose, A. and Tomaney, J. (eds) *Handbook of Local and Regional Development*. London: Routledge.

Christopherson, S. and Clark, J. (2010) 'Limits to the 'learning region': what university-centred economic development can (and cannot) do to create knowledge-based regional economies'. *Local Economy, 25*: 120–30.

City of Rotterdam Regional Steering Committee. (2009) 'The City of Rotterdam, the Netherlands: self-evaluation report', *OECD Reviews of Higher Education in Regional and City Development*. Paris. IMHE. Available at www.oecd.org/edu/imhe/regional development (accessed 24 July 2012).

Clark, B. R. (1996) 'Substantive growth and innovative organization: new categories for higher education research'. *Higher Education, 32*: 417–30.

Clark, B. R. (1998) 'The entrepreneurial university: demand and response'. *Tertiary Education and Management, 4*: 5–16.

Clark, B. R. (2003) 'Sustaining change in universities: continuities in case studies and concepts'. *Tertiary Education and Management, 9*: 99–116.

Clark, J. (2010) 'Coordinating a conscious geography: the role of research centres in multi-scalar innovation policy and economic development in the US and Canada'. *The Journal of Technology Transfer, 35*: 460–74.

Cochrane, A. (1999) 'Just another failed urban experiment? The legacy of the Urban Development Corporations', in Imrie, R. and Thomas, H. (eds), *British Urban Policy: An Evaluation of the Urban Development Corporations*. London: Sage Publications.

Cochrane, A. (2003) 'The new urban policy: towards empowerment or incorporation? The practice of urban policy', in Imrie, R. and Raco, M. (eds), *Urban Renaissance? New Labour, Community, and Urban Policy*. Bristol: The Policy Press.

Cochrane, A. and Jonas, A. (1999) 'Reimagining Berlin: world city, national capital or ordinary place?'. *European Urban and Regional Planning Studies, 6*: 145–64.

Coenen, L. (2007) 'The role of universities in the regional innovation systems of the North East of England and Scania, Sweden: providing missing links?'. *Environment and Planning C: Government and Policy, 25*: 803–21.

Cohen, A. M. (1998) *The Shaping of American Higher Education: Emergence and Growth of the Contemporary System*. San Francisco: Jossey-Bass Publishers.

Collinge, C. and Musterd, S. (2009) 'Deepening social divisions and the discourses of *knowledge* and *creativity* across the cities of Europe'. *Built Environment, 35*: 281–85.

Collins, F. L. (2010) 'International students as urban agents: international education and urban transformation in Auckland, New Zealand'. *Geoforum, 41*: 940–50.

Comunian, R., Faggian, A. and Li, Q. C. (2010) 'Unrewarded careers in the creative class: the strange case of bohemian graduates'. *Papers in Regional Science, 89*: 389–410.

Cooke, P. and Morgan, K. (1998) *The Associational Economy: Firms, Regions and Innovation*. Oxford: Oxford University Press.

Cooke, P., Uranga, M. G. and Etxebarria, G. (1998) 'Regional systems of innovation: an evolutionary perspective'. *Environment and Planning A, 30*: 1563–84.

Cooksey, D. (2006) *A Review of UK Health Research Funding*. London: HM Treasury.

Corburn, J. (2004) 'Confronting the challenges in reconnecting urban planning and public health'. *American Journal of Public Health, 94*: 541–6.

Corridor Manchester (2010) *Strategic Vision to 2020*. Manchester: Corridor Manchester.

Cross, E. and Pickering, H. (2008) 'The contribution of higher education to regional cultural development in the North East of England'. *Higher Education Management and Policy, 20*: 125–37.

Davies, A. R. and Mullin, S. J. (2011) 'Greening the economy: interrogating sustainability innovations beyond the mainstream'. *Journal of Economic Geography, 11*: 793–816.

Davies, J., Weko, T., Kim, L and Thulstrup, E. (2009) 'Finland', *OECD Reviews of Tertiary Education*. Paris: OECD.

de Hollander, A. E. M. and Staatsen, B. A. M. (2003) 'Health, environment and quality of life: an epidemiological perspective on urban development'. *Landscape and Urban Planning, 1*: 53–62.

Deas, I. and Ward, K. G. (2000) 'From the 'new localism' to the 'new regionalism'? The implications of regional development agencies for city-regional relations'. *Political Geography, 19*: 273–92.

Deas, I., Robson, B. and Bradford, M. (2000) 'Re-thinking the Urban Development Corporation 'experiment': the case of Central Manchester, Leeds and Bristol'. *Progress in Planning, 54*: 1–72.

Deem, R., Hillyard, S. and Reed, M. (2007) *Knowledge, Higher Education, and the New Managerialism: The Changing Management of UK Universities*. Oxford: Oxford University Press.

Deitrick, S. and Soska, T. (2005) 'The University of Pittsburgh and the Oakland neighborhood: from conflict to cooperation, or how the 800-pound gorilla learned to sit with – and not on – its neighbours', in Perry, D. C. and Wiewel, W. (eds) *The University as Urban Developer: Case Studies and Analysis*. Armonk: M. E. Sharpe.

Delanty, G. (2002) 'The university and modernity: a history of the present', in Robins, K. and Webster, F. (eds) *The Virtual University? Knowledge, Markets, and Management*. Oxford: Oxford University Press.

Department for Business, Innovation and Skills (2011) *Strength and Opportunity 2011: The Landscape of the Medical Technology, Medical Biotechnology, Industrial Biotechnology and Pharmaceutical Sectors in the UK*. London: HM Government.

Duke-Williams, O. (2009) 'The geographies of student migration in the UK'. *Environment and Planning A, 41*: 1826–48.

Duranton, G. and Puga, D. (2000) 'Diversity and specialisation in cities: why, where and when does it matter?'. *Urban Studies, 37*: 533–55.

Edquist, C. (ed.) (1997) *Systems of Innovation: Technology, Institutions and Organizations*. Abingdon: Routledge.

Edwards, B. (2000) *University Architecture*. London: Spon Press.

EcoCities (2011) *Four Degrees of Preparation: Greater Manchester Gets Ready for Climate Change*. Online. Available at http://www.adaptingmanchester.co.uk/ten-minute-read (accessed 24 July 2012).

Elton, L. (2000) 'The UK research assessment exercise: unintended consequences'. *Higher Education Quarterly*, *54*: 274–83.

Etzkowitz, H. (2003) 'Research groups as 'quasi-firms': the invention of the entrepreneurial university'. *Research Policy*, *32*: 109–21.

Etzkowitz, H. (2004) 'The evolution of the entrepreneurial university'. *International Journal of Technology and Globalisation*, *1*: 64–77.

Etzkowitz, H. and Leydesdorff, L. (2000) 'The dynamics of innovation: from national systems and mode 2 to a triple helix of university-industry-government relations'. *Research Policy*, *29*: 109–23.

Etzkowitz, H., Webster, A., Gebhardt, C., Terra, B. R. C. (2000) 'The future of the university and the university of the future: evolution of ivory tower to entrepreneurial paradigm'. *Research Policy*, *29*: 313–30.

Evans, J. (2011) 'Resilience, ecology and adaptation in the experimental city'. *Transactions of the Institute of British Geographers*, *36*: 223–37.

Evans, J. and Karvonen, A. (2010) 'Living laboratories for sustainability: exploring the politics and epistemology of urban transition', in Bulkeley, H., Castán Bronto, V., Hodson, M. and Marvin, S. (eds) *Cities and Low Carbon Transitions*. London: Routledge.

Evans, J. and Marvin, S. (2006) 'Researching the sustainable city: three modes of interdisciplinarity'. *Environment and Planning A*, *38*: 1009–28.

Faggian, A. and McCann, P. (2006) 'Human capital flows and regional knowledge assets: a simultaneous equation approach'. *Oxford Economic Papers*, *52*: 475–500.

Faggian, A. and McCann, P. (2009a) 'Universities, agglomerations and graduate human capital mobility'. *Tijdschrift voor Economische en Sociale Geografic*, *100*: 210–23.

Faggian, A. and McCann, P. (2009b) 'Human capital, graduate migration and innovation in British regions'. *Cambridge Journal of Economics*, *33*: 317–33.

Feldman, M. P. and Audretsch, D. B. (1999) 'Innovation in cities: science-based diversity, specialization and localized competition'. *European Economic Review*, *43*: 409–29.

Felsenstein, D. (1996) 'The university in the metropolitan arena: impacts and public policy implications'. *Urban Studies*, *33*: 1565–80.

Fielding, A. J. (1992) 'Migration and social mobility: South East England as an escalator region'. *Regional Studies*, *26*: 1–15.

Fincher, R. and Shaw, K. (2009) 'The unintended segregation of transnational students in central Melbourne'. *Environment and Planning A*, *41*: 1884–902.

Fischer. M. M., Revilla Diez, J. and Snickars, F. (2001) *Metropolitan Innovation Systems: Theory and Evidence from Three Metropolitan Regions in Europe*. Heidelberg: Springer.

Flint, K. (2001) 'Institutional ecological footprint analysis: A case study of the University of Newcastle, Australia'. *International Journal of Sustainability in Higher Education*, *2*: 48–62.

Florida, R. (2002) *The Rise of the Creative Class: And How it's Transforming Work, Leisure, Community and Everyday Life*. New York: Basic Books.

Florida, R., Gates, G., Knudsen, B. and Stolarick, K. (2006) *The University and the Creative Economy*, Online. Available at http://www.creativeclass.com/creative_class/2006/11/27/university-and-the-creative-economy/ (accessed 24 July 2012).

Fornahl, D., Hassink, R., Klaerding, C., Mossig, I. and Schröder, H. (2012) 'From the old path of shipbuilding onto the new path of offshore wind energy? The case of Northern Germany'. *European Planning Studies*, *20*: 835–55.

Freeman, C. (1995) 'The 'National System of Innovation' in historical perspective'. *Cambridge Journal of Economics*, *19*: 5–24.

Frenken, K., van Oort, F., Verburg, T. (2007) 'Related variety, unrelated variety and regional economic growth'. *Regional Studies*, *41*: 685–97.

Frost, C. (2011) 'Media Lab Culture in the UK'. Online. Available at http://www.artscouncil. org.uk/what-we-do/our-priorities-2011-15/digital-innovation/digital-resources/collaboration-and-freedom/essays-and-interviews/ (accessed 24 July 2012).

Gaffikin, F. (2008) 'Interface between academy and community in contested space: the difficult dialogue', in Wiewel, W. and Perry, D. C. (eds) *Global Universities and Urban Development: Case Studies and Analysis*. Armonk: M. E. Sharpe.

Galindo-Rueda, F., Marcenaro-Gutierrez, O. and Vignoles, A. (2004) 'The widening socio-economic gap in UK higher education'. *National Institute Economic Review*, *190*: 75–88.

Galloway, A. (2004) 'Intimations of everyday life: ubiquitous computing and the city'. *Cultural Studies*, *18*: 384–408.

Garmise, S. (1997) 'The impact of European regional policy on the development of the regional tier in the UK'. *Regional & Federal Studies*, *7*: 1–24.

Garnsey, E. and Heffernan, P. (2005) 'High-technology clustering through spin-out and attraction: the Cambridge case'. *Regional Studies 39*: 1127–44.

Geddes, M. (2000) 'Tackling social exclusion in the European Union? The limits to the new orthodoxy of local partnership'. *International Journal of Urban and Regional Research*, *24*: 782–800.

Geddes, M. (2006) 'Partnership and the limits to local governance in England: institutionalist analysis and neoliberalism'. *International Journal of Urban and Regional Research*, *30*: 76–97.

Genus, A. and Armstrong, A. (2011) 'Case study: developing low carbon neighbourhoods: a collaborative action research project in Newcastle'. Online. Available at http:// www.publicengagement.ac.uk/how/case-studies/low-carbon-neighbourhoods (accessed 24 July 2012).

Gerometta, J., Häussermann, H. and Longo, G. (2005) 'Social innovation and civil society in urban governance: strategies for an inclusive city'. *Urban Studies*, *42*: 2007–21.

Gertler, M. S. (2004) *Manufacturing Culture: The Institutional Geography of Industrial Practice*. Oxford: Oxford University Press.

Gertler, M. S. and Levitte, Y. M. (2005) 'Local nodes in global networks: the geography of knowledge flows in biotechnology innovation'. *Industry and Innovation*, *12*: 487–507.

Gertler, M. S. and Vinodrai, T. (2005) 'Anchors of creativity: how do public universities create competitive and cohesive communities?', in Iacobucci, F. and Tuohy, C. (eds) *Taking Public Universities Seriously*. Toronto: University of Toronto Press.

Gibbons, M., Limoges, C., Nowotny, H., Schwartzman, S., Scott, P. and Trow, M. (1994) *The New Production of Knowledge: The Dynamics of Science and Research in Contemporary Societies*. London: Sage.

Gibbs, D. and Jonas, A. E. G. (2001) 'Rescaling and regional governance: the English Regional Development Agencies and the environment'. *Environment and Planning C: Government and Policy*, *19*: 269–88.

Girardet, H. (1999) *Creating Sustainable Cities*. Totnes: Green Books Ltd.

Glaeser, E. L. (2005a) 'Review of Richard Florida's *The Rise of the Creative Class*'. *Regional Science and Urban Economics*, *35*: 593–6.

Glaeser, E. L. (2005b) 'Reinventing Boston: 1630–2003'. *Journal of Economic Geography*, *5*: 119–53.

Glaeser, E. L. and Saiz, A. (2004) 'The rise of the skilled city'. *Brookings-Wharton Papers on Urban Affairs*, 47–105.

Glaeser, E. L., Kallal, H. D., Scheinkman, J. A. and Shleifer, A. (1992) 'Growth in cities'. *Journal of Political Economy*, *100*: 1126–52.

Glasson, J. (2003) 'The widening local and regional development impacts of the modern universities – a tale of two cities (and north-south perspectives)'. *Local Economy*, *18*: 21–37.

Goddard, J. (2009) *Re-inventing the Civic University*. London: NESTA.

Goddard, J. and Chatterton, P. (1999) 'Regional Development Agencies and the knowledge economy: harnessing the potential of universities'. *Environment and Planning C: Government and Policy*, *17*: 685–99.

Goddard, J. and Puukka, J. (2008) 'The engagement of higher education institutions in regional development: an overview of the opportunities and challenges'. *Higher Education Management and Policy*, *20*: 11–41.

Goddard, J. and Vallance, P. (2011) 'Universities and Regional Development', in Pike, A., Rodríguez-Pose, A. and Tomaney, J. (eds), *Handbook of Local and Regional Development*. London: Routledge.

Goddard, J., Etzkowitz, H., Puukka, J. and Virtanen, I. (2006) 'Peer review report: the Jyväskylä region of Finland', *Supporting the Contribution of Higher Education Institutions to Regional Development*. Paris: OECD/IMHE. Online. Available at www.oecd. org/edu/imhe/regionaldevelopment (accessed 24 July 2012).

Goddard, J., Howlett, L., Vallance, P. and Kennie, T. (2010) *Researching and Scoping a Higher Education and Civic Leadership Development Programme*. London: LFHE.

Goddard, J., Vallance, P. and Puukka, J. (2011) 'Experience of engagement between universities and cities: drivers and barriers in three European cities'. *Built Environment*, *37*: 299–316.

Goddard, J., Robertson, D. and Vallance, P. (2012) 'Universities, Technology and Innovation Centres, and regional development: the case of the North-East of England'. *Cambridge Journal of Economics 36*: 609–27.

Goldstein, H. and Drucker, J. (2006) 'The economic development impacts of universities on regions: do size and distance matter?'. *Economic Development Quarterly*, *20*: 22–43.

Goodwin, M., Jones, M. and Jones, R. (2005) 'Devolution, constitutional change and economic development: explaining and understanding the new institutional geographies of the British state'. *Regional Studies*, *39*: 421–36.

Gornig, M. and Häussermann, H. (2002) 'Berlin: economic and spatial change'. *European Urban and Regional Studies*, *9*: 331–41.

Grabher, G. (1993) 'The weakness of strong ties: the lock-in of regional development in the Ruhr area', in Grabher, G. (ed.) *The Embedded Firm: On the Socio-Economics of Industrial Networks*. London: Routledge.

Grabher, G. (2001) 'Ecologies of creativity: the village, the group, and the heterarchic organization of the British advertising industry'. *Environment and Planning A*, *33*: 351–74.

Grabher, G (2003) 'Switching ties, recombining teams: avoiding lock-in through project organization?', in Fucs, G. and Shapira, P. (eds) *Rethinking Regional Innovation and Change: Path Dependency or Regional Breakthrough?* New York: Springer.

Grabher, G. and Stark, D. (1997) 'Organizing diversity: evolutionary theory, network analysis and postsocialism'. *Regional Studies*, *31*: 533–44.

Greenaway, D. and Haynes, M. (2003) 'Funding higher education in the UK: the role of fees and loans'. *The Economic Journal*, *113*: F150–F166.

Griffiths, R. (2006) 'City/culture discourses: evidence from the competition to select the European Capital of Culture 2008'. *European Planning Studies*, *14*: 415–30.

Griffiths, R., Bassett, K. and Smith, I. (1999) 'Cultural policy and the cultural economy in Bristol'. *Local Economy*, *14*: 257–64.

Groenendijk, J. (1998) 'Amsterdam, Utrecht, Groningen: universities' locational interests and urban politics', in van der Wusten, H. (ed.) *The Urban University and its Identity: Roots, Locations, Roles*. Dordrecht: Kluwer Academic Publishers.

Groen, J. A. (2004) 'The effect of college location on migration of college-educated labor'. *Journal of Econometrics*, *121*: 125–42.

Groen, J. A. and White, M. J. (2004) 'In-state versus out-of-state students: the divergence of interest between public universities and state governments'. *Journal of Public Economics*, *88*: 1793–1814.

Gumprecht, B. (2003) 'The American college town'. *The Geographical Review*, *93*: 51–80.

Gumprecht, B. (2007) 'The campus as a public space in the American college town'. *Journal of Historical Geography*, *33*: 72–103.

Gunasekara, C. (2006) 'The generative and developmental roles of universities in regional innovation systems'. *Science and Public Policy*, *33*: 137–50.

Haila, A. (2008) 'The University of Helsinki as a developer', in Wiewel, W. and Perry, D. C. (eds) *Global Universities and Urban Development: Case Studies and Analysis*. Armonk: M. E. Sharpe.

Hall, T. and Hubbard, P. (1996) 'The entrepreneurial city: new urban politics, new urban geographies?'. *Progress in Human Geography*, *20*: 153–74.

Ham, C. (2009) *Health Policy in Britain*, 6th Edition. London: Palgrave Macmillan.

Harding, A. (2007) 'Taking city regions seriously? Response to debate on 'city-regions: new geographies of governance, democracy and social reproduction'. *International Journal of Urban and Regional Research*, *31*: 443–58.

Harrison, J. (2010) 'Life after regions: the evolution of city-regionalism in England'. *Regional Studies*, DOI:10.1080/00343404.2010.521148.

Harrison, R. T. and Leitch, C. (2010) 'Voodoo institution or entrepreneurial university? Spin-off companies, the entrepreneurial system and regional development in the UK'. *Regional Studies*, *44*: 1241–62.

Harvey, D. (1989) 'From managerialism to entrepreneurialism: the transformation in urban governance in late capitalism'. *Geografiska Annaler. Series B, Human Geography*, *71*: 3–17.

Harvey, D. (2012) *Rebel Cities: From the Right to the City to the Urban Revolution*. London: Verso.

Hassink, R. (2007) 'The strength of weak lock-ins: the renewal of the Westmünsterland textile industry'. *Environment and Planning A*, *39*: 1147–65.

Hassink, R. and Klaerding, C. (2011) 'Evolutionary approaches to local and regional development policy', in Pike, A., Rodríguez-Pose, A. and Tomaney, J. (eds) *Handbook of Local and Regional Development*. London: Routledge.

Hastings, A. (1996) 'Unravelling the process of 'partnership' in urban regeneration policy'. *Urban Studies*, *33*: 253–68.

Haughton. G. (1997) 'Developing sustainable urban development models'. *Cities*, *14*: 189–95.

Healey, P. (2002) 'On creating the 'city' as a collective resource'. *Urban Studies*, *39*: 1777–92.

HEFCE (2011) *Decisions on Assessing Research Impact*. Bristol: HEFCE.

Hesmondhalgh, D. (2005) 'Media and cultural policy as public policy: the case of the British Labour government'. *International Journal of Cultural Policy*, *11*: 95–109.

Hilton, T. (1991) 'Art schools and urban culture', in Fisher, M. and Owen, U. (eds) *Whose Cities?* London: Penguin Books.

Hoare, A. and Corver, M. (2010) 'The regional geography of new young graduate labour in the UK'. *Regional Studies, 44*: 477–94.

Hodson, M. and Marvin, S. (2010) 'Can cities shape socio-technical transitions and how would we know if they were?'. *Research Policy, 39*: 477–85.

Hodson, M. and Marvin, S. (2012) 'Mediating low-carbon urban transitions? Forms of organization, knowledge and action'. *European Planning Studies, 20*: 421–39.

Holdsworth, C. (2009) '"Going away to uni": mobility, modernity, and independence of English higher education students'. *Environment and Planning A, 41*: 1849–64.

Howells, J., Ramlogan, R. and Cheng, S. L. (2008) 'The role, context, and typology of universities and higher education institutions in innovation systems: a UK perspective', *Discussion Papers and Project Reports, Impact of Higher Education Institutions on Regional Economics: A Joint Research Initiative*. Online. Available at http://ewds.strath.ac.uk/impact/PresentationsPublications/DiscussionPapers.aspx (accessed 24 July 2012).

Hubbard, P. (2008) 'Regulating the social impacts of studentification: a Loughborough case study'. *Environment and Planning A, 40*: 323–41.

Hubbard, P. (2009) 'Geographies of studentification and purpose-built student accommodation: leading separate lives?'. *Environment and Planning A, 41*: 1903–23.

Hudson, R. (2005) 'Rethinking change in old industrial regions: reflecting on experiences of the North East of England'. *Environment and Planning A, 37*: 581–96.

Hudson, R. (2010) 'Resilient regions in an uncertain world: wishful thinking or a practical reality?'. *Cambridge Journal of Regions, Economy and Society, 3*: 11–25.

Hudson, R. (2011) 'From knowledge-based economy to ... knowledge-based economy? Reflections on changes in the economy and development policies in the North East of England'. *Regional Studies, 45*: 997–1012.

Huggins, R. and Cooke, P. (1997) 'The economic impact of Cardiff University: innovation, learning and job generation'. *GeoJournal, 41*: 325–37.

Huggins, R. and Johnston, A. (2009) 'The economic and innovation contribution of universities: a regional perspective'. *Environment and Planning C: Government and Policy, 27*: 1088–106.

Huggins, R., Johnston, A. and Steffenson, R. (2008) 'Universities, knowledge networks and regional policy'. *Cambridge Journal of Regions, Economy and Society, 1*: 321–40.

Hughes, A., Kitson, M., Probert, J., Bullock, A. and Milner, I.(2011) *Hidden Connections: Knowledge Exchange between the Arts and Humanities and the Private, Public and Third Sectors*. Swindon: AHRC.

Hutton, T. A. (2006) 'Spatiality, built form, and creative industry development in the inner city'. *Environment and Planning A, 38*: 1819–41.

Iammarino, S. (2005) 'An evolutionary integrated view of regional innovation systems: concepts, measures and historical perspectives'. *European Planning Studies, 13*: 497–519.

Imrie, R. and Raco, M. (2003) 'Community and the changing nature of urban policy', in Imrie, R. and Raco, M. (eds), *Urban Renaissance? New Labour, Community, and Urban Policy*. Bristol: The Policy Press.

Imrie, R. and Thomas, H. (1999) 'Assessing urban policy and the Urban Development Corporations', in Imrie, R. and Thomas, H. (eds), *British Urban Policy: An Evaluation of the Urban Development Corporations*. London: Sage Publications.

Jackson, L. E. (2003) 'The relationship of urban design to human health and condition'. *Landscape and Urban Planning, 64*: 191–200.

Jacobs, J. (1969) *The Economy of Cities*. New York: Random House.

Johnston, R. J. (1989) 'The southwards drift: preliminary analyses of the career patterns of 1980 graduates in Great Britain'. *Geography*, *74*: 239–44.

Johnston, L. (2010) 'Regenerating through collaborative innovation: the changing role of universities in urban and regional regeneration'. *Journal of Urban Regeneration and Renewal*, *4*: 178–90.

Jonas, A. E. G., While, A. H. and Gibbs, D. C. (2011) 'Carbon control regimes, eco-state restructuring and the politics of local and regional development', in Pike, A., Rodríguez-Pose, A. and Tomaney, J. (eds) *Handbook of Local and Regional Development*. London: Routledge.

Jones, M. (2001) 'The rise of the regional state in economic governance: 'partnerships for prosperity' or new scales of state power?'. *Environment and Planning A*, *33*: 1185–211.

Jones, A., Williams, L., Lee, N., Coats, D., Cowling, M. (2006) *Ideopolis: Knowledge City-Regions*. London: The Work Foundation.

Karvonen, A. and van Heur, B. (forthcoming) 'Urban laboratories: experiments in rework-ing cities'. *International Journal of Urban and Regional Research*.

Keeble, D., Lawson, C., Moore, B. and Wilkinson, F. (1999) 'Collective learning processes, networking and 'institutional thickness' in the Cambridge region'. *Regional Studies 33*: 319–32.

Kellogg Commission on the Future of State and Land-Grant Universities (1999) *Returning to our Roots: The Engaged University*. Washington, DC: National Association of State Universities and Land Grant Colleges.

Kelly, U., McLellan, D. and McNicoll, I. (2011) *Making an Economic Impact: Higher Education and the English Regions*. Universities UK.

Kenyon, E. L. (1997) 'Seasonal sub-communities: the impact of student households on residential communities'. *British Journal of Sociology*, *48*: 286–301.

Kodrzycki, Y. K. (2001) 'Migration of recent college graduates: evidence from the national longitudinal survey of youth'. *New England Economic Review*, January–February: 13–34.

Kitagawa, F. (2004) 'Universities and regional advantage: higher education and innovation policies in English regions'. *European Planning Studies*, *12*: 835–52.

Kitagawa, F. (2012) 'City-regions, innovation and universities: the evolution and transition of UK urban governance institutions', in Cooke, P. (ed.) *Re-Framing Regional Develop-ment*. London: Routledge.

Krätke, S. (2004) 'City of talents? Berlin's regional economy, socio-spatial fabric and "worst practice" urban governance'. *International Journal of Urban and Regional Research*, *28*: 511–29.

Krücken, G. (2003) 'Learning the 'new, new thing': on the role of path dependency in university structures'. *Higher Education*, *46*: 315–39.

Kumar, K. (1997) 'The need for place', in Smith, A. and Webster, F. (eds) *The Post-modern University? Contested Versions of Higher Education in Society*. Buckingham: SRHE/Open University Press.

Kythreotis, A. (2010) 'Local Strategic Partnerships: a panacea for voluntary interest groups to promote local environmental sustainability? The UK context'. *Sustainable Development*, *18*: 187–93.

Lam, A. (2005) 'Organizational innovation', in Fagerberg, J., Mowery, D. C. and Nelson, R. R. (eds) *The Oxford Handbook of Innovation*. Oxford: Oxford University Press.

Larkham, P. J. (2000) 'Institutions and urban form: the example of universities'. *Urban Morphology*, *4*: 63–77.

Lawton Smith, H. (2007) 'Universities, innovation, and territorial development: a review of the evidence'. *Environment and Planning C: Government and Policy*, *25*: 98–114.

Leeke, M., Sear, C. and Gay, O. (2003) 'An introduction to devolution in the UK', *Research Paper 03/84*. London: House of Commons Library. Online. Available at www.parliament.uk/commons/lib/research/rp2003/rp03-084.pdf (accessed 24 July 2012).

Leicester, G. and Sharpe, B. (2010) *Producing the Future: Understanding Watershed's Role in Ecosystems of Cultural Innovation*. Bristol: Watershed.

Llobrera, J. T., Meyer, D. R. and Nammacher, G. (2000) 'Trajectories of industrial districts: impact of strategic intervention in medical districts'. *Economic Geography*, *76*: 68–98.

Löfsten, H. and Lindelöf, P. (2002) 'Science parks and the growth of new technology-based firms – academic-industry links, innovation and markets'. *Research Policy*, *31*: 859–76.

Loftman, P. and Nevin, B. (1995) 'Prestige projects and urban regeneration in the 1980s and 1990s: a review of benefits and limitations'. *Planning, Practice and Research*, *3/4*: 299–315.

Logan, J. R. and Molotch, H. L. (1987) *Urban Fortunes: The Political Economy of Place*. Berkeley: University of California Press.

Lounsbury, M. and Pollack, S. (2001) 'Institutionalizing civic engagement: shifting logics and the cultural repackaging of service-learning in US higher education'. *Organization*, *8*: 319–39.

Lowe, P. and Phillipson, J. (2009) 'Barriers to research collaboration across disciplines: scientific paradigms and institutional practices'. *Environment and Planning A*, *41*: 1171–84.

Lundvall, B.-Å. (ed) (1992) *National Systems of Innovation: Towards a Theory of Innovation and Interactive Learning*. London: Pinter.

Lundvall, B. and Borrás, S. (2005) 'Science, technology, and innovation policy', in Fagerberg, J., Mowery, D. C. and Nelson, R. R. (eds) *The Oxford Handbook of Innovation*. Oxford: Oxford University Press.

McCann, E. and Ward, K. (2010) 'Relational/territoriality: toward a conceptualization of cities in the world'. *Geoforum*, *41*: 175–84.

McIlrath, L. and Mac Labhrainn, I. (eds) (2007) *Higher Education and Civic Engagement: International Perspectives*. Aldershot: Ashgate.

Macintyre, C. (2003) 'New models of student housing and their impact on local communities'. *Journal of Higher Education Policy and Management, 25*: 109–18.

MacKinnon, D., Cumbers, A., Pike, A., Birch, K. and McMaster, R. (2009) 'Evolution in economic geography: institutions, political economy, and adaptation'. *Economic Geography, 85*: 129–50.

Madanipour, A. (2011) *Knowledge Economy and the City: Spaces of Knowledge*. London: Routledge.

Manchester City South Partnership (2008) *Strategic Development Framework*. Manchester: Manchester City South Partnership. Online. Available at http://www.corridorman chester.com/our-vision/why-the-corridor (accessed 24 July 2012).

Manchester: Knowledge Capital (2005) *Manchester: Knowledge Capital. Science City Programme*. Manchester: Manchester: Knowledge Capital. Online. Available at http:// www.manchesterknowledge.com/leading-change/manchester-science-city (accessed 24 July 2012).

Manchester: Knowledge Capital Partnership (2003) *Manchester: Knowledge Capital: A Place for Inspiration. A World of Opportunities*. Manchester: Manchester City Council/

Knowledge Capital Partnership. Online. Available at http://www.manchesterknow ledge.com/knowledge-bank/manchester-knowledge-capital-prospectus (accessed 24 July 2012).

Marcuse, P. and Potter, C. (2005) 'Columbia University's heights: an ivory tower and its communities', in Perry, D. C. and Wiewel, W. (eds) *The University as Urban Developer: Case Studies and Analysis*. Armonk: M. E. Sharpe.

Marginson, S., Weko, T., Channon, N., Luukkonen, T. and Oberg, J. (2008) 'Netherlands', *OECD Reviews of Tertiary Education*. Paris: OECD.

Markusen, A. (1996) 'Sticky places in slippery space: a typology of industrial districts'. *Economic Geography, 72*: 293–313.

Markusen, A. (2006) 'Urban development and the politics of a creative class: evidence from a study of artists'. *Environment and Planning A, 38*: 1921–40.

Markusen, A. and Gadwa, A. (2010) *Creative Placemaking*. Washington, DC: National Endowment for the Arts.

Marshall, J. N., Pike, A., Pollard, J. S., Tomaney, J., Dawley, S. and Gray, J. (2012) 'Placing the run on Northern Rock'. *Journal of Economic Geography, 12*: 157–81.

Martin, R. and Sunley, P. (2006) 'Path dependence and regional economic evolution'. *Journal of Economic Geography, 6*: 395–437.

Massey, D., Quintas, P. and Wield, D. (1992) *High-Tec Fantasies: Science Parks in Society, Science and Space*. London: Routledge.

Matthews, V. (2010) 'Aestheticizing space: art, gentrification and the city'. *Geography Compass, 4*: 660–75.

May, T. and Perry, B. (2006) 'Cities, knowledge and universities: transformations in the image of the intangible'. *Social Epistemology, 20*: 259–82.

May, T. and Perry, B. (2011a) 'Urban research in the knowledge economy: content, context, and outlook'. *Built Environment, 37*: 352–67.

May, T. and Perry, B. (2011b) 'Contours and conflicts in scale: Science, knowledge and urban development'. *Local Economy, 26*: 715–20.

Mayhew, K., Deer, C. and Dua, M. (2004) 'The move to mass higher education in the UK: many questions and some answers'. *Oxford Review of Education, 30*: 65–82.

MIER (2009) *Manchester Independent Economic Review: Innovation, Trade, and Connectivity*. Manchester: MIER. Online. Available at http://www.manchester-review.org.uk/ (accessed 24 July 2012).

Miles, M. (1997) *Art Space and the City: Public Art and Urban Futures*. London: Routledge.

Minton, A. (2003) *Northern Soul: Culture, Creativity and Quality of Place in Newcastle and Gateshead*. London: RICS/Demos.

Minton, A. (2009) *Ground Control: Fear and Happiness in the Twenty-First-Century City*. London: Penguin Books.

Mintzberg, H. (1980) 'Structure in 5's: a synthesis of the research on organization design'. *Management Science, 26*: 322–41.

Morgan, K. (2004) 'Sustainable regions: governance, innovation, and scale'. *European Planning Studies, 12*: 871–89.

Morgan, G (2006) *Images of Organization*. London: Sage Publications.

Mosey, S., Wright, M. and Clarysse, B. (2012) 'Transforming traditional universities structures for the knowledge economy through multidisciplinary institutes'. *Cambridge Journal of Economics, 36*: 587–607.

Moulaert, F. and Nussbaumer, J. (2005) 'The social region: beyond the territorial dynamics of the learning economy'. *European Urban and Regional Studies, 12*: 45–64.

Moulaert, F., Martinelli, F., Swyngedouw, E. and González, S. (2005) 'Towards alternative model(s) of local innovation'. *Urban Studies, 42*: 1969–90.

Mukkala, K., Ritsilä, J. and Suosara, E. (2005) 'Self-evaluation report of the Jyväskylä region in Finland', *Supporting the Contribution of Higher Education Institutions to Regional Development*. Paris: OECD/IMHE. Online. Available at www.oecd.org/edu/ imhe/regionaldevelopment (accessed 24 July 2012).

Munro, M., Turok, I. and Livingston, M. (2009) 'Students in cities: a preliminary analysis of their patterns and effects'. *Environment and Planning A, 41*: 1805–25.

Musson, S., Tickell, A. and John, P. (2005) 'A decade of decentralisation? Assessing the role of the Government Offices for the English regions'. *Environment and Planning A, 37*: 1395–1412.

Nature (2010) 'Save our Cities'. *Nature, 467*: 883–4.

Nelson, R. R. (ed.) (1993) *National Innovation Systems: A Comparative Analysis*. Oxford: Oxford University Press.

NHS Sheffield and Sheffield City Council. (2010) *Fairer Sheffield: Healthy Lives: Health Inequalities Action Plan 2010–2013*.

NIHR (2012) 'Collaborations for Leadership in Applied Health Research and Care (CLAHRCs)', *NIHR Briefing Documents*. Online. Available at http://www.nihr.ac.uk/ about/Pages/Briefingdocuments.aspx (accessed 24 July 2012).

Nijman, J. (1998) 'Urban change and institutional adaptation: the geographical identity of the University of Miami', in van der Wusten, H. (ed.) *The Urban University and its Identity: Roots, Locations, Roles*. Dordrecht: Kluwer Academic Publishers.

North, P. (2003) 'Communities at the heart? Community action and urban policy in the UK', in Imrie, R. and Thomas, H. (eds), *British Urban Policy: An Evaluation of the Urban Development Corporations*. London: Sage Publications.

Nowotny, H., Scott, P. and Gibbons, M. (2001) *Re-Thinking Science: Knowledge and the Public in an Age of Uncertainty*. Cambridge: Polity Press.

Oakley, K. (2006) 'Include us out – economic development and social policy in the creative industries'. *Cultural Trends, 15*: 255–73.

Oakley, K. and Selwood, S. (2010) *Conversations and Collaborations: The Leadership of Collaborative Projects between Higher Education and the Arts and Cultural Sector*. London: LFHE.

OECD (2005) 'Finland', *OECD Territorial Reviews*. Paris: OECD.

OECD (2007) *Higher Education and Regions: Globally Competitive, Locally Engaged*. Paris: OECD.

OECD (2010a) (Puukka, J., Wade, P., Asheim, B., Goddard, J. and Teichler, U.) 'Berlin, Germany', *OECD Reviews of Higher Education in Regional and City Development*. Paris: OECD. Online. Available at www.oecd.org/edu/imhe/regionaldevelopment (accessed 24 July 2012).

OECD (2010b) (Yelland, R., Dubarle, P., Holm-Nielsen, L., Asheim, B. and Timmerhuis, V.) 'Rotterdam, The Netherlands', *OECD Reviews of Higher Education in Regional and City Development*. Paris: OECD. Online. Available at www.oecd.org/edu/imhe/ regionaldevelopment (accessed 24 July 2012).

Oinas, P. and Malecki, E. J. (2002) 'The evolution of technologies in time and space: from national and regional to spatial innovation systems'. *International Regional Science Review, 25*: 102–31.

One NorthEast (2002) *Realising our Potential: The Regional Economic Strategy for the North East of England*. Newcastle upon Tyne: One NorthEast.

One NorthEast (2006) *Leading the Way: Regional Economic Strategy 2006–2016.* Newcastle upon Tyne: One NorthEast.

Orton, J. D. and Weick, K. E. (1990) 'Loosely coupled systems: a reconceptualization'. *Academy of Management Review, 15*: 203–23.

Ostrander, S. A. (2004) 'Democracy, civic participation, and the university: a comparative study of civic engagement on five campuses'. *Nonprofit and Voluntary Sector Quarterly, 33*: 74–93.

PACEC (2012) *Strengthening the Contribution of English Higher Education Institutions to the Innovation System: Knowledge Exchange and HEIF Funding: A Draft Summary Report for HEFCE.* Cambridge: PACEC. Online. Available at http://www.hefce.ac.uk/whatwedo/kes/heif/ (accessed 24 July 2012).

Parkinson, M., Champion, T., Evans, R., Simmie, J., Turok, I., Crookston, M., Katz, B., Park, A., Berube, A., Coombes, M., Dorling, D., Glass, N., Hutchins, M., Kearns, A., Martin, R. and Wood, P. (2006) *State of the English Cities.* London: Office of the Deputy Prime Minister.

Pearce, G. and Ayres, S. (2007) 'Emerging patterns of governance in the English regions: the role of Regional Assemblies'. *Regional Studies, 41*: 699–712.

Peck, J. (2005) 'Struggling with the Creative Class'. *International Journal of Urban and Regional Research, 29*: 740–70.

Peel, D. (2008) 'Varsity real estate in Scotland: new visions for town and gown', in Wiewel, W. and Perry, D. C. (eds) *Global Universities and Urban Development: Case Studies and Analysis.* Armonk: M. E. Sharpe.

Perkins, N., Smith, K., Hunter, D. J., Bambra, C. and Joyce, K. (2010) '"What counts is what works"? New Labour and partnerships in public health'. *Policy & Politics, 38*: 101–17.

Perry, B. (2007) 'The multi-level governance of science policy in England'. *Regional Studies, 41*: 1051–67.

Perry, B. and Harloe, A. (2007) 'External engagements and internal transformations: universities, localities, and regional development', in Harding, A., Scott, A., Laske, S. and Burtscher, C. (eds) *Bright Satanic Mills: Universities, Regional Development, and the Knowledge Economy.* Aldershot: Ashgate.

Perry, B. and May, T. (2010) 'Urban knowledge exchange: devilish dichotomies and active intermediation'. *International Journal of Knowledge-Based Development, 1*: 6–24.

Perry, D. C. and Wiewel, W. (2005) 'From campus to city: the university as developer', in Perry, D. C. and Wiewel, W. (eds) *The University as Urban Developer: Case Studies and Analysis.* Armonk: M. E. Sharpe.

Phillimore, J. (1999) 'Beyond the linear view of innovation in science park evaluation: An analysis of Western Australian Technology Park'. *Technovation, 19*: 673–80.

Pike, A. and Tomaney, J. (2009) 'The state and uneven development: the governance of economic development in England in the post-devolution UK'. *Cambridge Journal of Regions, Economy and Society, 2*: 13–34.

Pike, A., Rodríguez-Pose, A. and Tomaney, J. (2007) 'What kind of local and regional development and for whom?'. *Regional Studies, 41*: 1253–69.

Pollock, A. M., Price, D., Talbot-Smith, A. and Mohan, J. (2003) 'NHS and the Health and Social Care Bill: end of Bevan's vision?'. *British Medical Journal, 327*: 982–5.

Porter, L. and Barber, A. (2007) 'Planning the cultural quarter in Birmingham's Eastside'. *European Planning Studies, 15*: 1327–48.

Pratt, J. (1997) *The Polytechnic Experiment: 1965–1992.* Buckingham: SRHE/Open University Press.

Raco, M. (2000) 'Assessing community participation in local economic development – lessons for the new urban policy'. *Political Geography*, *19*: 573–99.

Rantisi, N. M. (2002) 'The local innovation system as a source of 'variety': openness and adaptability in New York City's Garment District'. *Regional Studies*, *36*: 587–602.

Rantisi, N. M. and Leslie, D. (2010) 'Materiality and creative production: the case of the Mile End neighbourhood in Montréal'. *Environment and Planning A*, *42*: 2824–41.

Rappaport, A. (2008) 'Campus greening: behind the headlines'. *Environment: Science and Policy for Sustainable Development*, *50*: 6–17.

Rees, W. and Wackernagel, M. (1996) 'Urban ecological footprints: why cities cannot be sustainable – and why they are a key to sustainability'. *Environmental Impact Assessment Review*, *16*: 223–48.

Regional Development Agencies Act (1998) London: The Stationary Office Limited. Online. Available at: http://www.legislation.gov.uk/ukpga/1998/45/contents (accessed 24 July 2012).

Rhoades, G. and Slaughter, S. (1997) 'Academic capitalism, managed professionals, and supply-side higher education'. *Social Text*, *15*: 9–38.

Richards, G. and Wilson, J. (2004) 'The impact of cultural events on city image: Rotterdam, Cultural Capital of Europe 2001'. *Urban Studies*, *41*: 1931–51.

Rodin, J. (2005) 'The 21st century urban university'. *Journal of the American Planning Association*, *71*: 237–49.

Rubin, I. S. (1979) 'Retrenchment, loose structure and adaptability in the university'. *Sociology of Education*, *52*: 211–22.

Russo, A. P. and Sans, A. A. (2009) 'Student communities and landscapes of creativity: how Venice – 'the world's most touristed city' – is changing'. *European Urban and Regional Studies*, *16*: 161–75.

Russo, A. P. and Tatjer, L. C. (2007) 'From citadels of education to Cartier Latins (and back?): The changing landscapes of student populations in European cities'. *Geography Compass*, *1*: 1160–89.

Russo, A. P., van den Berg, L. and Lavanga, M. (2007) 'Toward a sustainable relationship between city and university: a stakeholdership approach'. *Journal of Planning Education and Research*, *27*: 199–216.

Rykwert J. (2000) *The Seduction of Place: The History and Future of the City*. Oxford: Oxford University Press.

Sachs, J. D. (2004) 'Health in the developing world: achieving the Millennium Development Goals'. *Bulletin of the World Health Organization*, *82*: 947–9.

Schienstock, G. (ed.) (2004) *Embracing the Knowledge Economy: The Dynamic Transformation of the Finnish Innovation System*. Cheltenham: Edward Elgar.

Schreiterer, U. and Ulbricht, L. (eds) (2009) 'The City of Berlin, Germany: self-evaluation report', *OECD Reviews of Higher Education in Regional and City Development*. Paris: IMHE. Online. Available at www.oecd.org/edu/imhe/regionaldevelopment (accessed 24 July 2012).

Scott, A. J. (1997) 'The cultural economy of cities'. *International Journal of Urban and Regional Research*, *21*: 323–39.

Scott, A. J. and Storper, M. (2003) 'Regions, globalization, development'. *Regional Studies*, *37*: 579–93.

Secretary of State for Health (2010a) *Equity and Excellence: Liberating the NHS*. London: Department of Health.

Secretary of State for Health (2010b) *Healthy Lives, Healthy People: Our Strategy for Public Health in England*. London: Department of Health.

Sen, A. (1999) *Development as Freedom*. Oxford:Oxford University Press.

Shachar, A. (1998) 'The Hebrew University of Jerusalem: earthly planning in a heavenly city', in van der Wusten, H. (ed.) *The Urban University and its Identity: Roots, Locations, Roles*. Dordrecht: Kluwer Academic Publishers.

Shaw, K. and Fincher, R. (2010) 'University students and the "creative class"'. *Journal of Policy Research in Tourism, Leisure and Events*, 2: 199–220.

Shaw, K. and Greenhalgh, P. (2010) 'Revisiting the 'missing middle' in English sub-national governance'. *Local Economy*, 25: 457–75.

Shaw, K. and Theobald, K. (2011) 'Resilient local government and climate change interventions in the UK'. *Local Environment*, 1: 1–15.

Shaw, M., Dorling, D., Gordon, D. and DaveySmith, G. (1999) *The Widening Gap: Health Inequalities and Policy in Britain*. Bristol: The Policy Press.

Shearmur, R. and Doloreux, D. (2000) 'Science parks: actors or reactors? Canadian science parks in their urban context'. *Environment and Planning A*, 32: 1065–82.

Shorthose, J. (2004) 'The engineered and the vernacular in cultural quarter development'. *Capital & Class*, 28: 159–78.

Shutt, J., Pugalis, L. and Bentley, G. (2012) 'LEPs – living up to the hype? The changing framework for regional economic development and localism in the UK', in Ward, M. and Hardy, S. (eds) *Changing Gear – Is Localism the New Regionalism?* London: The Smith Institute.

Siegel, D. S., Westhead, P. and Wright, M. (2003) 'Science parks and the performance of new technology-based firms: a review of recent U.K. evidence and an agenda for future research'. *Small Business Economics*, 20: 177–84.

Siegfried, J. J., Sanderson, A. R. and McHenry, P. (2007) 'The economic impact of colleges and universities'. *Economics of Education Review*, 26: 546–58.

Simmie, J. (1998) 'Reasons for the development of 'islands of innovation': evidence from Hertfordshire'. *Urban Studies*, 35: 1261–89.

Slaughter, S. and Leslie, L. L. (1997) *Academic Capitalism: Politics, Policies, and the Entrepreneurial University*. Baltimore:The Johns Hopkins University Press.

Smaglik, P. (2010) 'From steel to science'. *Nature*, 463: 258–9.

Smith, D. P. (2008) 'The politics of studentification and '(un)balanced' urban populations: lessons for gentrification and sustainable communities?'. *Urban Studies*, 45: 2541–64.

Smith, D. P. (2009) 'Guest editorial: 'Student geographies', urban restructuring, and the expansion of higher education'. *Environment and Planning A*, 41: 1795–804.

Smith, D. P. and Holt, L. (2007) 'Studentification and 'apprentice' gentrifiers within Britain's provincial towns and cities: extending the meaning of gentrification'. *Environment and Planning A*, 39: 142–61.

Sotarauta, M. and Kautonen, M. (2007) 'Co-evolution of the Finnish national and local innovation and science arenas: towards a dynamic understanding of multi-level governance'. *Regional Studies*, 41: 1085–98.

Sporn, B. (1999) *Adaptive University Structures: An Analysis of Adaptation to Socioeconomic Environments of US and European Universities*. London: Jessica Kingsley Publishers.

Staber, U. and Sydow, J. (2002) 'Organizational adaptive capacity: a structuration perspective'. *Journal of Management Inquiry*, 11: 408–24.

Steinacker, A. (2005) 'The economic effect of urban colleges on their surrounding communities'. *Urban Studies, 42*: 1161–75.

Storper, M. (1995) 'The resurgence of regional economies, ten years later: the region as a nexus of untraded interdependencies'. *European Urban and Regional Studies, 2* 191–221.

Storper, M. (1997) 'The city: centre of economic reflexivity'. *The Service Industries Journal, 17*: 1–27.

Storper, M. and Scott, A. J. (2009) 'Rethinking human capital, creativity and urban growth'. *Journal of Economic Geography, 9*: 147–67.

Subotzky, G. (1999) 'Alternatives to the entrepreneurial university: new modes of knowledge production in community service programs'. *Higher Education, 38*: 401–40.

Swords, J. and Wray, F. (2010) 'The connectivity of the creative industries in North East England – the problems of physical and relational distance'. *Local Economy, 25*: 305–18.

Taylor, J. (2003) 'Institutional diversity in UK higher education: policy and outcomes since the end of the binary divide'. *Higher Education Quarterly, 57*: 266–93.

Tewdwr-Jones, M. and McNeill, D. (2000) 'The politics of city-region planning and governance: reconciling the national, regional and urban in the competing voices of institutional restructuring'. *European Urban and Regional Studies, 7*: 119–34.

Thomas, B., Pritchard, J., Ballas, D., Vickers, D. and Dorling, D. (2009) *A Tale of Two Cities: The Sheffield Project.* Sheffield: Social & Spatial Inequalities Research Group, Department of Geography, The University of Sheffield.

Thrift, N. and French, S. (2002) 'The automatic production of space'. *Transactions of the Institute of British Geographers, 27*: 309–55.

Tight, M. (2007) 'The (re)location of higher education in England (revisited)'. *Higher Education Quarterly, 61*: 250–65.

Tödtling, F. and Trippl, M. (2004) 'Like phoenix from the ashes? The renewal of clusters in old industrial areas'. *Urban Studies, 41*: 1175–95.

Tödtling, F. and Trippl, M. (2005) 'One size fits all? Towards a differentiated regional innovation policy approach'. *Research Policy, 34*: 1203–19.

Tomaney, J. (2002) 'The evolution of regionalism in England'. *Regional Studies, 36*: 721–31.

Travers, T. (2002) 'Decentralization London-style: The GLA and London governance'. *Regional Studies, 36*: 779–88.

Treado, C. D. (2010) 'Pittsburgh's evolving steel legacy and the steel technology cluster'. *Cambridge Journal of Regions, Economy and Society, 3*: 105–20.

Turner, P. V. (1984) *Campus: An American Planning Tradition.* Cambridge, MA: MIT Press. Online. Available at http://www.brynmawr.edu/cities/archx/campus/ (accessed 24 July 2012).

Turok, I. (2008) 'A new policy for Britain's cities: choices, challenges, contradictions'. *Local Economy, 23*: 149–66.

UKCRC (2008) *Strengthening Public Health Research in the UK: Report of the UK Clinical Research Collaboration Public Health Research Strategic Planning Group.* London: UKCRC.

Urban Task Force (1999) *Towards and Urban Renaissance.* London: Department for the Environment, Transport, and the Regions.

Uyarra, E. (2010) 'What is evolutionary about 'regional systems of innovation'? Implications for regional policy'. *Journal of Evolutionary Economics, 20*: 115–37.

Vallance, P., Goddard, J. and Kempton, L. (2011) *Research Impacts – The Perspective of the Academic Community: Summary of the Main Findings from an Online Survey.* Online. Available at http://www.ncl.ac.uk/curds/publications/publications/2011.

van den Berg, L. and Klink, H. A. V. (1996) 'Health care and the urban economy: the medical complex of Rotterdam as a growth pole?'. *Regional Studies*, *30*: 741–47.

van den Berg, L., van der Meer, J. and Pol, P. (2003) 'Organising capacity and social policies in European cities'. *Urban Studies*, *40*: 1959–78.

van der Wusten, H. (1998) 'A warehouse of precious goods: the university in its urban context', in van der Wusten, H. (ed.) *The Urban University and its Identity: Roots, Locations, Roles*. Dordrecht: Kluwer Academic Publishers.

Van Helleputte, J. and Reid, A. (2004) 'Tackling the paradox: can attaining global research excellence be compatible with local technology development?'. *R&D Management*, *34*: 33–44.

van Heur, B. (2010) 'The built environment of higher education and research: architecture and the expectation of innovation'. *Geography Compass*, *4*: 1713–24.

van Winden, W., Berg, L. van den. and Pol, P. (2007) 'European cities in the knowledge economy: towards a typology'. *Urban Studies*, *44*: 525–49.

van Winden, W., de Carvalho, L., van Tuijl, E., van Haaren, J. and van den Berg, L. (2012) *Creating Knowledge Locations in Cities*. Abingdon: Routledge.

Vedovello, C. (1997) 'Science parks and university-industry interaction: geographical proximity between agents as a driving force'. *Technovation*, *17*: 491–502.

Venetoulis, J. (2001) 'Assessing the ecological impact of a university: the ecological footprint for the University of Redlands'. *International Journal of Sustainability in Higher Education*, *2*: 180–96.

Vlahov, D., Freudenberg, N., Proietti, F., Ompad, D., Quinn, A., Nandi, V. and Galea, S. (2007) 'Urban as a determinant of health'. *Journal of Urban Health*, *84*: 16–26.

Wainwright, M. (2011) 'Newcastle hopes to tap deep heat with 2000m geothermal probe'. *The Guardian*, 23 February 2011.

Walsh, J. J. (2009) 'The University movement in the North of England at the end of the Nineteenth Century'. *Northern History*, *46*: 113–31.

Warburton, D. (2011) 'City leaders step in to save Newcastle's Science Central'. *The Journal*, 5 July 2011.

Ward, K. and Jonas, A. E. G. (2004) 'Competitive city-regionalism as a politics of space: a critical reinterpretation of the new regionalism'. *Environment and Planning A*, *36*: 2119–39.

Waters, J. L. (2012) 'Geographies of international education: mobilities and the reproduction of social (dis)advantage'. *Geography Compass*, *6*: 123–36.

Watson, D. (2007) *Managing Civic and Community Engagement*. Maidenhead: Open University Press.

Webber, H. S. (2005) 'The University of Chicago and its neighbors: a case study in community development', in Perry, D. C. and Wiewel, W. (eds) *The University as Urban Developer: Case Studies and Analysis*. Armonk: M. E. Sharpe.

Weber, R., Theodore, N. and Hoch, C. (2005) 'Private choices and public obligations: the ethics of university real estate development', in Perry, D. C. and Wiewel, W. (eds) *The University as Urban Developer: Case Studies and Analysis*. Armonk: M. E. Sharpe.

Weick, K. E. (1976) 'Educational organisations as loosely coupled systems'. *Administrative Science Quarterly*, *21*: 1–19.

While, A., Jonas, A. E. G. and Gibbs, D. (2004) 'The environment and the entrepreneurial city: searching for the urban 'sustainability fix' in Manchester and Leeds'. *International Journal of Urban and Regional Research*, *28*: 549–69.

While, A., Jonas, A. E. G. and Gibbs, D. (2010) 'From sustainable development to carbon control: eco-state restructuring and the politics of urban and regional development'. *Transactions of the Institute of British Geographers, 35*: 76–93.

Whitehead, M. (2007) 'The architecture of partnerships: urban communities in the shadow of hierarchy'. *Policy & Politics, 35*: 3–23.

Whitehurst, F., Siedlok, F. and Race, J. (2008) 'Reach-in and Reach-out: The story of the MSc in Pipeline Engineering at Newcastle University'. *International Small Business Journal, 26*: 709–33.

Wiewel, W. and Perry, D. C. (2005) 'Ivory towers no more: academic bricks and sticks', in Perry, D. C. and Wiewel, W. (eds) *The University as Urban Developer: Case Studies and Analysis*. Armonk: M. E. Sharpe.

Wiewel, W. and Perry, D. C. (2008) 'The university, the city, and the state: institutional entrepreneurship or instrumentality of the state?', in Wiewel, W. and Perry, D. C. (eds) *Global Universities and Urban Development: Case Studies and Analysis*. Armonk: M. E. Sharpe.

Wilkinson, R. (1996) *Unhealthy Societies: The Afflictions of Inequality*. London: Routledge.

Wilkinson, R. and Pickett, K. (2009) *The Spirit Level: Why Equality is Better for Everyone*. London: Penguin.

Wilkinson, T. (2011) 'Newcastle may see return to coalmining'. *The Independent*, 4 October 2011.

Williams, G. (1997) 'The market route to mass higher education: British experience 1979–1996'. *Higher Education Policy, 10*: 275–89.

Willmott, H. (2003) 'Commercialising higher education in the UK: the state, industry and peer review'. *Studies in Higher Education, 28*: 129–41.

Wright, M., Clarysse, B., Lockett, A. and Knockaert, M. (2008) 'Mid-range universities' linkages with industry: knowledge types and the role of intermediaries'. *Research Policy, 37*: 1205–23.

Yacobi, H. (2008) 'Academic fortress: the case of the Hebrew University on Mount Scopus, Jerusalem', in Wiewel, W. and Perry, D. C. (eds) *Global Universities and Urban Development: Case Studies and Analysis*. Armonk: M. E. Sharpe.

Yang, C., Motohashi, K. and Chen, J. (2009) 'Are new technology-based firms located on science parks really more innovative? Evidence from Taiwan'. *Research Policy, 38*: 77–85.

Yigitcanlar, T. and Velibeyoglu, K. (2008) 'Knowledge-based urban development: the local economic development path of Brisbane, Australia'. *Local Economy, 23*: 195 207.

Zeller, C. (2004) 'North Atlantic innovative relations of Swiss pharmaceuticals and the proximities with regional biotech arenas'. *Economic Geography, 80*: 83–111.

Zlotkowski, E. (2007) 'The case for service learning', in McIlrath, L. and Mac Labhrainn, I. (eds) *Higher Education and Civic Engagement: International Perspectives*. Aldershot: Ashgate.

Zukin, S. (1995) *The Cultures of Cities*. Oxford: Blackwell.

Index

Note: page numbers in **bold** type refer to figures and tables.